LATIN JAZZ

Currents in
Latin American
& Iberian Music

ALEJANDRO L. MADRID, SERIES EDITOR
WALTER AARON CLARK, FOUNDING SERIES EDITOR

Latin Jazz

THE OTHER JAZZ

Christopher Washburne

OXFORD
UNIVERSITY PRESS

Oxford University Press is a department of the University of Oxford. It furthers
the University's objective of excellence in research, scholarship, and education
by publishing worldwide. Oxford is a registered trade mark of Oxford University
Press in the UK and certain other countries.

Published in the United States of America by Oxford University Press
198 Madison Avenue, New York, NY 10016, United States of America.

Library of Congress Cataloging-in-Publication Data
Names: Washburne, Christopher, author.
Title: Latin jazz : the other jazz / Christopher Washburne.
Description: New York : Oxford University Press, 2020. |
Includes bibliographical references and index.
Identifiers: LCCN 2019048942 (print) | LCCN 2019048943 (ebook) |
ISBN 9780195371628 (hardback) | ISBN 9780197510841 (paperback) |
ISBN 9780197510858 (epub) | ISBN 9780197510865
Subjects: LCSH: Latin jazz—History and criticism.
Classification: LCC ML3506 .W37 2020 (print) | LCC ML3506 (ebook) |
DDC 781.65098—dc23
LC record available at https://lccn.loc.gov/2019048942
LC ebook record available at https://lccn.loc.gov/2019048943

For August and Isa, my angels and inspiration

Contents

Acknowledgments

THIS BOOK WOULD have never been possible without a whole village of extraordinarily generous and special people. I am blessed to have these friends, family members, colleagues, and bandmates in my life. Their contributions to the research and writing of this book were essential.

I first want to acknowledge the musicians I have collaborated with over the years who relentlessly advocate, sound out, and push the limits of beautiful possibilities of Latin jazz. I am most grateful to all the bandleaders who have invited me into their musical lives and taught me so much about the history of this music. It has been an honor to share the stage with the great masters Tito Puente, Mario Bauzá, Ray Barretto, Chico O'Farrill, and Eddie Palmieri. Each generously shared so much music and insight. I will be grateful forever. Many thanks to Irving Cancel and Richard Malcolm for introducing me to Latin jazz and giving me my first gigs in Boston. My long love for this music was launched on their bandstands. For that I will always be indebted. And thanks to Michele Rosewoman for challenging me to take the music even deeper into its roots. I am grateful to be able to share the stage with her. And special thanks to Bobby Sanabria for all of our collaborations and music making that has now stretched over the last twenty-nine years. His dedication to Latin jazz and generosity in sharing his wealth of knowledge are true gifts.

To all of the musicians that are part of my SYOTOS family (the Latin jazz band I have led for nearly thirty years): John Walsh, Ole Mathisen, Hector

Martignon, Leo Traversa, Vince Cherico, Oreste Abrantes, Ray Vega, Yeissonn Villamar, Barry Olsen, Harvie Swartz, Cristian Rivera, Chembo Corniel, Bernie Minosa, Bobby Sanabria, Renato Thoms, Claudette Sierra, Gabriela Anders, John DiMartino, Ruben Rodriguez, Ludwig Afonso, Diego Lopez, Jonathan Powell, Diego Urcola, Johnny Rodriguez, Louie Bauzó, Igor Atalita, Bobby Franchescini, Bobby Allende, Roberto Quintero, Samuel Torres, Obanilú Allende, Luisito Ayala, Herman Olivera, Alex Brown, Jimmy Delgado, Donald Nicks, Willard Dyson, Mitch Frohman, Alex Garcia, Hans Glawischnig, Steve Gluzband, Lincoln Goines, Armando Gola, Alex Hernandez, Cliff Korman, Brian Lynch, Eddie Martinez, Arturo O'Farrill, Willie Martinez, Ian McDonald, Dave Mead, Andre Mehmari, Jairo Moreno, Valerie Naranjo, Sebastian Nickoll, Alex Norris, Arturo Ortiz, Oscar Hernandez, Luis Perdomo, Edward Perez, Marcus Persiani, Max Pollak, Bobby Porcelli, Ivan Renta, Mario Rivera, Mario Rodriguez, Ernesto Simpson, Orlando Vega, Elio Villafranca, and Ben Wittman. Jamming with all of them has been a true blessing and the foundation for my love and dedication to this music. I am inspired nightly by their dedication and supreme musicality. Special thanks to Lois Griffith and Miguel Algarín at the Nuyorican Poets Café and Paul Stache and Frank Christopher at the Smoke Jazz Club for supporting us and inviting us to perform weekly for twenty-two years. Thanks to Carnegie Hall and Sarah Johnson, Joanna Massey, Manual Bagorra, Kate Pfaff, Ann Gregg, Jennie Wasserman, Mark Burford, Beth Snodgrass, Misty Tolle, Hillary O'Toole, Amy Mereson, Stephanie Cohen-Santiago, Lisa Halasz, Alan Sneath, Becky Hinkle, and Naomi Giges for giving us so many opportunities to perform over the years. Thanks to Brice Rosenbloom and Nada Taib for the great performance opportunities. And thanks to Randy Klein at Jazzheads Records and Jochen Becker at Zoho Records for believing in our music and putting it out there on seven recordings.

Thanks to Piers and Lucy Playfair for such innovative programming at the Catskill Jazz Factory, creating a space where I could sound out, perform, and dig deep into the performance history of the music that is the subject of this book. You made the Rags and Roots Band happen, and for that I will always be grateful.

To the Latin jazz DJs, advocates, producers, and cultural warriors Awilda Rivera, Gary Walker, Jose Cruz, Tomas Algarín, German Santana, Louis Lafitte, Jim Byers, Arturo Gomez, Janine Santana, Jesse "Chuy" Varela, Andy Harlow, Michael Bongard, Vicki Sola, Nicholas Marrero, Scott Thompson, Raul de Gama, and J. Michael Harrison,. Thanks for the continued spins and opportunities, and making sure the music is heard widely. And thanks to Harry Sepulveda for sharing his wealth of knowledge and making all of those mixed tapes for me. I am grateful to photographers Enid Farber, Joe Conzo Jr., Jack Vartoogian, and Hazel Hankin, who work tirelessly to capture the music as it is being made. I am so happy to be able to include their beautiful images in this volume.

Many thanks to Chris Rogers for sharing the amazing photos of his father, Barry Rogers; Gary Jefferson for his beautiful image of his father, Gene Jefferson; Eleonor Azpiazu for sharing photos of her father-in-law, Don Azpiazu; Marcello Piras for his generous sharing of Oscar Joost's original recording of "The Peanut Vendor"; Dan Morgenstern for sharing of his comprehensive and sage-like knowledge of jazz history; Richard Carlin for providing the opportunity to write about Latin music at the Apollo Theater; and the Hungarian Café for letting me sit there for hours writing and sipping ginger tea.

I want to express my thanks to my colleagues at Columbia University for being so supportive over the years: Ana Maria Ochoa, Aaron Fox, Kevin Fellezs, Alessandra Ciucci, George Lewis, Elaine Sisman, Walter Frisch, Giuseppe Gerbino, Susan Boynton, Ellie Hisama, Joe Dubiel, Fred Lerdahl, Brad Garton, Georg Haas, Magdalena Stern Baczewska, Jeff Milarsky, Peter Susser, Carol Becker, Farah Griffin, Paul Ingram, Michael Shadlen, and Robert O'Meally. I am lucky to work among such esteemed colleagues who continually inspire. I am grateful for the generous support of Beth Pratt, Erica Lockhart, Anne Gefell, Johanna Martinez, and Gabriela Kumar Sharma.

A number of graduate students at Columbia University have worked as research assistants for this project. Their diligence and hard work contributed greatly. I am most grateful to Melissa Gonzalez, Beatriz Goubert, Sara Snyder, Shannon Garland, Simon Calle, and César Colón-Montijo.

Special thanks to Ingrid Monson, Kay Shelemay, Richard Wolf, Virginia Danielson, and Katherine Hagedorn for their comments on earlier drafts and for their generous hospitality while I was teaching at Harvard as a visiting assistant professor.

I am grateful to Suzanne Ryan for her continued and patient support of this project despite the delays and obstacles, to the series editors Walter Clark and Alejandro Madrid, and to the three reviewers of this manuscript for their insightful and constructive comments and attention to details. Their work greatly enhanced this project.

To Mom, Shelley, and Rebecca, thank you for all your love, care, support, and guidance.

And last, August and Isa. I dedicate this work to you both. The research and writing took place over the entirety of your lives. You give me the love and hope that fuels my life and provides my inspiration to grow.

In 1517, Fray Bartolome de las Casas, feeling great pity for the Indians who grew worn and lean in
the drudging infernos of the Antillean gold mines, proposed to Emperor Charles V that Negroes
be brought to the isles of the Caribbean, so that they might grow worn and lean in the drudging
infernos of the Antillean gold mines. To that odd variant on the species *philanthropist* we owe an
infinitude of things: W. C. Handy's blues; the success achieved in Paris by the Uruguayan attorney-
painter Pedro Figari; the fine runaway-slave prose of the likewise Uruguayan Vicente Rossi; the
mythological stature of Abraham Lincoln; the half-million dead of the War of Secession; the $3.3
billion spent on military pensions; the statue of the imaginary semblance of Antonio (Falucho) Ruiz;
the inclusion of the verb 'lynch' in respectable dictionaries; the impetuous King Vidor film *Hallelujah*;
the stout bayonet charge of the regiment of "Blacks and Tans" (the color of their skins, not their
uniforms) against that famous hill near Montevideo; the gracefulness of certain elegant young ladies;
the black man who killed Martin Fierro; that deplorable rumba *The Peanut-Vendor* . . .
—JORGE LUIS BORGES, "The Remote Cause," in *The Cruel Redeemer Lazarus Morell* (1933)[1]

INTRODUCTION

The Other Jazz

JORGE LUIS BORGES uses this seemingly haphazard catalog of causal effects associated with the importation of enslaved African people in the New World to anach-
ronistically set up his short story "The Cruel Redeemer Lazarus Morell," about a
man who lives in the Deep South of the United States during slavery. This opening
passage adroitly captures the entanglement of culture, of people and events seemingly dispersed yet intrinsically connected through colonial encounters of the past
and the present—the global nature of human experience, even before mass-medi-
ation and cyberspace. Borges intriguingly intertwines and blurs the delineation of
the histories of the Americas (North and South) and the Caribbean, as well as between past and present, suggesting that the colonial encounters throughout history ensnare our experiences in myriad ways that have significant reverberations
in the present and in our conceptions of the past. The rhizomic connections he
constructs are unpredictable and barely traceable but are undeniable nonetheless.
His choice to include Moisés Simons's composition "El Manisero" ("The Peanut
Vendor") in his web of remote causes, a piece of music that is often looked upon
as the "catalyst" for what would become known as Latin jazz, is of particular interest.[2] Writing in 1933 in the aftermath of "The Peanut Vendor's" meteoric rise to
unprecedented international appeal, Borges, no doubt, experienced firsthand the

Latin Jazz. Christopher Washburne, Oxford University Press (2020). © Oxford University Press.
DOI: 10.1093/oso/9780195371628.001.0001

song's ubiquitous presence. The 1930 release of the song by Don Justo Azpiazú and his Havana Casino Orchestra rose to number one on the sales charts (the first Cuban band to hold that position),[3] only to be replaced in popularity by the numerous subsequent versions recorded by the pop and jazz stars of the day, such as Louis Armstrong, Guy Lombardo, and Duke Ellington. With more than 2 million copies in sheet-music sales, its feature in the film *Cuban Love Song* in 1931, and constant radio airplay and phonograph spins made the song almost unavoidable in daily cosmopolitan life, even in Buenos Aires. In particular, the often gimmicky arrangements and exotica stagings of the song on bandstands throughout the world must have been tiresome and even a bit alarming (in an Adornian sense) to this esteemed writer and cultural critic living in Argentina as he grappled with the implications of the nascent globalized pop-music market—thus, his descriptive choice, "deplorable." It was deplorable to some, especially Cuban elites who saw music from marginalized lower (and darker) classes come to represent their nation in the global imagination, a change incited from abroad. Their preferred genteel and sophisticated *danzón* was replaced by a street music known as *son pregón* but mislabeled as "rhumba" by RCA Victor executives more interested in capitalizing on exotic sounds from faraway places than understanding locally significant genre distinctions (even Borges gets the genre name wrong, though at least he spells "rumba" correctly).[4] Despite its "deplorability" and mislabeling, the song's international mass appeal made it one of the most commercially influential of the 1930s, an appeal that reverberated throughout the twentieth century and continues to do so into the present.

In the spirit of Borges, I take much liberty and indulgence and write . . . In 1930, the entrepreneurial vaudeville actress Marion Sunshine, feeling great pity for the financial woes of her husband (Eusebio Santiago Azpiazú), caused by the Depression, and for Broadway audiences' lack of opportunities to experience "real" Cuban music (which she imagined as the perfect antidote for the collapsing record, publishing, and entertainment industries), proposed to the opulent vaudeville Palace Theater (also suffering from the economic collapse) that they stage an afternoon of Cuban music featuring her brother-in-law's band, Don Justo Azpiazú and his Havana Casino Orchestra. She enlisted her husband as the band's manager for their North American tour. On April 26, 1930, after several successful uptown performances for Cuban and Puerto Rican audiences in New York City, the producers at the Palace agreed and presented one of the first occasions where a mainstream Broadway audience (read white) was exposed to "authentic" Cuban music, or so they imagined. For the third number of that fateful performance, Azpiazú directed his singer, Antonio Machín, to enter the stage wearing a Cuban street vendor's uniform, pushing a vending cart, and tossing bags of peanuts to the audience while singing "*Maní . . .*" In response, the crowd went nuts. To that odd variant on the species *staged authenticity* we owe an infinitude of things: the launching of the "rhumba" dance craze, replacing the foxtrot and the tango as the most popular dances; Cuba becoming a hegemonic force in new dance crazes for the next fifty or so years; Desi Arnaz wooing women with the flip of his thick flock of hair, while singing "Babalú" with a small conga drum strapped across his shoulder; the *I Love Lucy* show and the three-camera television shoot, which Arnaz invented and is still the industry standard today; Chano Pozo correcting the misconceptions created by Arnaz's superficial renditions of Cuban musical traditions by singing "Babalú" in a more genuine, respectful, and informed way with a large conga drum strapped across his shoulder; the Arthur Murray Dance Studios earning more than $14 million in profits during the Depression era by dedicating half of their classes to "rhumba"; Mario Bauzá being hired as the lead trumpet player in Chick Webb's band; Frank "Machito" Grillo proudly calling his band the Afro-Cubans way before anyone in the United States used the "Afro-" prefix; Pérez Prado's grunts while teaching everyone how to count to eight in Spanish; Dizzy Gillespie learning to play cowbell; Xavier Cugat's thirty-year gig at the Waldorf Astoria; life-size posters of Ricky Martin in adolescent girls' bedrooms in Ohio; T-shirts reading "More Cowbell"; Marc Anthony, Shakira, Christina Aguilera, Jennifer Lopez, and sundry other Caribbean and Latin Americans becoming US pop stars; Ry Cooder's "discovery" of the Buena Vista Social Club and his belief that his distracting twangy guitar noodling accompaniment was OK; new stylistic names such as Cubop, Afro-Cuban jazz, Afro-Latin jazz, and Latin jazz; the systematic omission of those terms and musicians associated with them in most jazz history books throughout the twentieth century; the inclusion of music associated with those terms in most sets of jazz played nightly throughout the twentieth and twenty-first centuries; and . . . the writing of this book.

This book is an exploration of Latin jazz through the lens of Borgesian entangled histories.

* * *

Jazz is a global music and transcultural in its stylistic scope. It has been so since its inception. No more is this apparent than in the form of jazz commonly known as Latin jazz. Latin jazz is a genre that embodies a nexus of intercultural exchange where African American traditions are blended with Caribbean and Latin American ones. Recently, there has been unprecedented interest in this music, both institutionally and within popular realms. This interest has increased the need to construct and record a viable historical narrative, documenting and structuring the complex genealogies of indebtedness and exchange. In spite of growing interest and popularity, this music and the musicians who make it are persistently marginalized, separated economically, politically, ethnically, and racially by the media, educational institutions, jazz producers and promoters, consumers, and musicians. The music is often segregated into allotted programming and promotional slots that neatly compartmentalize and pigeonhole, reserved exclusively for the exotic/the novel/the lightweight/the not real jazz/music for cats who can't play changes, and often billed with cliché terms, such as "hot," "fiery," or "caliente" (see Figure I.1). Though there are multiple reasons for this type of continued marginalization, it is important to note for our present discussion that economic concerns and the intense competitive environment of the jazz business are certainly key factors. Especially as the popularity of Caribbean and Latin American– inflected jazz styles grows, thus raising the economic stakes, strong resistance continues to fester among various groups within the jazz community who have benefited in the past from a more exclusive delineation of what jazz is. This marginalization has resulted in Latin jazz's systemic omission from jazz historical narratives, and to date, this style of music remains conspicuously underexplored in the scholarly literature.

What comes to mind are these questions: Is this book just another one of those instances where Latin jazz is sequestered so as not to interfere with the "real jazz," segregated from the mainstream, black-versus-white, US-centric jazz world? Should this music remain a separate category? Why is the music of Chico O'Farrill, Tito Puente, and Frank "Machito" Grillo rarely treated simultaneously with or

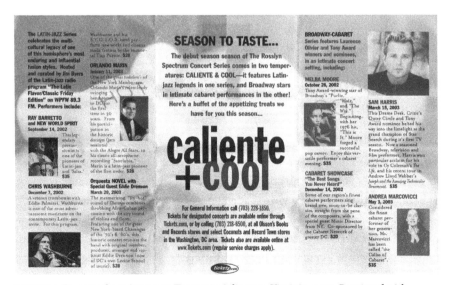

FIGURE I.1 Program from Spectrum Theater in Arlington, Virginia, 2002. Reprinted with permission from producer Jim Byers and the Spectrum Theater.

given equal weight to the music of Duke Ellington or Louis Armstrong? Should it be? This book explores these questions and serves as a corrective to the lacuna in jazz scholarship, acknowledging and celebrating the significant Caribbean and Latin American contributions to jazz.

This book is not a comprehensive historical study of the music (though one is desperately needed) but rather an issue-oriented historical and ethnographic study that focuses on key moments in the music's history in order to unpack the cultural forces that have shaped its development. The broad historical scope of this study, which traces the dynamic interplay of Caribbean and Latin American musical influence from eighteenth- and nineteenth-century colonial New Orleans through to the present global stage, provides an in-depth contextual foundation for exploring how musicians work with and negotiate through the politics of nation, place, race, and ethnicity in the ethnographic present. Specifically, I explore how genre and its associated imaginings are implicated in the construction of musical identities and boundary crossings through various performative and discursive practices in this overtly intercultural milieu. As the book's title suggests, Latin jazz is explored both as a specific subgenre of jazz and through the processes involved in its constructed "otherness."

WHAT IS LATIN JAZZ?

"Latin jazz" is an umbrella term for a genre of music that blends jazz with the musical practices, styles, and traditions of the Caribbean and Latin America. Historically, music from the Caribbean and Latin America has shared a common history with jazz, intersecting, cross-influencing, and at times seeming inseparable, as each has played a prominent role in the other's development. Early jazz musicians acknowledged this foundational connection. Most noted is pianist Jelly Roll Morton, who proclaimed, "If you can't manage to put tinges of Spanish in your tunes, you will never be able to get the right seasoning, I call it, for jazz."[5] In this context, "Spanish" refers to music coming from Spanish-speaking regions of the Caribbean and Latin America.

The Caribbean and Latin American influence on jazz remained prominent throughout the first half of the twentieth century, due, in part, to the growing presence of Caribbean and Latin American musicians participating in the US jazz scene. Some notable examples include Puerto Rican valve trombonist Juan Tizol, who performed with Duke Ellington; Cuban bandleader Frank "Machito" Grillo, who formed Machito and His Afro Cubans in 1938, a big band that employed and collaborated with many North American jazz musicians, including Stan Getz, Stan Kenton, Dexter Gordon, Harry "Sweets" Edison, Zoot Sims, Johnny Griffin, Buddy Rich, and Herbie Mann; Cuban trumpeter Mario Bauzá, who played with Chick Webb and later with Cab Calloway; Puerto Rican trombonist Fernando Arbello, who performed with Fletcher Henderson, Chick Webb, and Fats Waller; Puerto Rican tubist and bassist Rafael Escudero, who played on more than eighty recordings and performed with Fletcher Henderson, Louis Armstrong, and many others; trombonist Rafael Hernandez, who became one of Puerto Rico's most important composers and played in Luckey Roberts's band; and Cuban flautist Alberto Socarrás, who did session work for Columbia Records and performed in Benny Carter's band.[6] Socarrás is credited with recording the first jazz flute solo on Clarence Williams's 1927 release "Shooting the Pistol."[7] Simply put, these musicians, along with many others, brought extensive exposure of Caribbean and Latin American music styles to North American jazz musicians from the 1920s through the 1940s, providing the foundation for the emergence of what would eventually be labeled, "Latin jazz."

It was not until the mid-1940s, with the innovative work of Dizzy Gillespie, Chano Pozo, Mario Bauzá, Frank "Machito" Grillo, Stan Kenton, George Russell, and the like, that a separate stylistic label was deemed necessary to differentiate Caribbean and Latin American influenced jazz from other jazz styles. Previously, a separate style subcategory was not employed; instead, more specific terminology was used to delineate rhythmic variations played by jazz groups. These often included the names of dances that were associated with a song's rhythmic structure, such as the quadrille, rumba, stomp, and tango. Over time, these specific terms were used with less frequency as jazz became less associated with dance. By 1947, dance terms began to be replaced by the label "Cubop," and, later, "Latin jazz." Dizzy Gillespie popularized the term "Cubop" as a stylistic label, in part through his big band's acclaimed performance of the "Afro-Cubano Drums Suite" with Cuban percussionist Chano Pozo at Carnegie Hall in September 29, 1947, an event popularly referred to as the "birth of Latin jazz." The term "Cubop" itself, an elision of "Cuba" and "bebop," symbolized a new type of musical integration. The music drew inspiration equally from both styles to such a degree that it could no longer be labeled solely bebop or Cuban music. The name symbolized the new level of intercultural musical integration that differentiated the music from previous Caribbean and Latin American and jazz mixings. Though the Gillespie-Pozo collaboration was brief (1946–1948), due to Pozo's untimely death, its influence on jazz was profound. Gillespie's stature in the jazz community legitimized and set a precedent for greater incorporation of Caribbean and Latin American musical structures and principles into jazz music making. Latin jazz became an integral part of bebop where most players incorporated the rhythms and repertoire. Since the time of Gillespie and Pozo's initial collaboration, it has become rare to hear a jazz set without some form of Caribbean or Latin American influence directly derived from their efforts. Some non-Hispanic jazz musicians, such as Cal Tjader, George Shearing, Herbie Mann, and Stan Kenton, dedicated much of their professional energies to performing Latin jazz. As jazz musicians turned toward other Caribbean and Latin American music styles for inspiration and musical mixings, most notably Brazilian, the "Cubop" name proved too limiting and was eventually replaced by the more geographically inclusive "Latin jazz."

One of the earliest references to "Latin jazz" as a genre label came from writer David Drew Zingg in his liner notes for Tito Puente's 1956 release *Puente Goes Jazz* (Bluebird RCA 07863661482). He writes: "Here, in this album, you can witness the explosively exciting meld of African-Latin and African-North American music out of which is born a new form: Latin Jazz." Many other references followed in the ensuing years, most notably in the liner notes of vibraphonist Cal Tjader's albums. In 1958, for his release *Más Ritmo Caliente* (Fantasy 3262), the music is described as having a "Latin-jazz feeling." In the notes of *Cal Tjader Goes Latin* (Fantasy 3289, 1959), the music is referred to as "Latin/Jazz." And on his 1960 album *Demasiado Caliente* (Fantasy 3309), "Latin Jazz" is firmly affixed as the genre label. Attesting to the widespread use of the label by 1960, this was the same year that the Puerto Rican-Danish percussionist Juan Amalbert founded the Latin Jazz Quintet in Copenhagen.[8] Since 1960, Latin jazz has remained the substyle's most frequently used label, yet it remains highly contested. Other less frequently used labels include Afro Latin jazz, Afro-Cuban jazz, Caribbean jazz, and jazz Latin.[9]

For the purposes of this book, I have chosen to refer to this large and diverse body of music as "Latin jazz." This is the most commonly used and most widely known name for the music. However, I am not particularly comfortable with this choice, as I am cognizant of the vague and reductive nature of such a move. I often shy away from using it when describing my own music, as it simply erases the richly diverse traditions from which the music draws. I will explore the dilemma of genre naming throughout this book, but for now, the topic of this book is Latin jazz.

Despite the rich history of Caribbean and Latin American and jazz mixings briefly sketched above, the Caribbean and Latin American contributions to jazz are rarely discussed in jazz historical narratives. This book examines the reasons for this omission and why this is so problematic. I now turn to a brief historical and theoretical backdrop to explicate the framework within which I conducted my research.

* * *

This study positions all jazz as intercultural and transnational, as well as multivocal at its core. This is a political as much as a philosophical position and one that I have adopted in hopes of developing a more inclusive and realistic picture of the processes involved when musicians make jazz. At issue here is that much of early jazz research, both scholarly and journalistic, is colored by political, ethnic, and romanticizing agendas that disguise much of the complexities that underlie jazz music production. What is absent is a consideration of social forces and the interplay between various contextual factors, especially those that seem to counter a conception of jazz as art, as intellectual, as purely African American, and as an exclusively American music. The roles of commercialization, popular culture, globalization, and interculturality are downplayed or outright ignored.

In response to the systemic omission, absence, and silencing of Latin jazz and its innovators in historical narratives, I propose a new reading of jazz from a contextualist point of view, a reframing with an examination of the contexts from which jazz emerges, in order to question historical narratives that favor a chronological and linear approach, something to which traditional jazz history construction is prone. I also show that a conception of jazz as a global transnational phenomenon does not in any way detract from its "North Americanness," "African Americanness," nor blackness. Indeed, just the opposite is the case. Jazz employs an open-ended system of production, in and of itself reflective of a unique African American aesthetic, and the music's strengths derive from the richly diverse sources it draws upon. Latin jazz serves as the case study par excellence due to its intercultural roots associated with colonial New Orleans, the multivalent roles it has played throughout the history of jazz, its continued cross-fertilizing relationship with other jazz forms, and its ubiquitous international presence.

* * *

As jazz emerged from New Orleans in the early twentieth century, the city's ties to the Caribbean and its unique cultural mix served as an important component in the development of the music.[10] By way of his "Spanish tinge" comment, Jelly Roll Morton affirms the influence of the city's distinctive intercultural dynamic on early jazz. Coming from an early innovator who helped define the sound of jazz, his comment has served as mantra and justification for Latin jazz musicians to assert their place in jazz history and an impetus for closer scholarly examination of the music.[11] However, little attention has been given to the implications of such a statement. At its core resonates interculturality, firmly locating jazz in an "in between" space where peoples from diverse cultures rub up against one another. This is an interstitial space of significance, the space between colonizers and the colonized, black and white, black and creole, European and African, and the Caribbean and Latin America and the United States. This was the cultural climate of New Orleans in the eighteenth and nineteenth centuries from which jazz emerged.

Intercultural close encounters materialize into what Stuart Hall describes as a "creolized third space."[12] For Hall, the processes of creolization in the colonial setting are what define "Caribbeanness," and I would add "Latin Americanness" and "North Americanness." Many terms have been used to label the processes of cultural mixings in the Americas and the Caribbean, however Hall's choice of "creole" proves strategic and advantageous. Scholar John Szwed points out, terms such as "hybridity," "mestizaje," "cosmopolitanism," and "heterogeneity" are terminology of those who speak from positions of dominance. The view from the bottom is in striking contrast, with the use of words such, as "gumbo," "callaloo," and "creole." For this reason, Szwed, like Hall, prefers "creole" for the emergent products resulting from intercultural contact, precisely because it represents something new and calls into question concepts of descent and origin, because processes of creolization involve merging, dissolving, and ambiguous play that are decentered with no apparent fixed boundaries. It is organic to the Americas and the Caribbean. Szwed writes: "We benefit from a creolist view of society that rejects monolithic visions (even those that are pluralistic) of society as a sacred, political entity whose principal product is nationality, in favor of a notion of peoples in potentially equal, differing cultures, developing distinct ways of being and doing from ancestral sources, but also exchanging and sharing with each other and developing new forms, meanings, and interpretations."[13]

The key to understanding the processes of creolization is the specificity of the historical moment in which the cultural mixing takes place. In the case of early jazz, it was the confluence of slavery, colonialism, plantation life, postcolonialism, emancipation, and the tensions associated with processes connected to the indigenization of subjects with unequal power relations. It is where a new indigenous vernacular space, marked by a fusion of cultural elements drawn from the originating cultures, was permanently translated and indelibly marked upon every future iteration of the music.[14] Jazz is an expressive outcome of such encounters and processes.

Conceiving of New Orleans as a creolized space[15] and jazz as a creolized mode of expression, two distinct yet related narratives of the black Atlantic[16] are conjoined, that of the black Caribbean and that of black America (North, Central, and South). New Orleans is the key historical link between the two—connecting what I conceive of as a "black archipelago," which extends north along the Mississippi River, spreading across the United States with New York City as a centralized node, and extending down to the far reaches of South America, all by way of the Caribbean.[17] When expanding the conception of blackness in jazz beyond the confines of

United States, the limitations of the black/white binary, so prominent in the (US) cultural conceptions of race, become apparent. Delving into the interconnected reverberations of the cultural complexities involved in the music's history paints a different more nuanced picture. Using Hall's work as impetus, I seek to transform discussions of race from a simplified black/white binary so prominent in jazz writing into a black/brown/tan/mulatto/beige/white milieu, a blurred space that more closely resembles where jazz resides. I seek to expand the discussion of nation and place, recognizing the myriad diverse artistic spaces that were essential in the emergence of jazz and its continued development. Opening a more inclusive space, while attending to the complexities involved in the relationships of race, ethnicity, nation, and place, better recognizes the nuance and richness of the music's past and present.

The topic of Latin jazz is historically and geographically broad. Instead of attempting to superficially cover much of the music's history and global reach, I have chosen a more incisive tack, one that takes inspiration from scholar George Lipsitz's notion of "counter memory."

For Lipsitz, counter memory is a way of remembering and forgetting that starts with the local, the immediate, the personal, the particular, and the specific, then builds outward to reframe and refocus dominant historical narratives: "Counter memory looks to the past for hidden histories excluded from dominant narratives and forces revision of existing histories by supplying new perspectives about the past."[18] My research zeroes in on key musicians at pivotal moments who have defined and substantially impacted the development of the music despite the oppressed milieus in which they lived and worked. I focus on Latin jazz in New York City as my primary ethnographic site. In this way, New York as a creolized place, serves as a lens for issues that reverberate throughout the "black archipelago." New York–centricism, no doubt, is problematic when studying jazz as a global phenomenon, in that it cannot attend to locally inflected variations of Latin jazz iterations found throughout the world. However, since New York has been the most influential city in Latin jazz since the early twentieth century, carrying forward many of the traditions born and bred in New Orleans, and since much of jazz business and performance is centered in New York, I believe it can aptly serve as a productive microcosm for examining the wider global field. Further, the delimited scope of this study allows for delving deeper into specific issues that resonate globally. That said, much more work is indeed needed throughout the archipelago. Latin jazz scholarship is still in its early developmental stages.

* * *

My decision to focus on New York City also reflects my professional performance career. For the last thirty years, I have dedicated much of my artistic energy to performing and composing Latin jazz. I have led a New York City–based Latin jazz band, SYOTOS, since 1992. From 1992 to 2014, we held the longest weekly Latin jazz gig in the city's history, playing for twenty-two years consecutively. I have performed with almost every musician I discuss in this book, with the obvious exceptions of those who were no longer active when I arrived on the scene. I have performed on more than forty Latin jazz recordings, two of which received Grammy Awards and several others received Grammy nominations. I have toured internationally and extensively with Latin jazz groups. In fact, my first international performance tour was to El Salvador with trumpeter Frank Castaneda's Latin jazz group in 1988, just shortly after I had started playing Latin music while enrolled in New England Conservatory.

As a white musician born and raised in rural Ohio, steeped in blues and rock 'n' roll, and schooled in jazz and classical music, I had little exposure to Caribbean or Latin American music and culture before I began performing with salsa bands in Boston in the late 1980s. In Ohio, my only experience with Latin music was watching reruns of the *I Love Lucy* show and the one time I attended a Tito Puente performance at Peabody's Down Under, a local Cleveland music club. Reflecting back on those early introductions to Latin music, I realize that Desi Arnaz's on-air performances had almost no musical impact on me, except for introducing Cuban music as lighthearted and slightly comical entertainment. I sense that my impressions were not unique. Arnaz's role was important in that it exposed many people to some version of Cuban music, but it simultaneously caused harmful misconceptions that still remain today by masking the richness and depth of Cuba's musical traditions. It might have been the distancing effect of the black-and-white small-screen medium, couched in a sitcom with kitschy performances, more than the actual music that prevented me from connecting in a deeper way. The live performance of Puente was a whole different matter. I was immediately captivated by the mesmerizing harmonic vamps produced by pianist Sonny Bravo and bassist Bobby Rodriguez; the driving percussion produced by Puente's timbales, Johnny Rodriguez's bongos, and José Madera's congas; and the high-impact solos of saxophonists Mario Rivera and Bobby Porcelli. I was struck by how much groovier Santana's hit "Oye Como Va" sounded when played by Puente (who composed it). This strange but somehow familiar music resonated deeply within. In 1985, I did not imagine that within fifteen years, I would perform with Puente at Carnegie Hall, tour around the world with his band, come to understand that Santana had played "Oye Como Va" with a crossed-up clave that disrupted the rhythmic framework of the original, and grasp just how closely Puente's music was tied to the jazz and rock music that I had been listening to and playing for years.

When I played my first Latin dance gig in 1987, I felt like a complete outsider. But somehow my previous jazz training and my blues and rock performance experience eased my transition into the Latin music scene. It was an easy fit. My acceptance into the Latin dance scene was rather swift, attesting to a sincere openness of Caribbean and Latin American communities in Boston, and later in New York, to intercultural exchange. This is something for which I am most grateful. My acceptance was not unprecedented, though. Latin music bands in the United States typically have included white US-born horn players, a practice that was established in the 1940s during the mambo era. The expanded horn sections requiring a large supply of skilled players facilitated participation of many different ethnicities and cultural affiliations. In fact, arguably the most influential trombonist in Latin music was Barry Rogers, a longtime collaborator with Eddie Palmieri, who was of Jewish decent, born and raised in Brooklyn. I am grateful to him for paving the way for my participation.

The prominent role of the trombone and the captivating rhythms in Latin dance music compelled me to delve deeply into the study of the music. I soon began working several nights a week with a variety of Latin dance bands. Latin jazz, which combined the rhythms and performance conventions of Latin dance music with my jazz experience, was a logical next step in my exploration. It brought together two separate traditions that I loved (at least, at the time, I believed that they were separate). The ease with which I was able to perform Latin music, adapting quickly to the different rhythmic and aesthetic frameworks, made me pause and question why. Those first ponderings were the initial steps of a long research project that has now culminated in this book.

Shortly after embarking on serious study of Latin jazz, I became frustrated by how few resources were available and how little was written about the great Latin jazz musicians with whom I was performing. They were absent from most jazz textbooks, scholarly journals, and trade publications. Moreover, as I came to know and befriend many musicians from the Caribbean and Latin America, it was troubling to learn of their lack of opportunities in music scenes outside of Latin music. There was no reciprocating relationship to the one I enjoyed. There were few opportunities in the New York jazz scene for musicians from the Caribbean and Latin America. I felt compelled to do something to rectify this silencing and inequality. I decided to use my role as both musician and ethnomusicologist to document and advocate for change. Over the last years, some things have improved, but there is still much work to be done. I hope that this book can make a difference and provide wider recognition to the Latin jazz musicians so deserving of a place in jazz history.

The methodology I employ in this research adopts traditional modes of ethnomusicological inquiry by using performance as my central tool. This project does not solely draw upon this practice-based ethnographic framework; rather, I engage interdisciplinary strategies and historical research to yield more balanced and theoretically nuanced results in my analyses. Using my position as "constituent observer," I enter into areas of inquiry that are rarely touched upon in the scholarly literature, working from within musical arenas rather than from the outside looking in. My performance career serves as my entrée and my primary methodological strategy.

My central interests are at the heart of music making, where staged performance embodies the nexus of sound structure and social forces and where participants enact, imagine, construct, and maintain emergent identities and cultural affiliations. I am particularly focused on how discursive practices in performance events shape sound structure and aesthetics and, in turn, how sound can play an essential role in shaping cultural practices and lead to transformative change. At the same time, I feel it is essential to examine how present-day performance practices are historically situated, and thus I employ a "sonic archeological analysis" of performance events to demonstrate how resonances of the past (imagined or real) sonically shape our present sound environment.[19] Specifically, I have focused much of my effort on unpacking how processes of globalization, canonization, race relations, and genre construction are engaged, sounded out, and worked through in the act of making music and what insights those processes can offer into how societies are shaped. This book is built on my performance experience and explores deeply how Caribbean and Latin American music traditions are interconnected (in a Borgesian and deep structural sense) with music of the United States and, more specifically, jazz.

* * *

This book explores various theoretical framings as the primary avenue through which I approach a number of case studies. These frames, broadly speaking, include what I believe are the central tropes and social forces at play at the core of Latin jazz music making. They include the dynamics of intercultural exchange, the discursive practices associated with genre contestations, and the social forces involved in canonization. The beginning of this book maps out the various social terrains associated with Latin jazz and transparently demonstrates my particular biases, assumptions, and hypotheses. I connect how broader issues of economics, nation, race, and ethnicity are uniquely tied to various sonic manifestations and performance practices of Latin jazz throughout the twentieth century. The book then narrows its focus for each of the following chapters, highlighting historical moments, individual musicians, places, and events that have played key roles in the trajectory of this music.

In chapter 1, I explore how Latin jazz is positioned and named and the primary discursive contestations associated with the genre. I examine how musicians exert agency by manipulating generic boundaries as a negotiative tool.[20] With a focus on two prominent bandleaders as case studies, Arturo O'Farrill and Ray Barretto, I explore how discursive strategies, embodying a complex of subjectivities, serve as a lens into the fundamental political undergirding of intercultural production. What becomes apparent is that self-conceived notions held by musicians concerning how to label and perform this music prove to be neither static nor terminal in nature but rather must be imagined as mobile, fluid, and changeable, always strategic, and at times even seeming fickle. I explore the pendular, self-positioning discourse that makers of this music engage in, in order to navigate through and strategically position themselves within this at times adversarial milieu. I show how the politics of place, nation, class, economics, and race as well as the complex historical relationships inform their fluid dance of genre imaginings.

In chapter 2, I document the strong ties of the Caribbean and Latin America to the formative period of jazz and how that influence reverberated throughout the twentieth century. I argue that the strong foundational influence of Caribbean and Latin American music on pre-jazz styles makes the birth of jazz synchronous with the birth of Latin jazz. By building on the work of a number of scholars who have recently begun to tackle this complexity through historical studies of immigration patterns and the social and political development of New Orleans throughout the 1700s and 1800s and by conducting a sonic archeology of jazz styles throughout the twentieth century, reverberations of jazz's prehistory are uncovered and shown to resound loudly. Along with a discussion of the social history of New Orleans, I focus on the function of certain rhythmic cells in the jazz repertoire that are most typically associated with Caribbean and Latin American styles.

In chapter 3, I return to the discussion of "The Peanut Vendor" by using the song as a case study and lens into the New York City of the 1930s. I examine the role of the popular music industry in promoting "exotica" and "otherness" and how these practices established Cuban music and musicians as the domineering influence in mid-century Latin and jazz mixings. I explore the role of interculturality in 1930s New York jazz, challenging the traditional tropes found in historical narratives that posit jazz as a purely African American or North American music. A closer look at the contextual factors that led to these exchanges, I argue, calls for a rethinking of jazz as a transnational and global music. This chapter exposes the interracial, interethnic, international, and intercultural complexities and processes that undergird jazz performance practice and that serve as the primary driving forces in the evolution of the music. What becomes clear is that Caribbean and Latin American music and musicians have played significant roles in ways yet to be fully documented and understood.

Chapter 4 examines the relationship between African America, Latin America, and the Caribbean through the music and its associated performance practices realized on the stage of the Apollo Theater in Harlem from 1934 to the early 2000s. Through the lens of race, nation, and ethnicity, I explore the complex and often tenuous relations between the diverse peoples who colluded and collided on the stage of the Apollo to produce some of the most significant and influential contributions to popular cultural expression in the United States throughout the twentieth century. Though the Apollo is considered one of the most significant and influential venues in the twentieth century for African American music, studying the discourse and historical narratives concerning the theater's history and traditions reveals that the venue was also one of the most important Caribbean and Latin American stages in the United States throughout the century. Situated just blocks from one of the most vibrant Caribbean and Latin American neighborhoods in North America, Spanish Harlem or El Barrio, the Apollo was and continues to be a nexus for intercultural exchange between African American, Latin American, and Caribbean musics.

Chapter 5 discusses various ways the Caribbean and Latin American music styles continued to share a common history with jazz since through the 1940s to the 1960s, intersecting, cross-influencing, and at times seeming inseparable, as they have played seminal roles in each other's development. I explore three case studies: the collaboration of Dizzy Gillespie and Chano Pozo, Charlie Byrd and Stan Getz's *Jazz Samba* recording, and Mongo Santamaría's "Watermelon Man" recording. Yet in much of the jazz literature, these seminal roles have been diminished or downright ignored. The chapter explores the reasons for these omissions and the systematic "othering" of Latin jazz. I examine the forces at play in their continued exclusion, how this omission is tied to the economic marginalization of jazz, racism, nationalism, tensions between art and popular music, and canon construction, and I identify what is at stake when Latin jazz is included.

Chapter 6 is an ethnographic study of New York–based Latin jazz in the twenty-first century. Using five prominent bandleaders actively shaping the future of Latin jazz as case studies—Eddie Palmieri, Michele Rosewoman, Carlos Henríquez, Miguel Zenón, and Bobby Sanabria—I demonstrate how the historical specificities and developments discussed in the preceding chapters continue to reverberate and inform the music made in the present. Their voices and perspectives demonstrate how each of these musicians adopt unique strategies to navigate the terrain of inequity and adversity. They represent significant trends that will assert much influence on generations of musicians to come. Their combined perspectives suggest that Latin jazz is not, nor ever should have been, an "other jazz." Its presence can no longer be silenced or erased. All of the music and musicians associated with jazz deserve to be fully embraced and recognized.

Chapter 7 serves as the epilogue of this book and offers a new conception of jazz and Latin jazz that embraces a rhizomic model that accentuates the entanglement of the histories of the Caribbean and the Americas (North and South) and how all manifestations of jazz/Latin jazz are intercultural, transnational, and multivocal at their core. Conceived of in this way, Duke Ellington, Louis Armstrong, Tito Puente, Machito, Mario Bauzá, Dizzy Gillespie, Chano Pozo, and every other musician discussed in this book are unified and interconnected on the most fundamental and foundational level. The music is a product of the black, brown, tan, mulatto, beige, and white experience throughout the Americas and the Caribbean. By paying tribute to and celebrating the diversity of culture, experience, and perspectives that are foundational to jazz, the music's legacy is shown to transcend far beyond stylistic distinction, national borders, and the imposition of the black and white racial divide that has only served to maintain the status quo in the United States.

NOTES

1. Used by permission of Viking Books, an imprint of Penguin Publishing Group, a division of Penguin Random House LLC. All rights reserved. "The Cruel Redeemer Lazarus Morell," copyright © 1998 by Maria Kodama; translation copyright © 1998 by Penguin Random House LLC.; from *Collected Fictions*, vol. 3, by Jorge Luis Borges, translated by Andrew Hurley.

2. Roberts 1972, 39.

3. For more information about Azpiazú's first tour to New York City see Sublette 2004 and Powell 2007.

4. *Son pregón* is a variant of son, the predominant genre of Cuban popular dance music throughout the twentieth century. *Pregones* are melodically and topically based on the calls of street vendors and often feature sophisticated poetic constructs of double entendre and innuendo (see Díaz Ayala 1988).

5. Lomax (1950) 1973, 62.

6. For more information on Puerto Rican jazz musicians, see Serrano 2007.

7. Columbia Records (14241-D) and Paramount (DGF37).

8. Another important figure in this process of shifting the genre name to *Latin Jazz* is pianist George Shearing. A number of his albums released between 1957 and 1963, which were mostly Afro-Cuban-inflected jazz, included "Latin" instead of any reference to Cuba in their titles: *Latin Escapade* (Capitol T737, 1957), *Latin Lace* (Capitol T-1082, 1958), *Satin Latin* (MGM Records E4041, 1959), *Latin Affair* (Capitol T-1275, 1960), *Mood Latino* (Capitol ST1567, 1961), *Latin Rendezvous* (Capitol ST2326, 1963).

9. In chapter 1 of this volume, I explore the genre-naming contestations involved in Latin jazz and explore other labeling alternatives.

10. See Lomax 1950; Borneman 1969; Williams 1970; Fiehrer 1991; Gushee 1994; Washburne 1997; Ake 2002; and Brothers 2006.

11. Roberts 1979 provides one of the earliest examples of a writer exploring the "tinge." Note, however, that this publication came sixty-two years after the first jazz recording.

12. Hall 2003a.

13. Szwed 2005a, 233.

14. Hall 2003a.

15. See Hirsch and Logsdon 1992.

16. See Gilroy 1993a.

17. See Benítez-Rojo 1996 writing on the meta-archipelago of the Caribbean.

18. Lipsitz 1990, 213.

19. I use *performance practice* in this book not in the historical sense, as in the subdiscipline of historical musicology, but rather to refer to how musicians make music in the present; how they execute melodies, harmonies, rhythms, timbre, style, texts, embodied movements, and social contexts in performance; and how these conventions are intrinsically tied to genre and cultural affiliations.

20. See Bakhtin 1986; and Briggs and Bauman (1992) 2009.

WHY CALL IT LATIN JAZZ? AFRO-LATIN JAZZ, AFRO-CUBAN JAZZ, CUBOP, CARIBBEAN JAZZ, JAZZ LATIN, OR JUST . . . JAZZ

The Politics of Naming an Intercultural Music

BEGINNING IN THE mid-1990s, the growing appeal of Latin jazz prompted Wynton Marsalis, trumpeter and artistic director of Jazz at Lincoln Center, to program a number of Latin American- and Caribbean-themed concerts. They included "The Latin Tinge: Jazz Music and the Influence of Latin Rhythms" featuring Tito Puente, the Fort Apache Band, and Arturo Sandoval in March 1995; "Afro-Cuban Jazz" featuring Chico O'Farrill's Afro-Cuban Jazz Orchestra in November 1995; "Con Alma: The Latin Tinge in Big Band Jazz" in September 1998; and "The Spirit of Tito Puente" in November 2001 for the Jazz at Lincoln Center Annual Gala Concert.

At the 2001 Puente event, the Lincoln Center Jazz Orchestra (LCJO) and the Tito Puente Orchestra shared the stage, alternating numbers and at times performing together. Since Puente had passed away in 2000, his band was led by his longtime musical director José Madera and included seasoned veterans who had performed with Puente over the years, including saxophonists Mario Rivera, Bobby Porcelli, and Mitch Frohman; trumpeters Ray Vega and John Walsh; percussionist Johnny Rodriguez; pianist Sonny Bravo; bassist Ruben Rodriguez; and trombonists Lewis Kahn, Reynaldo Jorge, and myself. The LCJO was directed by Marsalis and included mostly younger accomplished musicians, none of whom had extensive experience playing Caribbean or Latin American music.

This concert was inspired by a collaborative recording Puente's band had done with the Buddy Morrow Big Band in 1960. The recording is titled *Revolving*

Latin Jazz. Christopher Washburne, Oxford University Press (2020). © Oxford University Press.
DOI: 10.1093/oso/9780195371628.001.0001

Bandstand and featured arrangements that seamlessly transition from swing to Latin rhythms.[1] Morrow's band was featured on the swing parts, Puente's band performed the Latin parts, and at times they played together. The bands were so well matched that it is difficult to hear the transitions between groups. Puente said that during the few live performances of the project, they would occasionally switch roles: "It was fun because my band always sounded just as good as Morrow's playing the swing parts, but his band could not play Latin that well."[2] History would repeat itself forty-one years later.

CASE STUDY 1: ARTURO O'FARRILL

During rehearsals for the 2001 concert, Marsalis became concerned about his band's lack of experience performing Latin music, so he hired Arturo O'Farrill, son of the influential Cuban composer and arranger Chico O'Farrill, as an assistant conductor and "Latin music coach" for his LCJO musicians. As work progressed with O'Farrill, Marsalis gained confidence in his band. During the final rehearsal, and to the surprise of the Puente musicians, Marsalis unilaterally decided to change plans and perform one of Puente's most famous originals, "Picadillo," solely with his own band instead of having Puente's band featured on that number. During the concert, the Puente veterans sat idly onstage watching as Marsalis's band struggled to execute the sharp rhythmic breaks that had made Puente famous among dancers. Immediately following this lackluster performance, the Puente band launched into a particularly inspired performance of the Latin jazz standard "Mambo Inn," which features both Latin and swing sections, leaving LCJO "in the dust," as the Puente musicians later proclaimed. It was apparent from the effusive response from the audience that the musicians were not the only ones who noticed the discrepancy between the two bands. (See Figure 1.1.)

Puente often complained of a double standard that required Latin musicians performing in the United States to have a strong grasp of jazz styles, while jazz players were not held to the same standard concerning their knowledge of Latin music.[3] Arranger and percussionist Madera concurs: "It is a well-known fact that a good jazz band cannot really play Latin dance music, but a good Latin big band, such as Machito or Puente or Tito Rodríguez could play jazz fairly well."[4] This disparity was clearly demonstrated that evening at Lincoln Center. Arturo O'Farrill recalls:

There was a benefit performance pairing Wynton's orchestra with Tito Puente's. Wynton had me lead a rehearsal of the Latin numbers. I wanted

FIGURE 1.1 The Tito Puente Orchestra (right) and the Lincoln Center Jazz Orchestra (left) with Wynton Marsalis (upper far left) and dancers performing at Avery Fisher Hall in November 2001 for the Jazz at Lincoln Center Annual Gala Concert. Photo © 2001 by Jack Vartoogian/ Front Row Photos.

them to play a Cuban phrase, but they just could not articulate it authentically. They would "jazz" it up. They could not "Afro-Cubanize" it. Wynton had this faraway look in his eye. I think that's when he realized that it takes a specialized group of musicians. It's a different approach—artistically, mentally, and emotionally.[5]

Shortly after the 2001 concert, Marsalis and the powers that drive Lincoln Center conceded the LCJO's lack of expertise and ability in performing Latin jazz and launched a second band in July 2002 that was solely dedicated to that body of music. O'Farrill was chosen to lead the new band. The programming at Lincoln Center is a powerful marketer for redisseminating the "jazz" word, especially through its effective educational programs. Marsalis and LCJO concertized internationally and presented numerous educational workshops. Similar programs were planned for O'Farrill's band. With unprecedented institutional support, O'Farrill was thrust from the shadow of his father into what was potentially the most powerful position in Latin jazz. Virtually overnight, this arena of jazz became historicized, worthy of preservation, and quasi–on par with the repertoire played by Marsalis's LCJO. Then came the problem of what to name this new band to differentiate it from Marsalis's group. The very choice of O'Farrill's leadership reflected the hegemonic position of Cuba in the development of the music throughout the twentieth century (O'Farrill is half Cuban and half Mexican and was raised in New York City). Cuba's influence was rooted in numerous historical factors, ranging from its rich musical heritage to a long economic relationship with the United States, its geographical proximity, the large Cuban immigration that brought numbers of exceptionally gifted and skilled performers, and of course, the success of that "deplorable rumba The Peanut Vendor." Further, Cuban musicians were some of the first important progenitors of pan-African explorations in jazz, prompting a number of intercultural collaborations that sought to sonically explore common musical heritages of African derived traditions. Jason Stanyek writes that it was Cuban percussionist Chano Pozo and trumpeter Dizzy Gillespie's musical ventures and "their ability to juxtapose different histories without sacrificing identities . . . as well as their reflexive use of notions of cultural difference as a basis of collaboration" that created the fulcrum of pan-Africanism and a dialogic space of interculturality in jazz.[6] Other Cuban musicians associated with these early intercultural explorations are Frank "Machito" Grillo, Mario Bauzá, and Chico O'Farrill (Arturo's father), among others.

Choosing the same instrumentation as the big band of Gillespie of the mid-1940s (that is, a jazz big band plus a three-piece Cuban percussion section) and hiring New York–based musicians seasoned in Afro-Cuban jazz styles, for all intents and purposes, O'Farrill's band was a fairly traditional Afro-Cuban jazz band. However, concerned with not promulgating a Cuban-centrism from such a powerful position, O'Farrill shied away from the more commonly used "Latin jazz" or "Afro-Cuban" labels and instead chose the name Lincoln Center's Afro-Latin Jazz Orchestra (LCALJO). O'Farrill said: "Wynton wanted 'Latin jazz' or 'Afro-Cuban' in the name of the band, but I did not think that these reflected the diversity of the music. So I chose a name that I had never heard used before in a band's name. As a Cuban, I find the Cuban-centrism offensive. It is a small view of the world. It does not reflect the global nature of the music. I have found great big-band traditions in Haiti, the Dominican Republic, and Mexico."[7]

Latin jazz, Afro-Cuban jazz, Cubop, Caribbean jazz, jazz Latin, and jazz are just a few examples of how this music has been labeled over the years. O'Farrill was cognizant of the implications and limitations of each. His naming predicament demonstrates how nationalistic, ethnic, geographic, and racial agendas inform discursive exercises of generic prescription. Moreover, the continual marginalization of the music heightened the stakes involved in the discourse concerning genre. The ramifications of nominal choices alone are significant in terms of the economic and cultural capital that each can potentially yield. Further, the burden of signification that each label carries, embodying a complex of subjectivities, yields productive analysis for scholarly inquiry, serving as a lens into the fundamental political undergirding of intercultural production. What becomes apparent is that self-conceived notions held by musicians concerning how to label this music prove to be neither static nor terminal in nature but rather must be imagined as mobile, fluid, and changeable, always strategic, and at times even seemingly fickle. In this chapter, I explore the pendular, self-positioning discourse that makers of this music engage, in order to navigate through and strategically position themselves within this at times adversarial milieu. I demonstrate that genres are not only performed but carefully imagined, constructed, and maintained in ways that reveal "the ideologies and power arrangements that underlie local impositions of generic order."[8] The politics of nation, class, economics, ethnicity, and race underpin a fluid dance of genre imaginings, as well as the complex relational dynamics of center and periphery, that is, mainstream and margin. Specifically, I examine two case studies of bandleaders who are positioned in divergent and revealing ways, namely, Arturo O'Farrill and Ray Barretto.

Before returning to the case studies, I want to explain how I am conceiving of the interactive social forces that undergird the music. The music and musicians associated with jazz and Caribbean and Latin American mixings operate on a stylistic continuum, with a sphere consisting of Caribbean and Latin American folk, traditional, dance, and popular forms, as well as their associated performance practices existing on one end of the spectrum and jazz forms and performance practices inhabiting the other (see Figure 1.2). These are obviously far from mutually exclusive generic entities, both having a closely shared history. Neither is bounded, and neither has an essentially pure or authentic past. In fact, there has been a continuous intercultural dialogue between practitioners of these styles since the inception of the music traditions we now locate under the auspices of the jazz tradition (roughly over the last hundred years). J. Lorand Matory has written about the misleading notions of Africa's unidirectional influence on diasporic styles, often conjured up solely to serve as root source material.[9] He critiques the limitation of such an outdated notion and instead points to the fundamentally dialogic

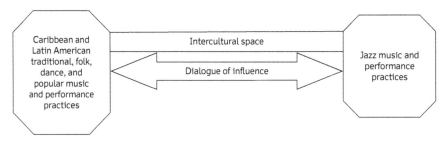

FIGURE 1.2 The Latin jazz continuum.

nature of the relationship between Africa on the one hand and the Americas and the Caribbean on the other, stating that these places have been and still remain in a state of constant exchange, rooted in real contacts by people and their artifacts operating within a living reciprocal relationship. The same can be said about the relationship of the musics located on this continuum, yet often with notions of Africa serving as the fundamental point of departure for intercultural exploration and stylistic mixing. It is the music that exists in between the two generic spheres located at either end of the continuum that I am presently focusing on, situated in the fluid intercultural space between both ends of the continuum, at times being weighted more heavily toward one side or the other but embodying enough stylistic diversity to be simultaneously excluded from both the "jazz" domain and the "Caribbean and Latin American" domain but indebted to and embedded in both, remaining in this dialectical middle ground, a multicultural one at that.[10]

Obviously, both spheres at the ends of this imagined continuum have at their core interculturality as a prominent productive and generative force. On the surface level one might ask, what isn't "intercultural music"? The pervasive and rather vague character of the term often reduces some of its explicatory power when considering the most basic meaning of the concept. What seems to be called for, though, is a theoretical specification of the very notion of interculturality. The truly intercultural artifact, I suggest, is not explicated by any simple reference to cross-generic or cross-stylistic origins (which would take us straight back to the stale insights of traditional historicist source studies) but that which retains at its core a certain level of fluidity and ambivalence in the way it is positioned in relation to these various cultural inputs. What is actually happening in this in-between shared space of real, lived experience is a dynamic field of forces at play where cultural difference and commonality are negotiated, battled, allied, and explored. In short, my use of the term "interculturality" must be seen in light of this dialectic movement between the two ends of the continuum.

At times, musicians delve into this interstitial space simply in search of fodder for innovation and change, exploring sonic alchemy, and some enter to assert their cultural roots; at other times, new affiliations and alliances are forged in this space fulfilling particular agendas. These agendas frequently are instigated by institutional urges of naming, labeling, and classifying, all of which are rather artificially static activities that tend to be relatively reductive in nature. But the naked fact of the functional necessity remains: due to economic and political pressures, we are repeatedly forced to specify generalities that essentialize music. Such classifying choices make a real difference in the lives of musicians, determining how they are produced, marketed, and programmed. Efficient labeling can mean the difference between making a living and not. Yet in reality, musicians rarely inhabit one place along this continuum but freely and fluidly migrate, changing positions even within one composition or from one song to the next. Thus, it is just as important to identify the counter-presence of resistance to generic sedimentation and acknowledge that most music thrives on the ability to remain operative and evasive within the fluidity of indeterminacy. Now, back to Arturo O'Farrill.

O'Farrill and Marsalis's "Afro-Latin" choice was particularly strategic, as it maintained the most commonly known label, "Latin jazz," as part of the name of the new band and at the same time referenced the concept of pan-Latinismo with "Latin" and pan-Africanism with the "Afro" prefix. The concept of pan-Latinismo was first associated with growing fervor for unity and ethnic revitalization that began in the 1960s among Latinx communities in the United States. In many ways, pan-Latinismo took inspiration from pan-Africanism, a unifying ideology and movement that promotes global solidarity among Africans and their descendants.[11] Both pan-Africanism and pan-Latinismo are intercultural concepts and frequent tropes that have been played out repeatedly as a way to negotiate a shared cultural space and are predicated on notions that the African diaspora and Latin American and Caribbean cultures, respectively, share essential commonalities. Both are part of a larger phenomenon of strategic pan-ethnic movements that have been fueled largely by political and economic pressures, promoting common unity for empowering a minority or marginalized group with mass mobilization toward a common goal. As such, both pan-Africanism and pan-Latinismo exist in constant tension with specific national, ethnic, class, and racial identification and distinction. By combining these two lineages, a shared sense of history and traditions are emphasized that bridge an ethno-racial divide within the United States, salving the wounds of two groups (black and Hispanic) that have often competed against each other for resources and opportunities. At the same time, the use of "Afro-Latin" suggests a challenge to an African American monopoly over blackness in the United States, acknowledging that race also matters within Latin American and Caribbean communities.[12]

Most important, the Afro-Latin appellation conjures a larger, more powerful coalition, that of a "circum-Atlantic" world. As Joseph Roach writes, "The concept of the circum-Atlantic world (as opposed to a transatlantic one) insists on the centrality of the diasporic and genocidal histories of Africa and the Americas, North and South, in the creation of the culture of modernity. In this sense, a New World was not discovered in the Caribbean, but was truly invented there."[13] This model of intercultural encounter offers an alternative historical narrative of American culture by emphasizing the truly astonishing multiplicity of cultural encounters in circum-Atlantic America and the adaptive creativity produced by the interactions of many peoples. Such a model provides a unifying conceptual framework for a black archipelago and a performance genealogy in which the perimeters of reciprocity become the center.[14]

Considering that Roach was writing about expressive culture in New Orleans, his discursive centering move comes uncomfortably close to challenging the origins of jazz as solely an expression of African American culture or, at least, calls for a redefinition of African American culture. Ironically, his centering strategy echoes those employed by Marsalis, who posits jazz as an essential and significant part of "American culture" (meaning the United States, in his case), a strategic and centering discourse that helped launched the Jazz at Lincoln Center program in the first place. Regardless of this possible ideological conflict with his boss, O'Farrill did not tread lightly in this regard, which may have contributed to the eventual demise of the Afro-Latin Jazz Orchestra (more on that later). O'Farrill stated, "The music [Latin jazz] was created here [in the United States], but it has the unfortunate stigma of being perceived as foreign. Latinos speak a different language, which makes it seem foreign to some people. It's not. It's as American as apple pie. Let's stop pretending it's a subset, a subgenre."[15] But then, a moment later in the same interview, a pendular discursive dance is revealed as O'Farrill backs away from following through with a logic that could have led to his own obsolescence at Lincoln Center: "Afro-Latin, Afro-Caribbean music is different enough from standard big band repertory that it deserves to be understood as a separate specialty and discipline."[16] This position, of course, strategically affirms the necessity for his LCALJO (see Figure 1.3) by emphasizing and maintaining a basic distinction between the music that was played by Marsalis's LCJO and that of O'Farrill's LCALJO. Thus, a specialized space on the continuum is reserved exclusively for "Afro-Latin jazz specialists," all the while maintaining the exclusive rights of Marsalis's band to the "jazz proper."

Acts of genre labeling are unavoidable necessities and serve the utilitarian needs of the economic strictures imposed by current music business practices involved in promotion, production, sales, and booking. However, I view this exercise of labeling as an act of discursive violence, because what it often cloaks and ignores, though simultaneously reflects, is a murkier layer located beneath the institutionalized game of naming, which involves the slippery complex of intercultural exchange. This exchange operates as a disruptive force, spawning new levels of heterogeneity and complexity, where commonalities are forged and collaborative space is created but where differences and diversities are de-emphasized or ignored and cultural specificity is erased. Thus, with all acts of naming, a discrepancy becomes apparent between actual lived experience and its idealized projection. In the case of the LCALJO, the concern for a delimited yet inclusive discourse had little specific relation to the diversity in cultural/national affiliations of the

FIGURE 1.3 Lincoln Center Afro-Latin Jazz Orchestra performing at Alice Tully Hall in 2002. From left to right: Mario Rivera, tenor; Arturo O'Farrill, piano; Erica von Kleist, alto; Bobby Porcelli, alto; Peter Brainin, tenor; Pablo Calogero, baritone; Milton Cardona, congas; Andy Gonzalez, bass; Jim Seeley, trumpet; Joe Gonzalez, percussion; Michael Philip Mossman, trumpet; John Walsh, trumpet; Ray Vega, trumpet; Felix Rivera, drums; Kenny Rampton, trumpet; Doug Purviance, bass trombone; Luis Bonilla, trombone; Reynaldo Jorge, trombone; Papo Vasquez, trombone. Photo © 2002 by Jack Vartoogian/Front Row Photos.

actual band members, which included six Puerto Ricans, two Dominicans, and one Costa Rican, along with eight Anglo Americans and one African American, all of whom resided permanently in the New York area.[17] O'Farrill was the only member with Cuban ancestry. No doubt, some of these musicians self-identified, to some extent, with the less specific Afro-Latin cultural affiliation, but certainly some did not. So on a basic participatory level, the Afro-Latin designation represented only a portion of the individual membership of the group. Moreover, most of the music they performed was firmly rooted in what is commonly referred to as Afro-Cuban traditions, and on the few occasions when non-Cuban-based music was programmed, they (quite revealingly) hired freelance ringers who specialized in those forms to compensate for the lack of expertise among the LCALJO members. Regardless, the discourse concerning the LCALJO remained strategically open throughout the group's tenure at Lincoln Center (2002–2007). The notion of required specialization and expertise served O'Farrill well by maintaining a privileged space for the LCALJO within the Jazz at Lincoln Center program; however, the broader implications of the band's name bore little resemblance to the actual music played.

There was also racial tension tied to the band's beginnings that is indicative of the systemic erasure and marginalization of the brown, tan, mulatto, and beige that this book addresses. O'Farrill relates:

> When Wynton came to the first rehearsal of the band, he asked me, 'Where are all the black people?' I wish I could hire all Latinos with dark skins, but that does not reflect who has made this music throughout history. You would often have Latin rhythm sections with Italian and Jewish horn sections. I base my hiring on artistic decisions. If there is a group of great Polish musicians who could play this music, I would have a bunch of Polish guys in the band. . . . Then maybe we would be playing Afro-polkas![18]

Marsalis's question suggests that his interpretation of "Afro" in the title simply meant "black," and the appearance of the new band required more black musicians to authentically stage the music. This was not the first time he had asserted such a position. In the beginnings of the LCJO, Marsalis had hired mostly young African American musicians in his band. When Lincoln Center board members first visited an early rehearsal, they requested that more diversity (meaning, where are all the white people?) be added to the band to better reflect their targeted audiences and subscription holders. According to several musicians, a white trombonist who was subbing during that particular rehearsal was subsequently hired as a permanent member of the band, while the African American musician he was replacing was fired. But what is most troubling is that in both cases, with the LCJO and the LCALJO, there were no questions posed, either by Marsalis or by the board members, about ethnicity, cultural affiliation, or nation. No member on the Lincoln Center board asked, "Where are all the Latinos?" because within the "jazz tradition," that has not been an issue or consideration. Not to mention that Marsalis had never hired a woman as a permanent member of the LCJO, and O'Farrill hired only one. For Marsalis, even Afro-Latin jazz was reduced to a black/white, US, male-centric thing. The imposition of a US-centric racial conception upon a music so closely tied to the Caribbean and Latin America, places with very different perspectives on race, represents a limited and narrow worldview of blackness and disregards the cultural history of the music that Marsalis and Lincoln Center sought to preserve. It is a violently reductive and irresponsible perspective, especially when asserted from the most powerful position in jazz. Here lies the heart of the problem that this book seeks to address. Even when Marsalis takes a positive step toward empowering Latin jazz, he simultaneously undermines the venture by the same forces and perspective that have marginalized the music for decades. Possibly, Marsalis believes that to do anything different would undermine his own centered position as arbiter for jazz, though I would argue that a global conception of blackness would only further empower his position, especially considering that he hails from the Caribbean city of New Orleans.

CASE STUDY 2: RAY BARRETTO

Conguero and bandleader Ray Barretto (Figure 1.4) provides a contrasting example to that of O'Farrill. Barretto led a hugely successful salsa band throughout the 1960s and '70s, but for the last twenty-five years of his life, he dedicated most of his performance energies to Latin jazz septets and sextets (Barretto passed away in 2006). He consciously hired musicians known as gifted jazz soloists but not considered specialists in Latin jazz, and he favored a traditional jazz quintet instrumentation (trumpet, saxophone, piano, bass, and drums) plus congas. Stylistically, his music inhabited a space on the continuum comparable to that of O'Farrill, favoring Afro-Cuban rhythms and styles. But as will be demonstrated, he positioned himself in a markedly different way.

FIGURE 1.4 Conguero Ray Barretto with bassist Jairo Moreno. Photo © 2011 by Enid Farber.

In 2003, Barretto was performing in France at the Jazz á Vienne Festival with his sextet. During a softer ballad, one drunken fan started shouting out requests for Barretto's most famous salsa tunes from the 1970s. Barretto attempted to ignore the disruption, but the fan's persistence caused him to stop the band. He exclaimed, "Do you see a singer onstage? Do you see timbales and bongos? This is a jazz band, and this is a jazz festival, and that is what we play . . . jazz! This music is for listening, not dancing. So shut up and listen, and you just might learn something." The fan became increasingly belligerent and continued to call out requests for salsa tunes, and several other audience members joined. Enraged, Barretto stood up (he was tall, with a muscular build, and had huge swollen hands, not an unassuming character) and shouted, to the audience's dismay, "Fuck you! And fuck all of France!" He then sat back down behind the congas and counted off the next tune, a straight-ahead swing tune with no pronounced Latin rhythms. According to Vince Cherico, who played drums for Barretto, the audience quickly simmered down by the end of that selection.[19] They played the rest of the concert without any further disruptions.

Barretto's downplaying of the Caribbean and Latin American influences heard in his music, while defending his musical choices to the French salsa fan, was the manifestation of a conscious self-positioning strategy that he employed on many occasions. For instance, when he negotiated for his annual week's engagement at the Blue Note Jazz Club in New York, he pleaded to share the bill with straight-ahead jazz musicians, such as Horace Silver or Johnny Griffin, and not to be paired with other musicians performing Latin jazz, such as Eddie Palmieri, Dave Valentine, or Poncho Sanchez. Regardless, he was rarely successful in this venture and mostly appeared on Latin-jazz-themed weeks. In other words, he did not want to be relegated to a separate marginalized space, or what he referred to as the "Latin jazz barrio."[20] He wanted his music to be included in the jazz sphere. This perspective is not surprising considering Barretto's background. Of Puerto Rican descent, born and raised in New York City, he musically matured playing next to jazz musicians, such as Philly Joe Jones, Art Taylor, Lou Donaldson, Red Garland, and Kenny Burrell. As a Nuyorican musician playing congas in the 1950s, an instrument that had not solidly become part of the jazz scene, inevitably he was seen as a liability. In spite of this, however, he developed a playing style that adapted itself to swing feels in an unprecedented way. The Cuban percussionists who came before him, such as Chano Pozo, had a comparatively more difficult time adapting to swing rhythm. Performing swing styles was not a regular part of their early musical experiences in Cuba. Barretto, on the other hand, was exposed early on to swing and even studied drum set. Though he never performed on drum set in his own bands, when he would come to the Latin jazz jam session I hosted for many years, he would frequently sit in on drums (never on congas) and he always requested that we play a medium swing jazz standard (never with a Latin rhythmic feel). In the liner notes of Red Garland's 1958 release *Manteca* (Prestige 7139), on which Barretto performs as a featured soloist, critic Ira Gitler attests to his accomplishments and adaptability: "A conga and the title might lead you to believe that this is an Afro-Cuban jazz album. This is not the case. Due to Barretto's rhythmic conception, the standards do not assume a Latin flavor, in spite of the instrument. Barretto, although of Latin descent, does not think, musically, like a Latin."

From this quote, we can surmise the type of racism the young Barretto faced and the hard work required to overcome such prejudice. In spite of his difficulties and his financially rewarding salsa career, he steadfastly believed that his alignment with jazz yielded greater prestige and cultural capital. One revealing example occurred while I was performing with his salsa band in California in 2003. I voiced a complaint with Barretto when the band did not receive individual hotel rooms, a common courtesy and something he could have easily lobbied for and obtained as the headliner at a large salsa festival. His response was, "What do you think this is? This is a salsa gig, not a jazz gig! In salsa, they do not treat musicians like they do in jazz. This is why I stopped playing salsa and prefer to play with my jazz band."[21] Regardless of the cause of this disparity in the treatment of musicians, for Barretto, there was a sharp social divide and disjuncture in the practices and expectations between the spheres associated with the continuum. And even though he was in a position to lobby for change, he chose not to and to maintain the status quo. Instead, he veered away from playing salsa (except when it financially made sense to be a salsa musician) and gravitated to jazz.

Though he referred to his own music as jazz, he did not disparage Latin jazz as a generic label. Rather, he was bothered by its misuse, especially by musicians who dabbled in mixtures but did not respect and maintain what Barretto referred to as the "true essence of both musical traditions" in their meldings. Though he did not provide specific names of musicians guilty of this misuse, he insisted, "I have no interest in being associated with those cats."[22] He felt that his music did represent the true essence of Latin jazz, but the widespread misrepresentation of the music by the industry and musicians forced him to distance himself from that label. He preferred to erase any doubt about where his music should be located: firmly within the jazz tradition. On the one hand, this clear distinction was at the expense of erasing his own rich cultural roots (at least discursively); on the other hand, it strategically centered Latin jazz as inseparable from the jazz tradition. And by extension, it served to acknowledge the significant contribution Caribbean and Latin American musicians have made to a music tradition held as something authentically "American."

* * *

Even though Caribbean and Latin American–inflected jazz styles have been performed since the birth of jazz, it was not until after Machito audaciously named his band the Afro-Cubans in 1940 and Gillespie coined the label "Cubop" for his collaborative work with Pozo in 1947 that musicians began to actively engage with the ideologies that underlie impositions of generic order associated with this body of music. During the postwar years, significant stylistic shifts reflected changes in the social landscape, particularly concerning issues of race, where members of an emboldened younger generation of innovative musicians were asserting difference and striving for artist independence from their forefathers. Labeling became an important signifying tool in this discourse. The term "Cubop" itself, an elision of "Cuba" and "bebop," symbolized a new type of musical integration. The appellation aptly symbolizes the new equipollent level of cross-cultural musical integration that differentiated the music from previous Cuban and jazz mixings (note the equal distribution of letters in this five-letter word, with two borrowed from each name along with sharing the middle letter). Gillespie and Pozo self-consciously foregrounded Cuban rhythms and styles in an unprecedented way which required jazz musicians to develop a deeper understanding and level of competency in Cuban styles. Machito's and Gillespie's influential positions ensured a significant presence of Caribbean and Latin American jazz exploration for future generations; however, their insistence on alternative generic labels located their pan-African explorations as something related to but not a part of jazz, ensuring a sense of otherness and alterity for generations.

The labels "Cubop" and "Afro-Cuban jazz" predominated until the early 1960s, when the less specific label "Latin jazz" came into fashion. This change was solidified by the US embargo against Cuba, beginning in 1960, which prevented continued exchange with Cuban musicians, and by a number of musicians who began exploring and incorporating musical traditions from many other places throughout the Caribbean and Latin America. The broader term "Latin jazz" aptly captured the growing diversity in musical styles as well as the diminished role of Cuban musicians working abroad. Since the 1960s, various other labels that refer to specific national, racial, or generic traditions have been used, such as "Afro-Colombian jazz," "Brazilian jazz," "mambo jazz," "Afro-Caribbean jazz," and "Afro-Puerto Rican jazz," to name just a few, but none has been as widely used as "Latin jazz." Regardless, the body of music to which these labels refer has been systematically marginalized ever since the labeling began, evidenced by a separate Latin jazz

Grammy category, distinct radio programming formats, and separate programming slots for festivals, clubs, and concert series. Some might argue that a separate Latin jazz Grammy and separate radio and concert programming are triumphs
that represent wider recognition and acceptance. Indeed, three of Barretto's
recordings received nominations in the "Best Latin Jazz Recording" category (he
won a Grammy for "Best Tropical Latin Performance" in 1989 for the song "Ritmo
en el Corazón" with Celia Cruz), and O'Farrill won a Grammy for "Best Latin Jazz
Recording" in 2009 and 2015. Most likely, neither musician would have won or
been nominated without these specialized categories, so both benefited from
the music's marked otherness.[23] Regardless, O'Farrill's and Barretto's discursive
engagements with generic order are the result of the historical legacy of labeling
introduced by Machito and Gillespie and the resultant marginalization of music
associated with that body of music.

   This institutionalized differentiation has exposed the music at its very core, and
on a foundational level, to the dynamic tensions of center and periphery, mainstream and margins. In this case, I am conceiving of the center as a location of
empowerment, authority, a privileged place (imagined or real), in terms of economics, nationalism, or cultural capital, and the periphery as a marginal location
of a somewhat disempowered difference, alterity, and otherness. There is a reciprocal relationship between the two (one needing the other for its existence), sus-
tained by a dialogic flow of energy and influence. This relationship is not static
and can easily be flipped. Like polarized magnets, center and margins never exist
in the same space but constantly remain polar opposites and at times can change
positions. Henry Louis Gates Jr. writes:

> The threat to the margin comes not from assimilation or dissolution—from
> any attempt to denude it of its defiant alterity—but, on the contrary, from
> the center's attempts to preserve that [and contain] alterity, which results in
> the homogenization of the other as, simply, Other. The margin's resistance
> to such homogenization, in turn, takes the form of breeding new margins
> within margins, circles within circles; an ever-renewed process of differentia-
> tion, even fragmentation. . . . For the very logocentricity of the center has, at
> least in certain spheres, conferred special authority on the marginal voice.[24]

I think Gates's perspective succinctly captures how musicians navigate their
positions along the continuum (and in stark contrast to the violence of generic
labeling), fluidly moving from center to periphery or choosing to remain at the
margins using a discourse of alterity to claim power or create space for innovation.
For musicians, a centered position is not always the most conducive for creativity,

and many would agree with the observations of Mikhail Bakhtin that "the most intense and productive life of culture takes place on the boundaries."[25] Moreover, musicians often adopt multiple musical identifications or subject positions, which are in sharp contrast to the "apparent 'unities' of collective experience," and thus may inhabit several contrasting positions within an imagined center/periphery and mainstream/margins relational framework.[26]

Imagined within this fluid framework of center and periphery, both O'Farrill and Barretto, each in his own way, attempt to attain a privileged position through divergent inscriptions of the logic of empowerment. In both instances, quite obviously, the act of positioning has led to strategic advantages, even at the cost of erasure and cultural denial. In Barretto's case, the center to which he aspires is the jazz mainstream, wanting his Latin jazz to be undifferentiated rather than set apart. O'Farrill deliberately exploits a marginal position, invoking powerful tropes of alterity (pan-Africanism and pan-Latinismo) to add credence and accentuating the advantages his position can potentially yield. O'Farrill and Barretto shared similar goals, not only seeking better performance opportunities and recognition but also advocating against the continued marginalization of Latin jazz. Each chose to pursue these goals from a differing vantage within a center/periphery framework. In the end, one could argue that Barretto's strategy had a greater impact; however, in fairness to O'Farrill, who is still in mid-career, it may be too early to tell.

Barretto's untiring advocacy from stages across the world (the incident in France being one example) and his performances with a number of renowned jazz musicians culminated in one of the most prestigious jazz awards, a National Endowment for the Arts Jazz Master Award in 2006. This was quite a remarkable accomplishment, especially considering that since the program's inception in 1982, only four of the 144 Jazz Master Award recipients have been musicians who primarily played Caribbean and Latin American–inflected jazz (Paquito D'Rivera in 2005, Barretto in 2006, Cándido Camero in 2008, and Eddie Palmieri in 2013). The fact that all of these awards have been granted within the last few years is significant, representing not only the growing popularity of Latin jazz but possibly also a relational shift between center and periphery and the long-overdue recognition of the Caribbean and Latin American contribution to jazz.

Throughout his affiliation with Lincoln Center, O'Farrill continued to advocate for recognition, both in terms of Afro-Latin jazz's relationship to jazz and within the inter-institutional dynamics of the Jazz at Lincoln Center program. O'Farrill stated:

Latin jazz is a misnomer. It doesn't exist. It's part of the same tree as jazz. Jazz and Latin are intertwined in ways that nobody has yet to even understand. In the music drawn from Latin roots we can find keys to both jazz's past and its future. . . . [It is as] worthy of attention as any genre. In fact, in some ways it's more so because it is a music that harkens closer to Africa than anything else in the current jazz pantheon.[27]

Words such as these challenge jazz's status quo and represent O'Farrill's growing frustration at working from his marginalized position. According to several musicians in the LCALJO, who wished to remain anonymous because they still perform regularly with his band, O'Farrill grew increasingly frustrated in his relationship with Lincoln Center, feeling that the LCALJO was not enjoying the same touring schedule and opportunities, or receiving commensurate compensation, as Marsalis's LCJO. He believed that once again, this disparity was just one more example of continued marginalization of Latin jazz. O'Farrill lamented: "Ultimately, as in the larger American culture, the Latin group became nothing more than a stepchild" at Lincoln Center.[28] When he lobbied for greater opportunity and compensation, he was duly fired, and the LCALJO was discontinued. Latin jazz performances are still programmed at Lincoln Center, but freelance musicians are now hired for each performance. Paquito D'Rivera and bassist Carlos Henríquez are employed to serve as musical directors for the events. O'Farrill continues to lead the Afro Latin Jazz Orchestra under the auspices of his own nonprofit organization, the Afro Latin Jazz Alliance, and as of the writing of this book, they were performing a few times a year at New York's Symphony Space.

* * *

Fabian Holt observes: "At a basic level genre is a type of category that refers to a particular kind of music within a distinctive cultural web of production, circulation, and signification. That is to say, genre is not only 'in the music,' but also in the minds and bodies of particular groups of people who share certain conventions."[29] The cases of both Arturo O'Farrill and Ray Barretto demonstrate how, within a distinctive cultural web of production, musicians actively resist, collude, and navigate within the dynamics involved in the framework of center and periphery and how musical genre serves as a communicative field of action, a highly contested arena where ethnic, national, geographic, economic, social, and racial affiliations are forged and identifications are created and erased. Both O'Farrill and Barretto demonstrate how individuals embrace conflicting desires and multiple subjective modalities, or what Katherine Pratt Ewing identifies as "shifting selves." She writes: "The individual takes on a history or histories through the construction of narratives in conversation with an interlocutor, aligns itself with ideologies, becomes the 'subject' of an ideology."[30] Their strategic "shifts" were fueled by the continued marginalization of their music. Ultimately, O'Farrill and Barretto show how the marginalization of this music presents both advantages and disadvantages to the musicians who make it. Studying how they chose to position themselves along the continuum and the discursive strategies involved in acts of self-positioning provides an opportunity to witness the multiplicity and complexities involved in the processes of intercultural production.

NOTES

Portions of this chapter were published as Washburne 2012.

1. RCA Victor LSP-2299.
2. Personal communication with author, October 1999.
3. Personal communication with author, 1998.
4. Personal communication with author, 2001.
5. Blumenfeld 2008.
6. Stanyek 2004, 89.
7. Interview with author, December 9, 2005.
8. Briggs and Bauman (1992) 2009, 238.
9. Matory 1999.
10. Kevin Fellezs has observed a similar dynamic in his research on jazz fusion. He borrows Isabol Armstrong's concept of the "broken middle" to posit fusion as an "overlapping yet liminal space of contested, and never settled, priorities between two or more musical traditions," a space that has "creative tension" and "possibilities" that "arrive . . . in the efforts to occupy multiple, sometimes contradictory positions" (Fellezs 2011, 8–9).
11. For more on pan-Latinismo, see Padilla 1985.
12. Román and Flores 2010, 3.
13. Roach 1996, 4.
14. Ibid., 189.
15. Meredith 2007, 70.
16. Ibid.
17. The personnel did fluctuate throughout the band's tenure at Lincoln Center; however, the racial and ethnic balance remained fairly stable.
18. Interview with author, December 9, 2005.
19. Personal communication with author, November 4, 2003.
20. Personal communication with author, September 2005.
21. Personal communication with author, May 23, 2003.
22. Ibid.
23. More Grammy categories have led to more Caribbean and Latin American musicians being nominated for awards and greater recognition for both individual musicians and Latin and Caribbean music in general. However, the separate categories keep Latin music as something different and perpetuate the "othering." See chapter 5 for a more in-depth discussion of the Grammys and Latin jazz.
24. Gates 1992, 315.
25. Bakhtin 1986, 2.

26. Born and Hesmondhalgh 2000, 33.
27. Blumenfeld 2008.
28. Ibid.
29. Holt 2007, 2.
30. Ewing 1997, 35.

> Now in one of my earliest tunes, "New Orleans
> Blues," you can notice the Spanish tinge. In fact,
> if you can't manage to put tinges of Spanish in
> your tunes, you will never be able to get the right
> seasoning, I call it, for jazz.
> —JELLY ROLL MORTON

> The relentless search for purity of origins is a voyage
> not of discovery but of erasure."
> —JOSEPH ROACH[1]

2

CARIBBEAN AND LATIN AMERICAN REVERBERATIONS AND

THE FIRST BIRTH OF LATIN JAZZ

New Orleans and the Spanish Tinge

THE ORIGINS OF jazz have proved to be contentious among musicians, critics, and scholars alike, and until recently, the Caribbean and Latin American influence was often omitted, overlooked, erased, or downright ignored. But considering that the development of jazz is intrinsically tied to the unique cultural climate of New Orleans, a city that played a crucial role in the emergence of African American culture and its expressive forms, examining this complex urban milieu makes it possible to bring jazz antecedents into much sharper focus. However, unpacking the heterogeneity involved in African American culture and jazz, especially in places like New Orleans, is a difficult and delicate terrain to navigate. As Ingrid Monson observes: "At the heart of the problem is that the inability to recognize the heterogeneity of musical elements found in jazz improvisation is deeply related to the heterogeneity of African American cultural experience. The jazz experience has always been more varied and cosmopolitan than the many narratives that have been written about it."[2] This chapter seeks to unpack some of that heterogeneity and to specifically elucidate the strong ties of the Caribbean and Latin America to the formative period of jazz and how that influence reverberated throughout the twentieth century.[3] I argue that the strong foundational influence of Caribbean and Latin American music on pre-jazz styles makes the birth of jazz synchronous with the birth of Latin jazz. By building on the work of a number of scholars who have recently begun to tackle this complexity through historical studies of immigration patterns and the sociopolitical development of New Orleans throughout the

Latin Jazz. Christopher Washburne, Oxford University Press (2020). © Oxford University Press.
DOI: 10.1093/oso/9780195371628.001.0001

1700 and 1800s, and by conducting a sonic archeology of jazz styles throughout the twentieth century, reverberations of jazz's prehistory will be uncovered and shown to resound loudly. Along with a discussion of the social history of New Orleans, I focus on the function of certain rhythmic cells in the jazz repertoire that are most typically associated with Caribbean and Latin American styles to demonstrate their omnipresence as "cultural phantasms" of jazz's past.[4]

Inspired by the work of Joseph Roach (1996), I have chosen "reverberation" as a way to understand the presence of the Spanish tinge in jazz. In its most simple form, the root of the word, "reverb," refers to ambient room sound. Whether in a live performance or a digital holograph of a past performance, reverb is universally added to sound systems, recordings, and broadcasts. Reverb can create the feeling of being in the same room as the musicians—but not just any room, one that has been sonically tuned for an optimal listening experience. Even personal stereo systems and listening devices often come with settings that allow listeners to superimpose their own reverb preferences onto the music in order to sculpt a personalized listening experience. Reverb is an essential element in all musical production and performance. For this study, though, I build on this mundane use and conceive of reverberations as a broader multileveled encounter with sound structure and as a way of hearing. Common definitions of reverberation reveal various shades of meaning:

1. To echo repeatedly. To resound, re-echo. To send back, return.
2. To have a far-reaching or lasting impact, especially as a result of being circulated widely.
3. To be reflected repeatedly off different surfaces.
4. To cause sound to bounce back, turn back on itself.

I embrace these definitions to demonstrate how the social, cultural, racial, and economic pasts echo repeatedly in the present, how Caribbean and Latin American influence on jazz has a far-reaching and lasting impact, and how jazz's sound structure reflects, bounces back, and turns back on itself with various shades and inflections that guide and reflect how we hear.

NEW ORLEANS AND THE ORIGINS OF LATIN JAZZ

New Orleans provides the best illustration of jazz's relationship with the Caribbean and Latin America, as its unique mix of European, African, Native American, Caribbean, Latin American, Creole, and African American cultures provided a complexity and thickness of culture that assured early jazz a wealth of inspiration. The city's cultural diversity generated constant musical innovation throughout the eighteenth, nineteenth, and early twentieth centuries that reverberated outward and asserted significant influence internationally. Its "Caribbean flavor" distinguished it culturally from other North American cities. Being governed in turn by the French (1718–1762 and 1800–1803) and the Spanish (1762–1800), New Orleans was culturally and economically aligned with the French and Spanish colonies in the Caribbean and Latin America. As one of the largest ports in North America throughout the 1800s and with its geographical proximity to the Caribbean and Latin America, it served as a gateway for intercultural exchange with the global south.

Admittedly, though, a New Orleans–centric study is problematically reductive, as it does not attend to the broad geographical scope involved in the emergence of jazz and Latin jazz. However, New Orleans was a central node of innovation in early jazz, and the musicians from that city traveled widely, disseminating their localized inflections that greatly influenced what jazz and Latin jazz would become. I now turn to a historical discussion to illuminate the unique diversity of New Orleans and its connection to the Caribbean and Latin America.

COLONIAL NEW ORLEANS

The close relationship of New Orleans with the Caribbean began with the first wave of enslaved peoples to reach its port. According to Lyle Saxon, Edward Dreyer, and Robert Tallant, in 1716–1717, roughly 3,500 enslaved peoples arrived from the islands of Guadeloupe, Martinique, and Saint-Domingue (the island that is now Haiti and the Dominican Republic). This initial importation infused New Orleans and the Lower Mississippi Valley with a nascent Afro-Caribbean black population that established neo-African belief systems and practices rooted in what would become known as voodoo, a legacy that is still present in New Orleans today. The enslaved West Indian peoples also brought a number of Afro-Caribbean music and dance traditions that would play foundational roles in the public performances in Congo Square in the ensuing years.

By 1718, the French had established New Orleans as a central hub for their slave trade; however, they soon found the enslaved people from the West Indies to be rebellious and troublesome because of their shared religious and cultural practices and began importing people only directly from Senegambia in West Africa.[5] According to Gwendolyn Midlo Hall, this choice set the French slave trade in New Orleans uniquely apart from other locations in North America, since most enslaved peoples from Senegambia were Bambara, and as they quickly outnumbered the enslaved peoples from the West Indies, a resulting cohesive formative enslaved culture of the Mississippi Valley and the Gulf Coast emerged. Moreover, the newly arrived Bambara bolstered the cultural cohesion among the enslaved communities by adopting and propagating the Afro-Caribbean religious, music, and dance traditions established by the first wave of enslaved peoples from the West Indies. Because of their large numbers, enslaved Senegambians were able to retain more of their cultural practices and thus became influential in defining an emergent Afro-Creole culture in the region and shaping local practices in New Orleans.

The geographical and socioeconomic similarities of Senegambia and the Lower Mississippi Valley are striking, as both were located on large rivers that served as major thoroughfares and gateways for cross-cultural trade and exchange. It was familiar territory to the Bambara. Hall describes the culture and socioeconomic climate of Senegambia as a crossroads where an array of diverse peoples and cultures mixed. The peoples from the region were primarily merchant class and were adept at navigating cultural difference and adopting beneficial aspects of the cultures they encountered. They excelled in adaptability. Hall writes that New Orleans was similar to Senegambia as a crossroads "where the river, bayous, and the sea were open roads, where various nations ruled but the folk continued to reign. They [Bambara] turned inhospitable swamplands into a refuge for the independent, the defiant, and the creative 'unimportant' people who tore down barriers of language and culture."[6] Their abilities were especially useful in eighteenth-century New Orleans, which was experiencing a scarcity of food and other resources. The resilience of the Bambara people and their ability to adapt by using virtuosic improvisational skills all the while suffering the inhumane conditions of enslavement were remarkable and ultimately provided the space and impetus for the birth of many African American music traditions, including jazz and Latin jazz.

One prime example of the Bambara's cultural retention and adaptability was how they transformed public culture and space in New Orleans. The most significant location was Place des Negres, also known as La Place Publique and commonly referred to as Congo Square. Taking advantage of article 5 of the French Code Noir, which exempted enslaved peoples from forced labor on Sundays and religious holidays, Louis XIV's support for creating public culture and performance, and the French administration's laissez-faire attitudes toward public Sunday gatherings of enslaved people, the dominant and entrepreneurial merchant-class Bambara lobbied for and established open-air markets. According to Jerah Johnson, participating in the New Orleans market economy enabled them to become a self-supporting group, and selling foodstuff served a real social need in a city suffering from food shortages.[7] The markets began in the 1730s, moving from various places before settling in Congo Square. With the exception of several interruptions caused by US government-imposed regulations, the Sunday market gatherings continued until just prior to the Civil War.[8]

The tolerant attitudes of the authorities toward the Sunday markets and gatherings of enslaved peoples were more aligned with the Catholic colonies of the French, Spanish, and Portuguese than with the evangelical English and allowed for a public assertion and formulation of an emergent Afro-Creole culture. For Roach, Congo Square represented an "unofficially designated auditora of cultural self-enunciation," a place in which everyday practices and attitudes could be legitimated, brought out in the open, reinforced, celebrated, or intensified.[9] This was especially the case with the "by-products of the square's market function," the accompanying dance and music practices that sounded out a blending of diverse African traditions that morphed into new Afro-Creole expressions.[10] These expressions were foundational in African American culture and its future musical expressions.

The open and highly adaptable Afro-Creole culture of the enslaved peoples (informed by the dominant Bambara culture) and their insistence on publicly asserting their voice and cultural practices in the face of adversity later served as the foundational tenets of jazz, a music that continues to be the voice of their legacy. Both the centrality of improvisation and the openness of the jazz aesthetic to incorporate a wide range of influences stem from the types of resilient practices of early Afro-Creole and African American culture found in Congo Square. And that openness is precisely how the Caribbean and Latin America became so influential in the emergence of jazz. The Caribbean, in particular, played a significant role in the new formations of cultural expression enunciated and experienced in Congo Square as a direct result of the Spanish rule.

POSTCOLONIAL NEW ORLEANS

When Thomas Jefferson acquired the Louisiana Territory from France in 1803, New Orleans had just completed twenty-eight years under Spanish administration (1762–1800). The period of Spanish/Cuban rule was extremely influential in the development of New Orleans as a Caribbean city. Governed directly from Havana, many colonial policies from the island were transplanted, such as building codes and design, increased slave importation (according to Ned Sublette, only one slave ship from Africa had arrived in thirty-eight years prior to the Spanish administration), and the French Code Noir was less strictly enforced, enabling more enslaved peoples to purchase their freedom through the system of *coartación*.[11] New Orleans had the highest concentration of free persons of color in the antebellum South. Johnson observes: "It was during the Spanish rule that Louisiana's free people of color achieved sufficient numbers and political importance that enabled them to mature into a community."[12] In their writings stemming from their travels in 1831–1832, both Alexis de Tocqueville and Gustave de Beaumont noted the remarkable status and achievements of the free persons of color in New Orleans in comparison with the rest of the United States.

The Spanish rule significantly re-Africanized and further Caribbeanized New Orleans due to increased trading with the Spanish Caribbean and a significant increase in population of freed people of color and enslaved peoples coming from the Caribbean. The increased population intensified the African culture and the relative freedom with which it was publicly practiced, differentiating New Orleans from any other place in North America. Sublette writes that the period of Spanish rule represented a "Kongoization" of New Orleans that enriched the dominant Bambara culture and established a strong connection with the heavily Kongo-inflected culture of Saint-Domingue.[13] This was significant because in the first quarter of the nineteenth century, just after the Spanish relinquished rule to the French (who then transferred it to the United States), about half the residents of New Orleans had been born or previously lived in Saint-Domingue. During the Haitian slave uprisings in the 1790s, persons of mixed blood (estimates range from 10,000 to 30,000 people) fled to Cuba. Many remained there until the Napoleonic wars erupted between France and Spain in 1809. Because of their French ancestry, many were forced once again to seek refuge in a foreign land. New Orleans was an attractive locale because of its proximity, similarity in climate, and Caribbean flavor.

The sudden population increase had a profound impact on the cultural, political, and economic landscape of New Orleans and the surrounding region. In 1791, the city's population was 4,897, a number that included 1,490 former enslaved peoples freed as a result of *coartación*. In 1806, the population had increased to more than 12,000, and by 1810, it was 24,552.[14] Half of this number represented refugees fleeing from the Napoleonic wars, coming from Cuba, Haiti, and Jamaica, and included people of European descent, African descent, mixed ancestry, and 3,000 former enslaved people who fled to New Orleans after participating in the Haitian rebellion (the population of the entire Louisiana Territory grew to 76,476, half being enslaved). Writing in 1830, Francois Barbé-Marbois observed: "Louisiana has been enriched by the disasters of St. Domingo [sic], and the industry that formerly gave so much value to that island, now fertilizes the Valley of the Mississippi."[15] Unlike in other US cities, the unique environment of New Orleans enabled the newly arrived refugees to retain their native languages and cultivate their cultural traditions, infusing local music with French, creole, African, and Caribbean traditions.

The refugees from Saint-Domingue are another key to understanding the unique cultural climate of New Orleans that has persisted to the present day. After immigrating, many remained in New Orleans and, as a highly educated class, assumed prominent places within the social fabric of the city, ensuring their profound and lasting influence.[16] As Thomas Fiehrer states, "it is the exceptional character of Saint-Domingue society . . . that accounts in large measure for Louisiana's celebrated cultural singularity."[17] Carl Brasseaux and Glenn Conrad add that "the smoldering embers of island identity in the New Orleans" were never fully extinguished over the years within this community.[18] The newly arrived maintained their island identity by actively asserting their cultural traditions, beliefs, and practices in their new homeland, especially concerning race and class.

Throughout the colonial period, New Orleans maintained a multicaste society (whites, creoles, free persons of color, and the enslaved peoples) and a more nuanced conception of racial difference (black, creole, mulatto, white, etc.) typically found throughout the Spanish and French colonies in the Caribbean and Latin America. The Saint-Domingue refugees reinforced and perpetuated this racial structure. This greatly delayed the adoption of the black/white binary conception of race found in the rest of the United States. As the country was working on the statehood of the Louisiana Territory, the refugees resisted assimilation by outright asserting their difference, maintaining their linguistic, religious, and cultural practices and establishing strong social, political, and economic networks through Freemasonry. As Roach writes: "Louisiana participated in the formation of the complex identities of the circum-Caribbean rim, even as it negotiated its incremental assimilation into the hypothetical monoculture of Anglo North America."[19] The resistance of the refugees strengthened the "Caribbeanization" of New Orleans and its surrounding environs. One key to understanding the foundational roots of jazz is this resistance to a black/white binary of race, as it maintained a space for the complexity of culture in New Orleans that reflected how real experience was manifested in everyday life. And as will be demonstrated, it provided a space for the convergence of influence that ensured an important role of the Caribbean and Latin America in jazz.

Demonstrating their political influence, the refugees successfully pressured William C. C. Claibourne, governor of the Territory of Orleans, to petition the US House of Representatives to pass a bill in 1809 allowing for an exception to the Act Prohibiting Importation of Slaves to the United States, which had gone into effect in 1808. The exception's sole purpose was to enable the newly arriving white elite refugees from Saint-Domingue to maintain their social status and wealth.

This was the only exception granted and the last legal importation of enslaved people into the United States.[20] Sublette contends that in addition to this importation, a number of pirated slave ships were being brought to Louisiana into the 1810s, though they remained largely undocumented. Collectively, this last influx of African and Afro-Creole enslaved peoples, both legal and undocumented, made New Orleans more closely tied to African culture than any other place in North America and continued the re-Africanization and Kongoization processes of the city.[21] As Hall writes; "New Orleans was a town with loose, flexible race relations and . . . the socially chaotic condition prevailing in the colony contributed to an unusually cohesive and heavily Africanized enslaved culture—arguably the most Africanized enslaved culture in the United States."[22] The music and dance traditions cultivated in New Orleans by the Saint-Domingue refugees and their enslaved peoples fundamentally reshaped the musical landscape of the city and, arguably, the United States.

CARIBBEAN REVERBERATIONS OF SAINT-DOMINGUE AND CONGO SQUARE

The musical influence of the Saint-Domingue refugees was vast. The proliferation of French theater, French lyric opera, and French ballet performances in the early 1800s reflected their preferences. Haitian and Cuban practices were incorporated into Mardi Gras celebrations. Their influence can be directly heard in the accompanying three-beat rhythm (♩. ♩. ♩), or what is known as the *tresillo* in the Spanish Caribbean, used by the roaming Mardi Gras Indian gangs. They revitalized balls and more seedy forms of entertainment, supporting a vibrant nightlife associated with live music, bars, gambling, prostitution, and other forms of debauchery—a legacy that continues today. They imported and popularized the contredanse and passepied, along with the Cuban *contradanza* and *danzón* among New Orleans audiences. These styles provided some of the rhythmic foundations found in ragtime and early jazz that make up the Spanish tinge to which Jelly Roll Morton refers. And speaking of Morton, a number of their descendants had a profound impact on the music scene. Composer Louis Moreau Gottschalk, director of the New Orleans French Opera Louis Placide Canonge, and composer and pianist Jelly Roll Morton are three prominent examples.

The music and dance cultivated in the gatherings of enslaved peoples in Congo Square provided the most striking manifestations of the New Orleans Africanized culture and the re-Africanization and Caribbeanization processes associated with the influx of enslaved peoples from Saint-Domingue and other Caribbean islands.

Many of the dances and instruments performed in the square throughout the late 1700s and 1800s were creolized variants derived from West African traditions. However, their names and practices were found primarily among enslaved populations throughout the Caribbean. Examples include dances, such as the *bomba*, the juba, the *calenda* (a version of the contredanse), the *chica*, and the *bamboula*, and instruments, such as the *banza*, the *bamboula*, and the marimba. The route these styles and instruments took from West Africa to Congo Square was certainly by way of Cuba, Saint-Domingue, and other Caribbean islands, being locally inflected and transformed along the way.[23] This is significant when considering that Congo Square serves as symbolic place of origin for the emergence of African American cultural expression. As Johnson writes: "No other single spot has been more often mentioned in scholarly speculations about the origins of jazz." It is no surprise that in the late 1960s, the park was renamed Armstrong Park, as a tribute the city's most famous jazz musician, Louis Armstrong. Johnson also believes that the activities of Congo Square represent a major point of origin for modern American dance.[24]

What becomes clear is that the foundations of African American cultural expression cultivated in New Orleans, real and imagined, are intrinsically tied to the Caribbean in significant ways. By conducting a sonic archeology of the actual musical sounds heard in Congo Square and by tracing how small rhythmic gestures reverberate over time, the foundational influence of the Caribbean comes into sharper focus, and mere symbolism, though significant in and of itself, can be transcended.

THE BIRTH OF LATIN JAZZ

The Caribbean-inflected music heard in Congo Square continues to reverberate in many forms. A prime example is the *bamboula*, a dance and the name of the cylindrical drums that accompany the dance. The *bamboula* was as one of the most popular and long-lasting dances performed in Congo Square, with versions reported from the 1780s through the 1860s. The primary rhythm of the dance, and its most identifiable musical element, features a long-short-long-long pattern (♩. ♪ ♩ ♩), or what is now commonly identified either as the tango or the habanera rhythm. Sublette claims that the rhythm as well as the word "tango" were being used and associated with the *bamboula* in Congo Square as early as 1786.[25] Robert Farris Thompson has traced the rhythm to the Kongo peoples in Africa, and in the Kikongo language, it is referred to as *mbila a makinu*, which is an incitation to dance.[26] The ubiquity and importance of this rhythm throughout the Caribbean and Latin America indicate that *mbila a makinu* traveled to Congo Square and other places in the "New World," through slave-trading routes. John Szwed provides other musical genres where this rhythm is prominent, including Umbanda in Brazil, Kumina in Jamaica, voodoo in Haiti, *gwo-ka* in Guadelope, *biguine* in Martinique, and the music of the Gullah singers of coastal South Carolina and Georgia.[27] In New Orleans, its Kongolese origins proved familiar to the influx of enslaved peoples from Saint-Domingue, and this is the key to its longevity and popularity.

The *mbila a makinu* was heard in Congo Square and throughout the Caribbean and Latin America decades before the tango and habanera emerged in the mid-1800s as the national dance musics of Argentina and Cuba, respectively. The adoption of this creolized African element as the iconic rhythm for two nationalist expressions demonstrates how Creole elites from those countries chose to sonically assert their independence from their Spanish colonizers. Their choice of a rhythm associated with the *bamboula* ensured that their national music was sonically independent from European traditions. The subsequent exportation of these two commercially successful musics and dances, the tango and the habanera, ensured that this rhythm continued to be disseminated widely and to resound globally.

The rhythm's connection to early jazz styles can be traced directly to the popularity among New Orleans audiences in the mid- to late 1800s of the habanera, the tango, and other versions of the rhythm and dance rooted in locally inflected historical trajectories, such as the *tango brasiliero* that was popularized by Brazilian composer Ernesto Nazareth and later transformed into the maxixe. Classical composers, such as Louis Moreau Gottschalk (1829–1869) and Georges Bizet (1838–1875), began adopting the popular rhythm. Two prominent examples are Gottschalk's *Bamboula*, or *Danse des negres* (Opus 2 for piano, written in 1844–1845), which was based on the rhythm and melody heard in Congo Square, and Bizet's popular "Habanera" aria from his 1875 opera *Carmen*. The music of Gottschalk and Bizet, along with "dance band" renditions of habaneras and tangos, were influential among ragtime composers. The rhythm appears in a number of ragtime pieces in the early 1900s, including Scott Joplin's (1868–1917) composition *Solace (A Mexican Serenade)*, written in 1909.[28] Joplin's parenthetical title referencing Mexico indicates that he associated the rhythm with the music of the "Spanish speaking south." He even includes a triadic harmonized melody that captures the sound of trumpets typically heard in Mexican brass band music, such as mariachi and *banda*. *Solace* provides insight into how ragtime composers asserted a broad globalized perspective that embraced the complexity of influences so central to the emergence of African American musical expression. Their cosmopolitan approach to music making reflected an aesthetic forged by the Afro-Creole culture performed in Congo Square and served as another precursive iteration of the open system of influence so central to the jazz aesthetic. The ragtime composers also reinforced the presence of the Caribbean and Latin America in African American musical expression.

Congo Square and the colonial encounter involving the Caribbean and Latin America continued to resound loudly well into the twentieth century, with abundant reverberations of the *mbila a makinu*. In the earliest jazz styles, the rhythm's presence in ragtime, along with the popularity of the habanera and the tango dance in the United States, prompted many pre-jazz and early jazz composers to incorporate the rhythm. W. T. Francis (1859–1916), whom Jack Stewart labels "one of an unbroken line of pianists-composers-arrangers who form a link between Louis Moreau Gottschalk and Jelly Roll Morton," began incorporating Latin American influences into his own compositions in 1885, using the habanera bass line in his composition "The Cactus."[29] The rhythm can be heard in the introduction of W. C. Handy's (1873–1958) "St. Louis Blues" (1914), the chorus of his "Beale Street Blues" (1917), and the piano version of his "Memphis Blues" (1912). Handy claims that he was inspired to incorporate the rhythm when he noticed how positively audiences responded when his band performed Sebastian Iradier's (1809–1865) famous habanera "La Paloma" and William H. Tyers's (1876–1924) composition "Moari" in 1909 (the original uses the *tresillo* rhythm in the bass line and was inspired by a Samoan song, though Handy's band played it with the habanera rhythm). He wanted his own compositions to yield the same desired effect.[30] Preferring the "habanera" label and using it as an example of the "Spanish tinge" in jazz, Jelly Roll Morton (1890–1941) incorporated the rhythm into a number of his compositions, including "New Orleans Joys," "Mamanita," and "Spanish Swat."[31] And trombonist Emile Christian (1895–1973) plays the rhythm as the bass line to accompany the cornet and clarinet duets on the 1920 recording of "I Lost My Heart In Dixieland" by the Original Dixieland Jazz Band.[32]

The rhythm also reverberates far beyond the jazz tradition. For instance, New Orleans brass bands adopted it as one of the signature rhythmic figures in their second-line beat, the iconic rhythm of street celebrations and parades for more than one hundred years. Its presence can be heard in the rhythm and blues of the 1950s. And today it serves as the fundamental beat and the most identifiable musical feature in reggaeton and can be heard on a number of hip-hop recordings. Reverberations of Congo Square continue to intrinsically mark our everyday sonic landscapes.

The connections to the Caribbean and Latin America in New Orleans music traditions were further reinforced in the late 1800s and early 1900s by the growing popularity of Cuban and Mexican music. This popularity was promoted by frequent travel by New Orleans based musicians to Cuba and by the numerous Mexican bands that performed in the city. For instance, Gottschalk, who dedicated much of his professional energies to documenting local traditions throughout the Caribbean and incorporating them into his own compositions, was a key figure in popularizing Cuban music. His multiple visits to Cuba inspired his popular "Ojos criollos: Danse cubaine," published in 1860, and he helped introduce and popularize the *contradanzas, criollos*, habaneras, and *claves* of Cuban composer Manuel Saumell (1817–1870) and the *danzas* of composer Ignacio Maria Cervantes (1847–1905). These imported genres, distributed through sheet-music sales, reintroduced and repopularized a number of Afro-Caribbean rhythms in New Orleans that played foundational roles in pre-jazz and early jazz. In addition to the habanera rhythm, the rhythms associated with these genres included the *cinquillo* (also known as the quintolet in Haiti) (♩♪♩♪♩), the *tresillo* (♩.♩.♩), and the *clave* (|♩.♩.♩ | (♩.♩♩♩ ♩ |). The influence of Gottschalk, Saumell, and Cervantes on ragtime composers is most evident in their ubiquitous syncopated melodies that use *cinquillo, tresillo*, and *clave*-derived rhythms. Just two of numerous examples are Scott Joplin's "The Entertainer" (1902) and "Easy Winners" (1901). The juxtaposition of these Caribbean-inflected melodies played against straight eighth-note bass lines gave the music its "ragged"-sounding rhythms which prompted the genre's name.[33] The rhythms were adopted by early jazz composers as well and served as the basis for a number of dance crazes. For instance, the *cinquillo* rhythm prominent in *danzones* and *contradanzas* became the identifying rhythm of the cakewalk, an African American dance popular in the late 1880s. The remnants of the cakewalk still reverberate in the modern jazz lexicon as a rhythmic break used as a cliché jazz ending.[34] Another example is the dance and rhythm known as the Charleston, named after the popular composition written by Cecil Mack and Jimmy Johnson in 1923. The Charleston adopts and alters the *tresillo* rhythm, creating a new variation by using the first two notes and omitting the last. The three-note rhythm (♩.♩.♩) is reduced to just two notes (♩.♩.♩). Another factor in the popularity of Cuban music was that African American members of the Onward Brass Band (a well-known and popular New Orleans band) were stationed in Cuba as members of the 9th Volunteer Army Immune Band during the Spanish American War (1898–1899). Sublette suggests that this may be an important link for Cuban influence in early jazz styles, as their stay coincided with the popularity of *orquestas típicas* in Cuba, playing *danzones,* habaneras, and early son. Upon their return to New Orleans, they no doubt brought back some of what they had heard, reinforcing the influence of Cuban music.[35]

The popularity of Mexican music was connected to numerous performances by visiting bands and by the immigration of influential Mexican musicians. Stewart has documented a number of Mexican bands that regularly performed in New Orleans throughout the late 1880s and early 1900s. Two examples include the Eighth Cavalry Mexican Band, under the direction of Encarnación Payen, which played at the World's Industrial and Cotton Centennial Exposition in 1884, and the Mexican National Band, under the direction of Malquiades Campos, which played for Armistice Day in 1920. The growing popularity of the visiting bands prompted Junius Hart to launch his publishing company in 1885 specializing in arrangements and transcriptions of Mexican music. By 1888, his catalog had grown to include 1,688 Mexican titles, making the music easily accessible to New Orleans–based bands.[36] The *tresillo* rhythm's prominent role in Mexican music served to solidify its presence in early jazz. The Mexican influence can also be heard in what Stewart labels the "mariachi sound," which features triadic two-part writing for trumpets playing with a brilliant and forceful sound.[37] This aesthetic preference is evidenced by Joe "King" Oliver's hiring of Louis Armstrong as a second cornet player in his Creole Jazz Band in 1922. Armstrong was renowned for his remarkable big sound and bringing a new aesthetic to jazz trumpet playing.

The visiting Mexican bands ranged from large ensembles (as many as one hundred members) to *orquestas típicas* (which had similar instrumentation to early jazz bands), and some musicians eventually stayed behind and participated in the burgeoning New Orleans jazz scene. This wave of immigrating Mexican musicians reinforced the Latin America influence. Bruce Boyd Raeburn has noted the sizable Hispanic and Latino populations living among Sicilians, Afro-French creoles, and African Americans and their adeptness at interacting across the racial spectrum in New Orleans, especially in "ethnically-diverse 'crazy quilt' neighborhoods [such as Tremé] that stimulated cultural interaction and exchange."[38] Stewart claims that Mexican-born saxophonists Florencio Ramos (1861–1931) and Leonardo Vizcarra (1860–1923) were two of the earliest resident saxophonists in New Orleans and are credited for introducing the saxophone to early jazz.[39] The prominent Tio family of Mexican-American clarinet teachers taught many of the great jazz clarinetists and developed a special technique that transformed jazz clarinet playing.[40] The family included two brothers, Papa (Luis) Tio (1862–1922) and Lorenzo Tio Sr. (1867–1908), who were both born in Mexico, and Lorenzo Tio Jr. (1893–1933), who was born in New Orleans.[41] Their students included Sidney Bechet, Johnny Dodds, Omer Simeon, Barney Bigard, Jimmie Noone, and Louis Cottrell Jr., among many others.

* * *

With his "Spanish tinge" comment, Jelly Roll Morton chose to acknowledge the significant influence that "other" musics of the New World exerted on jazz, thereby challenging notions of American exceptionalism. But Morton was not the first to comment on the Spanish tinge. In 1898, African American composer Benjamin Harney published a book titled *Ben Harney's Rag Time Instructor*. In the introduction, he stated: "Ragtime or Negro dance time originally takes its initiative steps from Spanish music, or rather from Mexico, where it is known under the head and names of *Habanera, Danza, Seguidillo*, etc."[42] And in 1938, even Duke Ellington commented: "When I came into the world, Southern Negroes were expressing their feelings in rhythmic 'blues' in which Spanish syncopations had a part."[43] As Szwed writes: "What Jelly Roll [as well as Harney and Ellington] saw as an enduring and integral part of American music, later commentators would dismiss as an imported craze.... But in retrospect, it appears that Morton was correct. Those who ignored him erected a false evolutionary perspective that emphasized jazz as a radical break from the musical past, and by excluding the whole range of folk, ritual, and foreign musics from jazz history, all of the music of the United States was grossly oversimplified."[44]

Unpacking the Spanish tinge as a concept integral to jazz has been slow in coming. Morton, among others, discussed the Spanish tinge in the 1930s, but it was not until years later that scholars would begin to explore the significance of the concept. Writing in 1956, Marshall Stearns pioneered the acknowledgment of broader Caribbean influence on early jazz with a focus on the habanera rhythm, or what he labeled the *tangano* rhythm, and he identified the presence of various West Indian traditions in New Orleans and how they influenced early jazz.[45] Ernest Borneman, writing in the 1950s, and John Storm Roberts in the 1970s broadened the discussions and theories about the Spanish tinge, with Borneman focusing on creole motifs and beats and their connection to European colonial history and Roberts documenting how the influence manifests broadly across numerous musical styles in the United States.[46] In the 1990s, Lawrence Gushee and Fiehrer championed a "Spanish tinged hypothesis," which argued for considering the roots of jazz as "Afro-Latin-American."[47] And by the early 2000s, a larger number of scholars had contributed valuable insights into the Spanish tinge concept and its connection to New Orleans. For instance, David Ake explored the tinge's connection to the diversity of creole culture in New Orleans and how it disrupts notions of the black/white racial binary.[48] Charles Garrett builds on Ake's work and in studying Jelly Roll Morton demonstrates how the tinge extends beyond the incorporation of rhythmic cells and was fully incorporated into his repertoire and professional affiliations and integral to his own cultural self-identification.[49] Sublette and Pamela Smith document in great detail the tinge's connection to

Cuba.[50] Szwed explores the truly global implications and broad reach of the concept.[51] And the work of Raeburn comprehensively builds on this previous work and moves to adopt a more nuanced and complex conception of the Spanish tinge. He looks at specific musicians in New Orleans and their experiences in negotiating race, class, ethnicity, economics, and stylistic melding to demonstrate the complexity undergirding Morton's original statement. From Raeburn's perspective, the Spanish tinge not only is apparent in the rhythmic cells but also was a strategic tool used by New Orleans musicians as a "racial masquerade to thwart segregation when it got in the way of their musical interests." It also was a product of hybrid vernacular cultural systems "that informed the regional market and how they were used by musicians to exchange ideas and generate work" and as a "functional imperative" for musicians to employ whatever musical ideas and tools were necessary to provide a competitive edge and generate work.[52] The theoretical broadening of the Spanish tinge that this body of work represents enables a more nuanced perspective on African American culture and expression. It allows for a space for and acknowledgment of the brown, tan, beige, and mulatto in jazz and in the cultural landscape of the United States. Building on the work of these scholars, I now turn to more specific examples in jazz to demonstrate how the "foreign musics" continue to reverberate and trace how Caribbean and Latin American rhythms continue to resound in jazz throughout the music's first one hundred years.

THE REVERBERANT RHYTHMS

The Spanish tinge in jazz encompasses much more than rhythmic cells; however, they serve as a useful lens to uncover how the social, economic, and political histories of New Orleans are sonically embedded in music and how that past continues to reverberate from within the sonic landscape of jazz. The rhythmic cells that reverberate Caribbean and Latin American influence in jazz are interrelated in a number of ways suggesting a common source or lineage. Both the existence of habanera, *tresillo, cinquillo*, and *clave* types of rhythms throughout West Africa and the functional similarity of the *cinquillo* and the *clave* in Cuban and Haitian music to bell patterns in many West African music traditions as rhythmic organizing principles strongly point to origins in West Africa. Indeed, the *tresillo, cinquillo*, and *clave* share a common ancestor in the ubiquitous bell patterns found in West African music. An example is the following pattern in 12/8 meter: (♩♩♪♩♩♩♪) or [2 + 2 + (1 + 2) + 2 + (2 + 1)]. Like the bell patterns, the rhythmic cells all consist of groupings of threes and twos that divide measures unequally. The *cinquillo* has a [(2 + 1) + (2 + 1) + 2)] division of an eight-beat measure, the *tresillo* has a (3 + 3 + 2) division of an eight-beat measure, and the two-measure son *clave* has the *tresillo* in one measure with the other consisting of a quarter rest, followed by two quarter notes and a quarter rest (3 + 3 + 2) (2 + 2 + 2 + 2). The *clave* is most likely derived from the African bell pattern above. By replacing the eighth notes in the pattern with rests, the *clave* configuration in 6/8 is apparent (♩ ♩ 𝄾 ♩ ♩ ♩ 𝄾). A similar relationship is shared between the *tresillo* and the *cinquillo* rhythm. By omitting the second and fourth strokes of the *cinquillo*, the *tresillo* rhythm is revealed.

As rhythmic organizing principles, these rhythmic cells can serve as the scaffolding upon which all musical parts are built. They are the rhythms the musicians and dancers must feel internally throughout a performance in order to coordinate with one another (similar to feeling the beats 2 and 4 in swing). For instance, the *cinquillo* is central to the *danzón*; its Haitian relative and most likely its precursor, the quintolet, is key to many Haitian styles; and the *clave* is the predominant rhythmic organizing principle in a variety of Cuban music styles.

The etymology of *clave* is of interest to this study as it possibly provides a more direct connection of musical practice to the history of the slave trade. In Spanish, the word literally means key, clef, code, or keystone. Fernando Ortiz believed that the word *clave* was derived from *clavija*, meaning a wooden peg, reflecting the appearance of the instrument that plays the rhythm, called *claves*.[53] *Claves* are two wooden sticks that produce a high, piercing sound when hit against each other. *Clavija* is also the name of the wooden pegs that held the sails in place on ships from the colonial period. One theory of how this instrument came to play such a prominent role in Cuba was tied to the absence of drums on slave ships. Forcing the enslaved peoples to dance during the harsh transatlantic crossing was one strategy traders used to maintain the physical health of their captives. In lieu of drums, *clavijas* were used to play bell patterns to rhythmically organize the dance. In the colonies, this practice continued, and the rhythms morphed into what we recognize as *clave*.

The acknowledgment of all these rhythmic cells in pre-jazz and early jazz styles is nothing new; however, their connection to the Caribbean and Latin America is often overlooked or erased by both scholars and musicians attributing them as simply "African." As noted, they are certainly derived from West African music traditions; however, they were profoundly transformed in the Caribbean and Latin America before arriving in New Orleans. For example, when discussing the syncopation in the melody of Scott Joplin's "Maple Leaf Rag" (1899), Gunther Schuller draws upon the work of Borneman and boldly states: "Once again we encounter the polymetric—or in this case—bimetric approach of the African native forced into the simple 2/4 pattern of European marches. Ernest Borneman states quite accurately that this 3 + 3 + 2 pattern is 'unmistakably African in origin and approach.'"[54] Schuller's claims are typical of his era of research but also ironic considering that Borneman was an early champion of recognizing the Caribbean and Latin American influence and was one of the first to call for rethinking the historical study of jazz by approaching it as an "Afro-Latin music tradition." Borneman's argument was based on the numerous recordings throughout jazz history that incorporate "Creole beats" and "motifs," such as habanera, *cinquillo, tresillo*, and *clave*.[55] The decontextualized quoting of Borneman's perspective is one way the erasure of the Caribbean and Latin America is perpetuated. In another instance, Schuller identifies the *gankogui* pattern of the Ewe peoples of Ghana as the antecedent to the Charleston.[56] The *gankogui*'s 3 + 3 + 2 pattern is identical to the *tresillo* rhythm. By making this connection, whether valid of not, Schuller is omitting decades of the *tresillo*'s presence and transformations in New Orleans, which was more directly influential on jazz than a remote performance tradition in Ghana.

Bassist and educator Richard Davis echoed Schuller's point of view. When I studied jazz improvisation with Davis as an undergraduate at the University of Wisconsin, he began one lecture with this statement: "To play with the right swinging feel in jazz, you need to learn the Charleston rhythm. It is the fundamental root of swing." Davis later explained that he believed this rhythm was from Africa and was directly tied to the roots of jazz. As we collectively practiced soloing exclusively with this rhythm, my classmates and I were unaware of its significant history and how the rhythm reverberated a legacy connected to the Caribbean and Latin America. Davis is considered one of the most prominent jazz educators in the Midwest, and he taught at the university for close to forty years. How does such a message that omits the Caribbean and Latin American connection reverberate over time to the thousands of students in his classes, many of whom have become prominent jazz educators at universities across the United States? Another example is Benny Powell, trombonist with the Count Basie Orchestra. While commenting on improvising background figures behind soloists, or "riffing," with Basie's band, Powell stated: "The rhythms we played during the riffs were African. That is what is African about the music. They come from Africa." However, one of Basie's signature riffs, known as the "Woodchopper's Ball riff," which can be heard on his 1938 recording of "Doggin' Around," is identical to the *clave* rhythm.[57] When I suggested a possible Caribbean connection, Powell became more adamant and said that these rhythms in jazz have nothing to do with Cuba or the Caribbean.[58] I am not suggesting that Schuller, Davis, or Powell conspired to erase the Caribbean and Latin American influence in jazz through their assertions of an African lineage but rather that they were simply reiterating widely accepted perspectives that were shaped over time by a complex of issues tied to race, class, economics, ethnicity, and nationalism, among others. Nonetheless, perpetuating such a stance reverberates over time, resulting in misattribution and reductive simplification. This is how historical legacies are prone to erasure, forgetting, and fading over time. One aim of this study is to remember and to acknowledge. I now survey excerpts from the jazz repertoire throughout the twentieth century to illustrate the omnipresence of these rhythmic cells and the diversity of their use.

ANALYSIS OF THE MUSIC SOUND STRUCTURE

Certain aspects of jazz performance practice (e.g., individuality of expression, constant variation, sparing use of repetition, and patterns set up to be broken) inherently change the function of these rhythmic cells when heard in jazz, compared to their function in Caribbean and Latin American music, and manifest in a variety of ways. This is especially the case with *clave*, as its adherence is central to later distinctions between jazz and Latin jazz. In Cuban music, for instance, the rhythm and its governing rules are more strictly adhered to. In jazz, as discussed below, this is not the case.

Clave refers not only to the specific rhythmic patterns but also to the underlying rules that govern this organizing principle. Concerning these rules, Steven Cornelius uses the analogy of a keystone, the wedge-shaped stone that is placed at the top of an arch which locks all the other stones in place, to describe the function of the *clave* in relation to all the other parts in the music.[59] When the rhythmic structure of a composition fits into a configuration that does not clash or cross with the *clave*, the piece is said to be "in *clave*." The following general guidelines help determine if a musical phrase is in *clave* and, if so, to which measure of the *clave* it corresponds:

1. Accented notes correspond with one or all of the *clave* strokes.
2. No strong accents are played on a non-*clave* stroke beat if they are not balanced by equally strong accents on *clave* stroke beats.
3. The measures of the music alternate between an "on the beat" and a "syncopated beat" phrase or vice versa, similar to the *clave* pattern.
4. A phrase may still be considered in *clave* if the rhythm starts out clashing but eventually resolves strongly on a *clave* beat, creating rhythmic tension and resolution.[60]

Since the *clave* is two measures in length, either the three-stroke or the two-stroke measure can appear first, and they are labeled "3-2" or "2-3," accordingly.

The most common appearance of *clave* as a rhythmic organizing principle in jazz is found in the brief rhythmic breaks and common rhythms in many jazz settings. They are often played by a soloist or are arranged for the entire ensemble. Mark

FIGURE 2.1 Examples of commonly found jazz breaks within a 2-3 *clave* rhythm framework.

FIGURE 2.2 Drum-break introduction from Louis Armstrong's "Tiger Rag."

FIGURE 2.3 Piano comping rhythm from Miles Davis's "Two Bass Hit," fourth chorus, A section.

Gridley, in his widely used jazz textbook *Jazz Styles: History and Analysis*, provides a list of some of the most common syncopated rhythms found in jazz.[61] Although this list is not comprehensive, fifteen of his twenty-six examples correspond to the *clave* strokes, are considered to be in *clave,* and could easily be performed in a Cuban music setting. Several of those rhythms are notated in Figure 2.1. The corresponding *clave* rhythm appears on the top staff, with the rhythms appearing on the lower staffs. Note that each example has accented notes on *clave* beats. Another example is the drum-break introduction to Louis Armstrong's "Tiger Rag," where the accented beats correspond to *clave* strokes and the second measure is the *cinquillo* rhythm (Figure 2.2), a rhythm that also conforms to rules governing *clave.*[62]

The rhythmic cells also appear in "comping" patterns, the accompaniment to solos played by the rhythm section (piano, guitar, bass, and drums). Figure 2.3 is a frequently heard rhythmic phrase taken from Red Garland's piano comping on Miles Davis's "Two Bass Hit."[63] The first four measures are the *tresillo* pattern minus the last beat—the Charleston rhythm.

A third type of use occurs in repetitive horn riffs like the ones discussed above by Benny Powell. Figures 2.4 and 2.5 are two riffs played by the brass in the final two choruses of "Toby" recorded by the Bennie Moten band of the 1930s. In both examples, at least one rhythm from each bar corresponds to a *clave* stroke, and the second riff is the *cinquillo* rhythm minus the first note—the cakewalk rhythm.[64] The corresponding *clave* rhythm is notated on the second staff in both examples.

A fourth type of use is when the actual melody corresponds to the *clave* rhythm. Figure 2.6 shows the first eight bars of Duke Ellington, Irving Mills, and Henry Nemo's "Skrontch."[65] In 1938, it was the Cotton Club Parade's dance finale, with singer Ivie Anderson exhorting everyone to learn this new dance. It is unusual for a jazz composition to remain strictly within the *clave* configuration for such a long section. Perhaps this reflects Ellington's familiarity with Caribbean musical practices and a strategy to compete with the popularity of the *clave*-based conga dance craze of the late 1930s.

A more typical example is the melody of Thelonious Monk's "Rhythm-a-ning," which only partially adheres to *clave*.[66] The first half of the melody falls into the

FIGURE 2.4 First riff from the final chorus of the Bennie Moten Band's "Toby."

FIGURE 2.5 Second riff from the final chorus of the Bennie Moten Band's "Toby."

FIGURE 2.6 A section from the melody of Duke Ellington's "Skrontch."

FIGURE 2.7 First four measures of the melody of Thelonious Monk's "Rhythm-a-ning."

FIGURE 2.8 First four measures of the melody of Dizzy Gillespie's "Salt Peanuts."

FIGURE 2.9 First nine measures of Seymour Simons and Gerald Marks's "All of Me."

clave rhythm (Figure 2.7), but the second half of the A section and the entire B section avoid the *clave* configuration. Similarly, the main melodic figure from Dizzy Gillespie's "Salt Peanuts" is in *clave* (Figure 2.8).[67] This melodic phrase is one of the most frequently quoted motives in Latin jazz soloing. Its *clave* rhythm enables its adaptability to both jazz and Latin music settings, and playing it serves as a homage to a great musician who was an advocate for jazz and Caribbean music mixings.

The last type of use occurs in the phrasing that particular performers employ. One example is Armstrong's interpretive phrasing of the first eight measures of Seymour Simons and Gerald Marks's standard "All of Me."[68] Notice how the original rhythm of the melody (Figure 2.9) is transformed and performed with accents placed on beats that correspond to the *clave* rhythm (Figure 2.10). This example demonstrates the third guideline listed earlier, where the measures alternate between "on the beat" phrasing and more syncopated measures. Armstrong favored this formula throughout his career, both in the statement of melodies and in his solos. Peter Ecklund, among others, has observed Armstrong's penchant for "displacing the notes of the melody into rhythmic figures that cross the barlines, often in complex three against two patterns that can be found in Cuban music."[69]

FIGURE 2.10 First nine measures of Louis Armstrong's rendition of "All of Me."

FIGURE 2.11 First three measures of Jelly Roll Morton's introduction to "Maple Leaf Rag."

FIGURE 2.12 Main melodic motive from King Oliver's Creole Band's, "Jazzin' Babies Blues."

FIGURE 2.13 Main melodic motive from Miff Mole's Band's "Crazy Rhythm."

Another brief instance of this type of rhythmic phrasing occurs in Jelly Roll Morton's rendition of Scott Joplin's "Maple Leaf Rag," where *clave* figures are interspersed throughout. Figure 2.11 is from the introduction that Morton composed based on Joplin's original.[70]

Early jazz recordings provide the most examples of these rhythmic cells. Often the principal melodic figure of a composition fits the *clave* configuration. Because the composition was built around the motive, much of the performance had rhythms corresponding to the *clave* rhythm. Figure 2.12 and Figure 2.13 provide examples from the repertoire of King Oliver's Creole Band and Miff Mole's

Band, respectively, where the notated two-bar phrases are repeated frequently throughout the recordings.[71]

* * *

The Caribbean and Latin American influence extends far beyond the simple presence of rhythmic cells and into the realm of aesthetics involved in the jazz performance. Don Rouse has pointed out that on a substantial number of recordings, "the four-four rhythm precedes the all-out, ride-out, or 'hot' choruses in which the band reverts to Caribbean cross-rhythms."[72] In other words, the Caribbean and Latin American influence played a central role in early jazz's "hot aesthetic," that of building energy and excitement throughout a performance to entice dancers to take it to the next level. The most famous example is Armstrong's Hot Five 1926 recording of Kid Ory's "Muskrat Ramble," where the *tresillo* is the most prominent rhythm throughout the final chorus.[73] Though he did not identify the Caribbean or Latin America specifically, Martin Williams noted that the unique character of New Orleans music was specifically its "greater rhythmic resourcefulness," which contributed to "greater emotional range. . . . Thus in New Orleans jazz, African American music underwent an all important change which redirected its course and gave it a way to continue and grow. Of that much we can be certain."[74] Raeburn concurs, adding: "Morton's remarks on 'seasoning' may, in fact, have been referring to something more inchoate than the 'Spanish tinge' as we now conceive it, adumbrating a broader sensibility that later became standardized in jazz discourse as 'hot' (meaning exciting, expressive, and 'from the heart')."[75] In this light, it is not surprising that words such as "hot," "spicy," and "tasty" remain common descriptive terms for the preferred aesthetic in Cuban dance music.

Similar to the habanera rhythm, *clave* reverberates beyond jazz in other musical styles that emerged from the cultural milieu of New Orleans. For instance, Peter Narváez, writing about New Orleans blues traditions, states: "New Orleans was a gateway to the Caribbean and Latin America where barrelhouse and honky tonk blues pianists coexisted with their jazz and ragtime counterparts; its cosmopolitan milieu nurtured cultural distinctiveness that emerged in musical styles— one of these was a form of blues with the rhythmic underlay of *clave*."[76] Drummer Warren "Baby" Dodds also commented about the connection between the blues and the Caribbean and Latin American influence: "The Blues were played in New Orleans in the early days very, very slow . . . but in a Spanish rhythm."[77] Much like the *bamboula, clave*'s influential reach extends beyond blues into brass-band music and hip-hop as well, encompassing a truly wide stylistic swath.

* * *

The examples I have presented here represent only a minuscule portion of the repertoire where habanera, *clave, cinquillo,* and *tresillo* rhythms occur. The abundance of these rhythms dispels any notion that their presence is coincidental. The frequency of these rhythms in early jazz suggests that the Caribbean and Latin American influence was so tied to its developmental stages that the rhythms became a part of the rhythmic foundation of jazz. Over the years, jazz musicians have intuitively turned to these rhythms to provide rhythmic vitality, using phrases that were accepted as part of the jazz lexicon.

As jazz became less associated with dance throughout the twentieth century, the prominence of these rhythmic figures diminished. Early jazz and swing (1917–1945) provide countless examples, but with the advent of bebop, the rhythms were used less frequently, with the exception of music influenced by Gillespie's and Pozo's Cubop. Finding examples from the avant-garde of the 1960s and jazz fusion of the 1970s is considerably more difficult. The rhythms' waning presence in new jazz styles may merely point to other, more recent influences in this constantly evolving and globalized music tradition. Paul Berliner writes: "Just as jazz was born from an amalgam of African, European, and African American musical elements, it has continued the practice of absorbing different musical influences. Jazz remains a characteristically open music system capable of absorbing new traits without sacrificing its identity."[78] Note that once again, the Caribbean, Latin America, and any mention of Afro-Latin are absent in Berliner's description, even though he rightly points out the fundamental system that is responsible for bringing a wide range of influences into jazz in the first place, and it is also responsible for the ebb and flow of the presence of the rhythmic cells over time. At the same time, the variety of rhythmic gestures in jazz obviously points to more influences than just the Caribbean and Latin American rhythmic principles. I am not suggesting that the rhythm in jazz is solely Caribbean and Latin American but a statement that the rhythm in jazz solely is African is equally problematic and oversimplistic. Neither statement embraces the rich and complex social fabric that sonically reverberates every time jazz is played.

Gillespie and Pozo are often credited with bringing Afro-Cuban rhythms into jazz. Considering that Cuba had already played a significant role in the musical traditions of New Orleans for close to 175 years prior to the Gillespie and Pozo collaboration, it's more accurate to state that they revitalized the Caribbean and Latin American influence in jazz, amplifying the reverberations of its past influence. Trumpeter Wynton Marsalis concurs: Gillespie "didn't just represent what's modern either—the greatest artists have a dialogue with the entire history of the form, not just with those aspects that are prevalent in their particular time. That's the point of the entertaining he presented: Dizzy was trying to consolidate aspects of the jazz tradition. . . . It's like the Latin music he was into—that's always been in jazz, that's what Jelly Roll called 'the Spanish Tinge.' Dizzy opened up another audience for jazz by exploring it though, and he opened up jazz to something else."[79] As Marsalis's comment acknowledges, the birth of jazz and Latin jazz happened at the same time, not as separate entities (or twin siblings) but rather as one singular musical form. Jazz is a music that reverberates its legacy, the roots of which extend back to the first wave of enslaved peoples coming from the Caribbean in 1716.

NOTES

1. Roach 1966, 6.
2. Monson 1994, 311.
3. The chapter builds on some of my previously published research that can be found in Washburne 1997.
4. José Gonzalez Alcantud labels the reoccurring figures and sounds of Andalusia's Muslim history in music as "cultural phantasms" (Gonzalez Alcantud 2002).
5. Saxon, Dreyer, and Tallant (1945) 1987, 224–225.
6. Hall 1992b, 85, 87.
7. Johnson 1992, 18, 42.
8. See Cale 1971. See also Debien and Le Gardeur 1992.
9. Roach 1966, 28.
10. Johnson 1991, 121.
11. Sublette 2004, 106.
12. Johnson 1992, 52.
13. Sublette 2008, 105, 109.
14. Kendall 1922, 85. Natalie Dessens reports differing figures, with the population in 1785 as 5,028 and in 1810 as 17,242. She also reports that the Saint-Domingue refugees increased the white population by 43 percent, free people of color by 34 percent, and by 38 percent in the enslaved population. Despite their differences, both sources document a dramatic population increase. Dessens also claims that the first boat carrying the refugees reached New Orleans on May 12 1809, and by January 1810, a total of 9,059 refugees had arrived. Dessens 2007, 1, 27, 35.
15. Barbé-Marbois 1830, 354.
16. La Chance 1992, 259; Brasseaux and Conrad 1992, x.
17. Fiehrer 1992, 7.
18. Brasseaux and Conrad 1992, xviii.
19. Roach 1966, 10.
20. For more information, see La Chance 1992.
21. Sublette 2008, 265. John Hope Franklin estimates that up to 250,000 enslaved peoples were illegally imported into the United States between 1808 and the Civil War (Franklin 1948).
22. Hall 1992b, 64.
23. For more information about the dances in Congo Square, see Dessens 2007, 154; Fiehrer 1992, 24; Hunt 1988, 78; Stearns 1956, 27.
24. Johnson 1992, 3.
25. Sublette 2008, 123, 287.

26. Thompson 2005, 115.

27. Szwed 2005b.

28. Jelly Roll Morton's claim that Gottschalk's most popular operatic transcription "Miserere" was used in a cutting piece by ragtime players attests to the composer's influence. Starr 1995, 448.

29. Stewart 1994, 9.

30. Handy 1941, 97–98.

31. For more examples, see Szwed 2005b.

32. RCA Victor 815 (December 1, 1920).

33. The Cuban influence extends beyond these rhythms and can be heard in harmonic progressions and bass lines as well, but for the purposes of this chapter, I focus on rhythmic cells.

34. Stewart 1999.

35. Sublette 2004, 324–325.

36. Stewart 2007, 3, 6.

37. Ibid., 5.

38. Raeburn 2012, 23.

39. Stewart 2007, 4.

40. The technique combined the Albert fingering system with a double lip embouchure and the use of soft reeds.

41. Kinzer 1996, 279–283; Roberts 1972.

42. Roberts 1999, 10.

43. Ellington 1938, 14, 18.

44. Szwed 2005b.

45. Stearns 1956, 33.

46. Borneman 1959a; Borneman 1959b; Roberts 1979.

47. Gushee 1994; Fiehrer 1991.

48. Ake 2002.

49. Garrett 2008.

50. Sublette 2008; Smith 1986.

51. Szwed 2005a; Szwed 2005b.

52. Raeburn 2012.

53. Ortiz (1935) 1984.

54. Schuller 1968, 24.

55. Borneman 1959a; Borneman 1959b; Borneman 1969.

56. Schuller 1968, 19–20.

57. *The Smithsonian Collection of Classic Jazz, Volume 2* (RD 033-2 A5 19477), first issued on Decca 1965, matrix 63920-A.

58. Personal communication with author, 1995.

59. Cornelius 1991, 15.

60. For more on *clave*, see Washburne 2008.

61. Gridley 1978, 428–429.

62. Louis Armstrong, "Tiger Rag," *Ambassador Satch* (Columbia Records CL840, 1955).

63. Miles Davis, "Two Bass Hit," *Milestones* (Columbia Records CL 1193, 1958).

64. Bennie Moten, "Toby," *Count Basie in Kansas City: Bennie Moten's Great Band of 1930–1932* (RCA Victor LPV 514, 190, 1932).

65. Duke Ellington, "Skrontch," *Duke Ellington: An Explosion of Genius (1938–1940)* (Smithsonian Collection P6 15079 R018, 1938).

66. Thelonious Monk, "Rhythm-a-ning," *Criss Cross* (Columbia Records CK 48823, 1958).

67. Dizzy Gillespie, "Salt Peanuts" (Guild Records 1003, 1945).

68. Louis Armstrong, "All of Me," *Ambassador Satch* (Columbia Records CL 840, 1955).

69. Ecklund 2001, 96.

70. Jelly Roll Morton, "Maple Leaf Rag," *Smithsonian Collection of Classic Jazz* (Smithsonian Collection PC 11891).

71. King Oliver's Creole Band, "Jazzin' Babies Blues" (Okeh 4975, matrix 8403-A, 1923); and Miff Mole, "Crazy Rhythm," *Thesaurus of Classic Jazz Vol. 3* (Okeh 41098, matrix 400895-B, 1928).

72. Rouse n.d. Other examples he provides include "Hear Bouncing Around," "Louisiana Swing," and "Mamma's Gone, Goodbye" (Piron's New Orleans Orchestra, Victor and Okeh, 1923); "New Orleans Stomp," "Ain't Gonna Tell Nobody," and "Buddy's Habits" (King Oliver's Jazz Band, Columbia and Okeh, 1923); "Frankie and Johnny" (Fate Marable, Okeh, 1924); and "Sweet Mumtaz" (Russell's Hot Six, Vocalion 1010, 1926).

73. Louis Armstrong's Hot Five, "Muskrat Ramble" (Okeh, matrix 9538, 1926).

74. Williams 1967, xiii.

75. Raeburn 2012, 29.

76. Narváez 1994, 219.

77. Gara 1992, 11.

78. Berliner 1994, 489.

79. Mandel 1993, 26.

3

THE SECOND BIRTH OF LATIN JAZZ

Louis Armstrong and Duke Ellington Do the Rumba

THROUGHOUT THE TWENTIETH century, musicians from the Caribbean, Latin America, and the United States turned to one another for innovative inspiration. Their long-term interrelationship was rooted in a complex of social factors that colored their intercultural exchanges and how people have thought about them. I now return to "The Peanut Vendor" to explore one such exchange. The performance of Don Azpiazú and his Havana Casino Orchestra at the RKO Palace Theater in 1930 and RCA Victor's subsequent release of Azpiazú's version of "The Peanut Vendor" profoundly changed the course of jazz. The successes of the concert and the recording provided the groundwork for what would later be identified as Latin jazz and reinvigorated the long-established intercultural connection between Havana and New York City.

Using "The Peanut Vendor" as a case study, I explore the role of interculturality in 1930s New York jazz, challenging the traditional tropes found in historical narratives that posit jazz as a purely African American or North American music. A closer look at the contextual factors that led to these exchanges, I argue, calls for a rethinking of jazz as a transnational and global music. As Jerome Harris writes, "Given the multicultural elements that underlie both jazz and the country in which it developed, perhaps the image of jazz as exclusively black . . . has never completely matched the reality."[1] This chapter exposes the interracial, interethnic, international, and intercultural complexities and processes that undergird jazz performance practice and that serve as the primary driving forces in the evolution of the music. What will become clear is that Caribbean and Latin American music and musicians have played significant roles in ways yet to be fully documented and understood.

Latin Jazz. Christopher Washburne, Oxford University Press (2020). © Oxford University Press.
DOI: 10.1093/oso/9780195371628.001.0001

This chapter stands in clear opposition to much early jazz research which is colored by political, ethnic, and romanticizing agendas that disguised much of the complexities involved in jazz music production. Robert Walser has observed: "Musicological treatments of jazz have been chiefly devoted to legitimatization—the main argument having been that jazz is worthwhile because its improvised solos demonstrate organic unity and motivic coherence. . . . Organicism and the elevation of jazz musicians to the status of artist served as a way for writers to approach jazz from a modernist stance—art for art's sake."[2] Composer, conductor, and jazz scholar Gunther Schuller provides a prime example. Schuller's strategy was to demonstrate how jazz musicians adopted similar techniques and processes of the "great" classical composers of the Western canon. For instance, he presented saxophonist Sonny Rollins as a virtuosic improvising composer ("composing in real time"), analyzing the uncanny motivic coherence and development built into his improvisations.[3] Duke Ellington, on the other hand, is presented as a prolific composer of extended works, on par with the great composers of the Austro-German tradition because of his use of compositional techniques and forms associated with classical music (e.g., fantasies, symphonies, concertos, etc.).[4] Schuller's approach was good-intentioned and reflective of the early generation of jazz scholars/writers who were fierce advocates for the acceptance of African American music and musicians as legitimate objects for serious study.

The battle for the recognition of jazz as art, as serious artistic expression, and as a valuable cultural contribution was long and hard fought. The earliest Ph.D. dissertations on jazz were not produced until the 1970s, more than fifty years after the release of the first jazz recordings. Schuller was on the forefront of this struggle. In 1969, as the newly appointed president of New England Conservatory in Boston (his tenure lasted from 1967 to 1977), he established the first degree-granting jazz studies program at a major conservatory and a pioneering Third Stream Studies program that explored the melding of jazz and classical traditions.[5] His Eurocentric approach to jazz analysis served him well, as it bridged cultural and disciplinary divides, easing the resistance from musicologists and the board of trustees at an institution that had exclusively offered classical-music training for years. In many regards, his strategy was successful beyond the confines of New England Conservatory, as his work and programs contributed to the eventual inclusion of jazz in the academy at large (note the numerous jazz studies programs now at universities and conservatories around the world) and the regular jazz programming at many institutions associated with classical music, such as Lincoln Center, Carnegie Hall, and the Kennedy Center. These changes are worthy of celebration, and early jazz scholars deserve credit for their contributions to the cause. At the same time, however, we must not lose sight of the problematic limitations and consequences of this type of jazz scholarship, especially concerning its impact on Latin jazz.

Schuller's analyses, like much of early jazz scholarship, impose a methodology rooted in Western classical music traditions and a Eurocentric value system and philosophy of artistic expression that are problematically narrow, myopic, and arguably racist.[6] It results in much reductive distortion and erasure, especially in regard to Latin jazz and to musicians from the Caribbean and Latin America who are rarely mentioned in the writings of Schuller (and with very few exceptions, just about every other jazz writer working before the 1990s). Their collective work focuses on only a small and narrow part of jazz, and the portion it does address is filtered and predetermined through the privilege of the (mostly) white male writers. The voices of the musicians remain colonially silent. Early jazz scholarship is yet another white (mis)appropriation of black music. What is absent is a consideration of contextual, discursive, and social forces, especially those that seem to counter a conception of jazz as art, as intellectual, as purely African American, or as an exclusively American music. Processes of globalization, economics, interculturality, and the role of popular culture, in turn, are downplayed or outright ignored. The repercussions of the limited purview abound, especially concerning Latin jazz. When jazz programs began developing at universities and conservatories in the wake of Schuller's influence, no Latin jazz ensembles or courses specifically focused on Latin jazz were included; instead, big bands and small combos focused on straight-ahead, bop, modal, and free jazz proliferated. Early jazz history textbooks excluded any mention of Latin jazz or musicians who dedicated much of their professional lives to the music. The inclusion of Latin jazz in higher education did not appear with any regularity until the late 1990s, more than sixty years after "The Peanut Vendor" was recorded. And still today, these ensembles and courses tend not to be part of the required curricula; rather, they remain mere optional electives.

Ronald Radano and Philip Bohlman offer a solution to counter these past methodological trends. They call for a new musicological approach that does not disavow past legacies but rather embraces the "modes of critical reflection and analytical rigor" that older models yield. At the same they advocate for establishing a new relation to the prior racial supremacy by adopting "a darker complected, self-reflexive avenue of exploration of a mulatto 'new.'"[7] With Radano and Bohlman's suggestion in mind, I revisit the singular event of the Azpiazú concert and the reverberations of its immediate aftermath and propose a new reading from a contextualist point of view that encompasses a multilayered historical and social perspective, a reframing with an examination of the contexts from which the event emerged. I conduct a sonic archeological analysis to demonstrate how, on a granular level, jazz resounds its transnational and intercultural past and how its open-ended system of production functions and serves to provide the music with innovative vitality. I begin with an exploration of the contextual factors that contributed to the success of "The Peanut Vendor" and then proceed to the analysis of the music's structure.

CASE STUDY 3: DON AZPIAZÚ AND "THE PEANUT VENDOR"

As demonstrated in chapter 2, due to their geographical proximity, Cuba and the United States maintained strong economic and intercultural ties for hundreds of years. By the late 1800s, robust trade between the port cities of Havana and New Orleans, along with growing international sheet-music sales, had introduced Cuban music genres, such as the habanera and the *danzón*, to a fairly broad audience across the United States. The relationship between the music of Cuba and that of the United States was renewed and further bolstered by the new developments in networks of exchange of the early twentieth century. This was especially the case for music, because by the late 1920s, both Havana and New York had become important centers for the international music industry.

Developments in transnational dissemination networks (radio, film, and the recording industry) and in transportation, trade, and communication accelerated the international exchange of musical traditions and ideas. Consuming, performing, and dancing to popular music coming from "faraway places" (other than Western Europe), became more the norm than the exception, as an unprecedented access was facilitated through mass media, tourism, and travel. Cuba's proximity made it one of the most convenient and familiar "faraway places," and subsequently, it became the most popular "exotic" music in the United States, and also in Europe, by the end of the 1920s. Exploring how Cuba's music traditions, when transplanted in new cultural contexts, were reproduced and subsequently reimagined, mistranslated, and refashioned prove illuminating. In the analysis that follows, I trace the acoustic dislocation, respatialization, and recontextualization of "The Peanut Vendor," or what Steven Feld refers to as "schizmogenesis," to demonstrate how race, otherness, and interculturality undergird the reimagining process.[8]

In the 1920s, the symbiotic relationship between Cuba and the United States deepened in profound ways as performance opportunities in Havana grew for bands based in US, catering to a newly established and thriving tourist industry. Resorts typically featured a mix of performers from the United States and Cuba.

Havana was introduced to the newest jazz and popular music styles from the United States, which, in turn, spawned a number of highly successful local jazz bands and a variety of early Cuban music and jazz mixings.[9] At the same time, many Cuban-based bands traveled to New York City to record and perform in Spanish Harlem, infusing New York with the newest Cuban dances and styles.[10] A significant number of Cuban musicians stayed, emigrating to the United States and becoming active in the New York music scene. These developments established an unprecedented and vibrant feedback loop of cross-influence and cross-fertilization that profoundly impacted the music in both locales. Don Azpiazú and his Casino Orchestra and his performance practices were products of this deepened feedback loop of influence.

Leading up to April 26, 1930, the date of the Azpiazú performance at the RKO Palace Theater in New York, there was growing fascination (some might say fetishization) with performed "exotic otherness" among both US and European audiences. The exotica in vogue focused on staged primitivism and blackness, the roots of which can be traced to the influence of the World's Fair (*Exposition Universelle*) exhibitions of 1889 in Paris and the artistic movements that emerged in its aftermath in the 1910s and 1920s.[11] The movements began in high-art circles but soon influenced middle- and working-class tastes, and performances (and images) of "primitive blackness" began captivating mass audiences.[12] The artwork of Georges Braque, André Derain, Amedeo Modigliani, and others; the popularity of Josephine Baker in Paris; and the "jungle" music of Duke Ellington performed at the Cotton Club in New York for white audiences are just some of many manifestations of this phenomena. Starting in the 1910s, dances from "other places" grew in popularity among white audiences and white performers. Figure 3.1 shows an advertisement in the *New York Times* for the Paradise Ballroom at Reisenweber's Columbus Circle from March 9, 1917. The event is titled "Seance Tea Dances" and promises "An Entire Novelty," with activities that include "Gypsie crystal gazing," Ouija boards, and "the Original 'Jazz' Dance and the Cuban Danzon will be introduced by Miss Perot and Mr. Anderson," accompanied by none other than the Original Dixieland Jazz Band (ODJB), the first recorded jazz band made up of white musicians from New Orleans. Presumably, the ODJB played Cuban *danzones* for the event; however, they made no recordings of Cuban music. Regardless, this is one of the earliest examples of North American "jazz groups" playing Cuban music in New York, and the ad demonstrates how "otherness" and exotica were central in popularizing jazz to white audiences in the early twentieth century.

Though many of the exhibitions and performances were problematically racist and imbued with exoticized fantasy, they did yield some positive results for the

TO-DAY   TO-DAY

Daily at 4:30——An Entire Novelty

"SEANCE TEA DANCES"

(Devised by John Murray Anderson·)

Karma . . . *in Mediumistic Dances of the Orient*
Tencita Guerra . . . . *Gypsie Crystal Gazer*

Original "Jazz" Dance and Cuban Danzon
OUIJA BOARDS WILL BE PROVIDED

Will Be Introduced by Miss Perot and Mr. Anderson
IN AMERICA'S MOST BEAUTIFUL BALLROOM

"PARADISE"

AT REISENWEBER'S COLUMBUS CIRCLE

Under Directions of

Miss Grace Field.

Exhibition Dances by	Additional Divertissements by
Miss Field & Mr. Wm. Reardon	Miss Perot & Mr. Anderson.
"FASHION'S A LA CARTE"	The Original Dixieland
Orchestra	"JAZZ" Band
direction of Emil Coleman	
AFTERNOONS AT 4:30	Evenings at 11:30.

FIGURE 3.1 Advertisement for jazz and Cuban *danzón* event with the Original Dixieland Jazz Band at the Paradise Ballroom in New York City, from the *New York Times*, March 9, 1917.

performers who were able to capitalize on the opportunities in entrepreneurial and creative ways. Many Cuban performers became particularly adept at staging their "otherness," "blackness," and "primitivism" for the wave of visiting tourists in Havana seeking an authentic Cuban experience. Some performers took advantage of that experience when traveling abroad, complicitly staging "Cuban otherness" and "exoticized blackness" to gain a foothold on international touring circuits and for obtaining recording and publishing contracts. Exploitative and racist as it may have been, the economic and commercial pressures faced by musicians were often the strongest driving force in their decisions to participate in somewhat demeaning performance practices. What is most often overlooked in historical analyses is that music is not only an expressive art but also a business, and a gig . . . is a gig. Most musicians did not, and still do not, have the means to turn down work, especially musicians of color who were/are forced to navigate a prejudicial working environment. Economics as a strong force in the lives of musicians must not be underestimated. The more marginalized the musicians and the music they play, the stronger the force. Performing otherness and exotica allowed Cuban musicians to corner a particular market and meet the entertainment industry's demand. Musicians associated with "The Peanut Vendor," such as composer Moisés Simons, vocalist Rita Montaner, and bandleader Don Azpiazú, greatly benefited and enjoyed international success with their renditions and stagings of "authentic" Cuban music.

In 1922, Moisés Simons (1889–1945), while working in Spain, received a commission to write songs for a Cuban music revue. Catering to Spanish middle-class expectations of romanticized Cuban street life, Simons composed "The Peanut Vendor" for the show. The song, with its melody based on a street vendor's call, is generically known as a *son pregón*, a popular dance music with inventively poetic lyrics that capture the sonic environment of urban street life. He borrowed heavily (some say stole) from street-vendor calls he had heard in Cuba and composed a simple, straightforward diatonic melodic line with a cleverly syncopated hook, all performed over a two-chord harmonic vamp.[13] The lyrics, with their seemingly romantic imagery conjuring a "simple" and "provincial" island life, resonated with audiences living in bustling urban centers of Europe. Even though Simons composed this song thousands of miles from his native land and for the purposes of the Spanish audience, the lyrics simultaneously attended to the poetic conventions typical of *pregones*, which are laced with double entendre and street slang fully accessible only to Cubans. With a wink, Simons places a joke fully on the consuming "others" by writing racy and suggestive lyrics with opaque references to sex (more about this shortly) that would have been banned outright had anyone in Spain, and later in the United States, understood the full meaning of the song. Shortly after composing "The Peanut Vendor," he returned to Havana to lead a highly accomplished jazz band that performed at the Plaza Hotel and featured some of the best early Cuban jazz musicians, such as trumpeter Julio Cueva and flutist Alberto Socarrás (who would later emigrate to New York, lead a highly successful recording career, and establish the flute as a viable solo instrument in jazz).[14] Simons's stylistically agile composing and performing abilities enabled him to cater to diverse audiences simultaneously, garnering success globally.

Actress and vocalist Rita Montaner (1900–1958), another Cuban performer capitalizing on the popularity of exotica in Europe, performed in Paris in Josephine Baker's Revue. She began including "The Peanut Vendor" in her repertoire in the mid-1920s and was the first to record it (in 1928). She played a key role in introducing the song to US audiences when she began regularly performing at New York's Plaza Hotel, appearing with Xavier Cugat at the Apollo Theater, and in 1931 performing on Broadway with singer Al Jolson.[15] Her successes sparked the interest of US music publisher Herbert Marks, who subsequently purchased "The Peanut Vendor" in 1929 while honeymooning in Havana. His widely distributed sheet-music sales, Montaner's recording and performances, and the subsequent "North Americanized" versions with English lyrics (which lacked any suggestive or salacious content) played by dance bands throughout the late 1920s ensured widespread familiarity of the song prior to Azpiazú's concert. In 1930, this internationally popular melody did not require any introduction to mainstream US audiences. It was already a piece of transnational music steeped in the global market—"world music" before such a label was coined.

In the post-WWI years, jazz had garnered considerable economic and cultural interest abroad as a style associated with the victorious United States and as a music of a "primitive black other." Cuba was not immune to the global fascination of jazz, and it had a lasting musical impact on local music and dance expression. Writing in 1939, Cuban scholar Emilio Grenet assesses jazz's impact. I quote him at length because he also opines that jazz's popularity in Cuba was the key to Cuban music's success internationally. Though he does not mention Azpiazú, this excerpt speaks directly to the success of "The Peanut Vendor":

> In the year 1916 the first group of American negroes surprised us with the stridencies and acrobatics of the jazz band and the dynamism of their disarticulated dances. . . . Jazz submerged our *danzón* into the most absolute oblivion and during several years it was not used at dances. . . . The best orchestras were imported from the United States; our flutists packed away their instruments to adopt the saxophone, while the kettle drummers gave themselves over to the grotesque jugglings of the American drummer. At the same time that the *danzón* was denaturalized by the use of foreign airs, Cuban *canciones* were danced with fox-trot rhythm. We cannot deny, however, that cultivation of jazz made possible the triumph of our *rumba*. Cuban music with the American accent of the saxophone was as interesting a melodic element for Americans as their trombone glissandes [sic] and their acrobat drumsticks had been for us.[16]

Don Justo Angel Azpiazú (1893–1943), a seasoned Cuban bandleader working in Havana, was one of the first to develop equal competence in Cuban music and jazz styles. More important, he was a pioneer in the mixing of those two styles. His abilities, along with his light skin, gained him entrée into the upscale and prestigious hotel circuits in Havana. Strongly influenced by jazz performance practice, Azpiazú expanded the traditional Cuban conjunto (typically a sextet or septet) to a fourteen-piece big band (modeled on the Fletcher Henderson band, one of the most successful New York jazz bands of the 1920s). Azpiazú's band included brass, woodwinds, guitar, banjo, violins, piano, and bass, mixed with Cuban

FIGURE 3.2 Press photo of Don Azpiazú from 1931. Courtesy of Eleonor Azpiazú.

percussion (i.e., maracas, timbales, guiro, *claves*, cowbells, and bongos). He hired vocalists who adopted the popular smooth crooning style of Al Jolson and Rudy Vallee. He sculpted a refined performance practice that gently translated Cuban music for tourists by combining familiarity with a sense of "authenticity"—a staged exotica that was not too foreign or threatening. His version of Cuban music was couched in jazz big-band instrumentation and arranging techniques, while accompanied by an array of traditional Cuban rhythms, melodies, and percussion instruments (an early version of what would later define Latin jazz as a separate genre). His press photo of 1931 (Figure 3.2) is particularly telling. He strikes a relaxed, smiling, and friendly pose. He is dressed in traditional Cuban performance garb and surrounded by Cuban percussion instruments, while holding a *clave* stick like a cigar. The photo was taken in New York and was used for promotion outside of Cuba. His jazz big band and the music they performed are absent, and in this photo, all things Cuban serve as the contextualizing props. It captures what set Azpiazú apart and foregrounds what specifically marks him as other and exotic.

In contrast, the press photo of his Havana Casino Orchestra (Figure 3.3) displays all of the familiar trappings employed in promotional materials for jazz big bands

FIGURE 3.3 Press photo of Don Azpiazú and his Havana Casino Orchestra, circa 1930. Courtesy of Eleonor Azpiazú.

of the 1930s, with the band posing onstage in performing positions and an array of instruments on display. What sets this image apart from those of other jazz bands of the day were the Cuban outfits, the bag of "Hot Peanuts" displayed prominently in the lower left corner (a carefully positioned prop allotted equal visual weight to the musical instruments), and, more subtly, the mixed race of the band. Azpiazú was clever and cutting-edge in his pursuits and used his success to break down not only stylistic divides but also racial and societal barriers. He was one of the first bandleaders to employ dark-skinned musicians and add street elements to his musical mix in high-society performance venues, pioneering changes in the performance practice of bands across Cuba. His performance at the Palace Theater marked one of the first occasions when a racially integrated band performed in New York at an exclusively white venue, predating Benny Goodman's celebrated integrated group of 1936, often referred to as the "first integrated jazz band" (Figure 3.4).

In the United States, nationality trumped the racial distinctions of the day, allowing Afro-Cubans access to opportunities where African Americans were barred. The presence of dark-skinned Cubans was an aberration for most white North Americans, who were unsure of just how to position them. For instance,

FIGURE 3.4 Benny Goodman's band in 1936. From left to right: Lionel Hampton, Gene Krupa, Teddy Wilson, and Benny Goodman. Courtesy of Phoebe Jacobs.

when Mario Bauzá toured in the southern United States with black jazz groups, the bands would send him into "white only" restaurants to buy food for everyone. When the white owners or patrons would protest, he would respond in his thick Cuban accent that he was not black but Cuban, and he usually would be served. At the same time, he experienced much prejudice in his daily life in Cuba and credited his decision to emigrate to the United States to his experiences in Harlem, where he witnessed African Americans living in a community relatively free of racial strife. At the same time, however, his presence along with other Afro-Cubans in New York introduced African American musicians to a different model of blackness that would exert profound influence just one decade later (I explore this in greater detail in chapter 4).

The success of Azpiazú's performance at the Palace Theater was rooted in his finely tuned staging of "authenticity" that relied on his heavy use of Cuban percussion, along with his choice of singer Antonio Machín to deliver the songs. Machín was one of the first Afro-Cubans to perform with white jazz orchestras in Cuba, starting with Azpiazú at the Casino Nacional in the mid-1920s. So Machín and Azpiazú were experienced in performative mediation and negotiation involved in staging race within a prejudiced society. As Robin Moore writes, black and mulatto

entertainers, such as Machín and Montaner, "served as cultural mediators performing rumbas in a 'sophisticated' manner yet with an 'aura of authenticity.' They
translated working class musical expression into a form acceptable to the middle-
class public" both in Cuba and abroad. They crossed social boundaries of race and
class to an unprecedented degree.[17] The "authentic" Cuban performance heard at
the Palace Theater in April 1930, then, was a much filtered and tempered one. The
song was delivered by a dark-skinned Cuban singing in Spanish and dressed as a
street vendor (exotic in and of itself), but his smooth crooning style (sometimes
he was referred to as the "Rudy Vallee of Cuba") along with his good looks were familiar US popular music practices. And to top off the performance, Machín entered
the stage pushing a vendor's cart and tossing bags of peanuts to the crowd while
singing. The mix of gimmickry, familiarity, authenticity, and exotica capitivated
the audience and launched a new era in global popular music and a new level of
engagement with Cuban music in jazz.

What the audience thought they heard at the Palace Theater was authentic
Cuban music, though the name, conventions, and history of the specific styles
remained unknown to most. Contributing to the impression of authenticity was
the assumption that Machín was singing a Spanish version of the well-known and
rather trite English lyric. Written by Marion Sunshine and L. Wolde Gilbert and
published in the United States in the years prior to the Palace Theater performance,
the English version depicts a provincial setting of Cuba street life that resonates
musical innocence and simplicity. Here are a few examples of the English lyric: "In
Cuba, each merry maid wakes up with this serenade. Peanuts! They're nice and
hot! . . . If you haven't got bananas don't be blue, peanuts in a little bag are calling
you. . . . The Peanut Vendor's on his way. At dawning that whistle blows through
ev'ry city, town, and country lane, you'll hear him sing his plaintive little strain . . ."

Ironically and unbeknownst to the audience, the Spanish lyric content arguably was the only unmediated and most "authentic" aspect of the Azpiazú performance. *Son pregones* draw on rich poetic traditions in Cuban popular music
and are known particularly for their wit and double entendre (a necessary device
to circumvent censorship in Cuba's conservative Catholic society).[18] "The Peanut
Vendor" is an archetypal example and is laced with suggestively erotic imagery
and clues to the obscured meaning of the song. The Spanish lyrics that Machín
sang at the Palace Theater, written by Simons and Montaner, offer an alternative
perspective under the guise of a street vendor's plaintive song, where scenes of
innocent provinciality are replaced by titillating prurience. In the Spanish version, only native speakers familiar with the slang and the poetic conventions of
the genre would have recognized the double meaning of the idiomatic phrase that
serves as the song's hook, *Si te quieres por el pico divertir, cómete un cucurruchito de*

maní ("If you want through your mouth to be amused, eat a small paper cone of peanuts"). Cristóbal Díaz Ayala has pointed out that *pico* can be interpreted as either "mouth" or as "yoni" and *cucurrucho de maní* ("cone of peanuts") as "phallus."[19] Other suggestive lyrics include phrases such as "Darling, do not lie down to sleep, without eating a paper cone of peanuts" and "when the street is empty, sweetheart, the peanut man intones his song, and if the girl hears that singing, she calls from her balcony, give me your peanuts!"[20] At the Palace Theater, the racy meaning of the lyrics was lost on the non-Spanish-speaking audience. One wonders how a black man singing about sex to white audiences in 1930 would have been received. Regardless, the array of exotic Cuban percussion introduced that night, surrounded by the familiar trappings of big band instrumentation and performance practice (Azpiazú's arrangement even ends with a trio of clarinets, the signature sound of the popular Henderson band) and led by a bandleader seasoned in staged exotica, provided just enough "otherness" in this musical cocktail to appeal broadly. The success of "The Peanut Vendor" was noticed by the attending RCA Victor executives, which, in turn, led to their historical decision to record Azpiazú's band performing the song.

In the 1920s, RCA Victor was a company on the vanguard of producing records that crossed national and ethnic boundaries. Its focus on Caribbean and Latin American styles greatly popularized the music among international audiences and established new norms in the world music industry, something that Angel Quintero Rivera describes as a "transference from the national to the nomadic."[21] Due to Cuba's proximity, the company began sending representatives to Havana regularly to scout for new talent and recording possibilities. By 1930, they had amassed hundreds of recordings of Cuban music, so the decision to record Azpiazú's band performing "The Peanut Vendor" was in line with the trajectory of RCA Victor's business plan. However, the decision was also viewed as a risk due to Azpiazú's heavy use of traditional Cuban percussion instruments and his inclusion of unadulterated Cuban rhythms, both of which were relatively unfamiliar to non-Cuban audiences at the time. Recorded on May 13, 1930 (matrix 62152, disc 22438) (just days after the Palace Theater appearance), Azpiazú's "The Peanut Vendor" was not commercially released until September 1930 due to the trepidation of RCA Victor executives concerned about whether the US public was ready for such "authentic" Cuban music. Indicative of its lack of confidence in the recording's potential, RCA Victor never explored the true meaning of the lyrics or the song's genre label. Consequently, it mislabeled the genre and then misspelled the mislabel, marketing the song as "rhumba." *Son pregones* are quite different from traditional rumba, an Afro-Cuban genre featuring drums and voice and associated with black urban street culture.

To the surprise of many, "The Peanut Vendor" quickly rose to number one, outselling the most popular artists. Estimates range up to 2 million copies sold in the first two years after its release, and the song produced more than $100,000 in royalties for Simons within the first fifteen years of its publication.[22] The accompanying dance became a big international craze, firmly establishing the RCA Victor's mislabel as the widely accepted name of the music and the dance (the mislabel was eventually used even in Cuba). The success of the song and the dance firmly established a long tradition of Cuban dance styles reaching the US shores, transforming popular music for decades. Some of the Cuban dance crazes that followed in the wake of rhumba were the conga, mambo, cha-cha, and salsa.

"The Peanut Vendor" earned Azpiazú an unprecedented level of international success, especially for a Cuban bandleader. He subsequently appeared in several Hollywood films, including *Swing High* and *Cuban Love Song* (a 1931 production starring Jimmy Durante, Lawrence Tibbett, and Lupe Vélez, in which he was featured performing "The Peanut Vendor"), toured throughout the United States and Europe, and eventually landed a nightly gig at the prestigious Rainbow Room in New York, alternating sets with the Casa Loma Orchestra. His success paved the way for many more Cuban bands to tour internationally, and New York was a major hub on that circuit.

"The Peanut Vendor's" meteoric rise led to its ubiquitous presence in the musical soundscape of the early 1930s, both in the United States and abroad (witness Jorge Luis Borges, in the opening of this book's introduction). Within a matter of weeks, numerous jazz and pop stars recorded their own versions, such as the California Ramblers, Red Nichols, Duke Ellington, Louis Armstrong, Paul Whiteman, Xavier Cugat, Nathan Glantz and His Orchestra, and a newly established group calling themselves the Manisero Orchestra.[23] Four versions charted in the United States in 1931: Don Azpiazú (number one), the California Ramblers (number five), Red Nichols (number five), and Louis Armstrong (number fifteen). (Armstrong's version was reissued in 1941 and recharted at number twenty-five.) On the international scene, the Berlin-based Oscar Joost und seine Orchester recorded the song in July 1931, and the song was used by the New Zealander animated-film maker Len Lye as the theme in his 1933 *Experimental Animation* (aka *Peanut Vendor*). The first Cuban release after the song became a hit in the United States was in 1931, by the Hermanos Castro Jazzband, a group Ned Sublette identifies as the "first Cuban *banda grande* (big band)." Their arrangement featured an inventive mash up of W. C. Handy's "St. Louis Blues" with "The Peanut Vendor."[24] The juxtaposition of two seminal songs that feature overt cross-stylistic mixing provides a provocative Cuban perspective on the centrality of Cuban styles and their influence on jazz (Handy's original version of "St. Louis Blues," published in 1914, uses the Cuban habanera bass line and rhythm). In this inventive Cuban version, "The Peanut Vendor" is given equal weight to that of Handy's hit song, and in the process, the two-chord vamp of the Simons tune is transformed into an extended blues form— an intriguing early manifestation of global jazz.

The growing public demand for performances of the song and its commercial potential prompted jazz musicians and producers to create their own versions and to search for other Cuban songs to incorporate into their repertoire, essentially transforming jazz repertoire and performance practices in the process. After the success of "The Peanut Vendor," the Savoy Ballroom and other Harlem dance halls began featuring two bands per dance, a rhumba band alternating sets with a swing band. In the early 1930s, this became a standard practice. In many ways, the advent of the swing era was synchronous with the rise of Latin music in the United States, and it often took place in the same locations and for the same audiences. This enabled much more cross-fertilization than has been recognized. Reading histor- ical and biographical studies of prominent bandleaders in the 1930s, such as Benny Goodman and Artie Shaw, the Latin-music bands that performed side by side with them night after night are rarely mentioned and are virtually erased from the his- torical record. However, the presence of the Latin music bands and the increased demand for their music had a huge impact on the business of music. The music industry responded quickly by publishing sheet music of numerous Caribbean and Latin American compositions and arrangements. For instance, the E. B. Marks catalog included more than 600 Caribbean and Latin American songs in the early 1930s, most of which were Cuban.[25] And in 1931, the Gretsch Percussion Company started producing a line of rhumba percussion instruments, responding to the new demand for bongos, *claves*, maracas, guiros, cowbells, and timbales.

I now turn to two case studies, Louis Armstrong and Duke Ellington, to ex- plore in greater detail the relationship of "The Peanut Vendor" and jazz in the early 1930s.

* * *

Since jazz's inception, jazz artists have taken material from pop music and made it their own, and "The Peanut Vendor" was no exception. Louis Armstrong and Duke Ellington quickly capitalized on the song's success and recorded it within a few months of Azpiazú's release—Armstrong on December 23, 1930, and Ellington on January 20, 1931. Their expeditious decision to record and perform "The Peanut Vendor" demonstrates the close relationship between popular music trends and jazz repertoire choices. Strategies to record the most popular music of the day often blurred distinctions between "jazz" (or "swing") and "pop," especially in the 1930s. When jazz becomes pop, and vice versa, the neat conceptions of jazz as art music posited by scholars (à la Schuller) are complicated. Further, when jazz's source materials are drawn from foreign places, the conception of jazz as purely "African American," or simply "American," becomes paradoxical. "The Peanut Vendor" presents a challenge to conventional jazz historical narratives. The complexity of popular tastes and trends must in some way be accounted for through a broadened investigative scope where the dynamic processes of value operative in pop culture are accounted for. "The Peanut Vendor" offers an opportunity to do just that.

In the case of "The Peanut Vendor," an exoticized, though mediated and whitened, version of Afro-Cuban music emerged from the transnational context of the global marketplace and was strategically introduced and marketed in a way, and in a time, that catered and appealed to popular tastes. Appropriating such influences from a wide range of sources was part and parcel of the jazz aesthetic and a familiar mode for innovation and change within jazz. But as access to broader global sources was facilitated through radio, recordings, and travel, the scope of influence and possibilities exponentially expanded. Closely examining how two important figures in jazz, Armstrong and Ellington, contended with this broadened scope sheds light on the various divergent strategies for the innovative intercultural exploration that was so central in shaping the sound of jazz for generations to come.

CASE STUDY 4: LOUIS ARMSTRONG

According to Schuller, it was Armstrong's intrepid manager Joe Glaser's "battle plan" to record all of the newest songs to bolster Armstrong's popularity.[26] It is no surprise, then, that the most popular song of the year would prompt an expeditious Armstrong rendition. Armstrong's "The Peanut Vendor," recorded in Los Angeles on December 23, 1930, typifies the strategy of infusing otherness and exotic sounds into jazz for novelty and popular appeal. However, because it was completed so soon after Azpiazú's release, the haste of Glaser's plan can be heard in the production. Exploring which elements of Azpiazú's arrangement remain and which are omitted is particularly revealing.

Instead of a completely new and unique approach, Armstrong's rendition (it is unclear who arranged his version) relies heavily on the Alfredo Brito arrangement that Azpiazú performed, with some parts copied outright. For instance, Armstrong's version is in the same key of G major, uses the same two-chord harmonic movement throughout, adopts a similar overall form, and incorporates Brito's brass and saxophone riffs along with his accompaniment figure played by a trio of clarinets.

The clarinet trio was the signature sound of the Fletcher Henderson band, a sound that was familiar to New York audiences in 1930. Brito's appropriation of the trio strategically couched unfamiliar Cuban musical elements within a recognizable and identifiable popular sound. It was a softer and less threatening introduction to otherness and cultural difference (a practice that Azpiazú often employed). Including the same arranging choice in Armstrong's version is a bit perplexing, considering that Henderson's band was a competitor. On the one hand, it may just reflect a lackadaisical attitude toward this recording, since no new arrangement was attempted. On the other hand, these appropriating practices play an essential role in jazz production that serve to connect this intercultural music to the larger domain of the black circum-Atlantic. Paul Gilroy writes:

> The contemporary musical forms of the African Diaspora work within an aesthetic and political framework which demands that they ceaselessly reconstruct their own histories, folding back on themselves time and again to celebrate and validate the simple, unassailable fact of their survival. This is particularly evident in jazz, where quotes from and parody of earlier styles and performers make the past actually audible in the present . . . the stylistic voices of the past are valued for the distinct register of address which each offers.[27]

Armstrong's appropriation of the clarinet trio (voices/sounds) of the past, albeit the recent past, serve to acknowledge, validate, and pay tribute to Henderson (his former boss and mentor) and Azpiazú simultaneously. It was a subtle but powerfully validating gesture coming from one of the biggest stars in jazz. The conscious triangulation of the music of Azpiazú, Henderson, and Armstrong affirmed and reverberated a connected tradition and shared history tied to the black circum-Atlanticexperience and reified the "black archipelago," which in this case extends from Havana to New York and on to Los Angeles.

The Armstrong recording, however, conspicuously omits the "authentic" Cuban elements that made the Azpiazú arrangement so popular in the first place. The entire performance employs a swing eighth-note feel instead of a straight eighth feel typically heard in Cuban music and does not include Cuban percussion or rhythms associated with son. The absence of percussion and Cuban rhythms is not completely unexpected, because instruments were difficult to purchase in 1930 (Gretsch did not start mass-producing them until 1931), and Cuban percussionists were not yet regular fixtures on the jazz scene. Jazz musicians from the United States had not yet had many opportunities to learn, perform, and master contemporary Cuban styles.[28] Without Cuban percussion or rhythms, the producers felt that not enough exoticism, otherness, or novelty sounded for Armstrong's version to be competitive. So instead, castanets were then added, playing pseudo-Latin rhythms, and were sonically mixed in the foreground, much like the Cuban percussion in the Azpiazú recording. This was a curiously uninformed choice considering that in Cuba, castanets are most associated with the music of the colonizers rather than the colonized, a detail overlooked for the sake of commercial appeal. Moreover, the straight rhythmic feel of the castanets clashes with the swing feel played by the rest of the band, and, indicative of attitudes in the 1930s where percussion was viewed as ancillary at best, no credit on liner notes or any subsequent discography is given to the percussionist. Regardless, Armstrong's "The Peanut Vendor" garnered substantial commercial success.

In spite of the absence of Cuban sounds, it is clear that Armstrong was familiar with Azpiazú's recording, as his trumpet and vocal phrasings mimic Machín's phrasing and tone throughout. As in Machín's version, every phrase sung by Armstrong (and played on trumpet, for that matter) is rhythmically organized by the 2-3 *clave* pattern, a practice essential in Cuban son, even though his band members were not adhering to that rhythmic configuration. However, unlike Machín, Armstrong chose either to ignore or to not learn the English or Spanish lyrics and, instead, firmly imprints his own artistic stamp by sculpting an original improvisatory lyric and scat rendition. His new lyrics change the word *maní* (peanut) to (what could possibly be considered stereotypical) "Marie," transforming the song into a declaratory love song, while his new lyrics are interspersed with scatting vocables:

Marie, Marie . . . *Bah bah dah dee dee inn bah du dah dah no, whah dah bah dah dah lohm nah bah dah noh.* That's when I love with all my dear. That's when I *day bah yee*, Marie. *Bah bah bah dee bah dee bah dee* now. *Bah dee dee bah dee bah dee bah ee* now. *Bah dah dee bah too bah too* oh my dear. That's when I know Cuban is *en len low.* When Spanish *hal* may be. When my Spanish my one ish heart, Marie. Oh Spanish, Spanish, *dup dup*, Spanish, Spanish, Spanish. *Bana bud dee in bud dee in bud dee in bud dee in ban dah duh.* Marie, Marie."

The words "Cuban" and "Spanish" jump out of the scatted *bahs* and *dahs*, possibly suggesting (with a wink of his eye) that Armstrong is scatting playfully in Spanish. Trite as his rendition may seem at first, there is a profound connection to the original, and his unique artistic identity is marvelously maintained in a way that only Armstrong could pull off while simultaneously attending to novelty.

Despite its commercial success, most jazz historians all but write off Armstrong's version. For instance, Schuller writes:

On "The Peanut Vendor" . . . Armstrong gives up. He evidently felt he could add nothing to this tune (which has no changes, being a one chord G major piece) other than a muted theme statement which almost anyone could have played, and a scatty vocal with pseudo-Mexican allusion. . . . It is an interminable song, and very likely there was no time for a full-fledged Armstrong solo; or else he felt he could not function against the background of sloppily, stiffly played castanets and horrendously out of tune guitar strumming.[29]

One wonders how closely Schuller actually listened to this cut, especially since it clearly is a two-chord piece (dominant to tonic) and has no "pseudo-Mexican allusion," nor does it have anything to do with Mexico. Was it Schuller who gave up? He is correct about the accompaniment and the absence of a trumpet solo, but that did not seem to deter its popular appeal. More important, it may be true that the muted theme statement could be played by "almost anyone," but it wasn't. Armstrong, arguably the most important jazz soloist in 1930, did it, and that is what makes this piece so significant.

Regardless, "The Peanut Vendor" is rarely included on Armstrong compilations and is not written about seriously by most jazz scholars. The erasure of "The Peanut Vendor" from jazz historical narratives is rooted in two factors: otherness and commercialism. Cuban music's reinfiltration into jazz in the 1930s challenges claims of jazz as a purely African American or an exclusively American music, a long-established driving force in jazz scholarship. House Resolution 57 from the US Congress in 1987 aptly captures this position: "Jazz has achieved preeminence throughout the world as an indigenous American music and art form . . . a uniquely American musical synthesis and culture through the African-American experience. . . . [J]azz is hereby designated a rare and valuable national American treasure." Caribbean and Latin American music and musicians contaminate conceptions of a pure "American" or African American jazz and thus are not worthy of acknowledgment in liner notes and are better left out of neatly constructive linear historical narratives. "The Peanut Vendor's" broad commercial appeal challenges the conception of jazz as art music. Jazz critic Rudy Blesh, writing in 1946, captures this position, which has been reiterated continually throughout the music's history: "Commercialism is a cheapening and deteriorative force, a species of murder perpetrated on a wonderful music by whites and by those misguided negroes who, for one or another reason, choose to be accomplices to the deed. . . . Commercialism is a thing not only hostile, but fatal to jazz."[30] In this regard, Armstrong's "The Peanut Vendor" was viewed as a hostile infiltration, a pandering to popular tastes for commercial appeal, and an aberration not worthy of note.

CASE STUDY 5: DUKE ELLINGTON

Recording in New York on January 20, 1931, just on the heels of the Armstrong release, Ellington offers an alternative and, in some ways, a more imaginative approach. As a consummate composer, arranger, and visionary, he seizes on "The Peanut Vendor" as an opportunity to assert a uniquely creolist perspective that blends a number of Caribbean and African American styles in unprecedented ways. Even though he had vocalists working regularly with his band, Ellington adeptly avoids any issues of lyrics and language by offering a purely instrumental arrangement. He is less concerned with inserting exotic sounds for novelty, so no Cuban or extraneous percussion instruments are included. Instead, drummer Sonny Greer adapts the rhumba beat to his drum set, which he plays throughout most of the recording. Greer's rhythm is superimposed onto a bass line that alternates between walking swing and a traditional Cuban *tumbao* pattern (the *tresillo* rhythm). The arrangement begins transposed to the more horn-friendly key of F major. And as in Armstrong's arrangement, the horns play with a swing eighth-note feel throughout, at times clashing with the straighter feel of the rhythm section. Staying true to Azpiazú's opening melodic statements, Ellington keeps the original call-and-response form, with Freddie Jenkins playing the main melodic statements on solo muted trumpet and Barney Bigard playing the improvisatory responses on clarinet. After the first statement of the melody, Ellington departs from the Azpiazú arrangement by adding a modulation to A-flat major and launching into a newly composed calypso section that introduces completely new material not directly related to the Simons composition. As a transition back to the melody, Ellington plays a Harlem stride-piano interlude using the original vamp heard on the Azpiazú recording before returning to the melody orchestrated for the full band and with newly composed interludes. The arrangement returns to the calypso before ending with the original melody. This innovative mash-up of swing, Cuban rhumba, Trinidadian calypso, and Harlem stride demonstrates what Jocelyne Guilbault calls "diasporic musical inter-culture" and attests to Ellington's familiarity with Caribbean styles and his conception of how they are tied intrinsically to African American musical expression.[31] In Ellington's "The Peanut Vendor," the black archipelago stretches from Havana to Port of Spain and on to Harlem.

Erected in 1997 on the corner of East 110th Street and Fifth Avenue in Manhattan, arguably the most important intersection in Latin jazz history (more on that in chapter 4), stands a cenotaph for Edward "Duke" Ellington (Figure 3.5). His statue towers over a newly constructed traffic circle, recently named Duke Ellington Circle. Ellington is depicted standing upright next to a piano atop a towering pedestal supported by three columns decorated with three muses on each,

FIGURE 3.5 Cenotaph of Duke Ellington located on the corner of East 110th Street and Fifth Avenue in New York City. Photo by author.

representing all nine muses in Greek mythology. Ellington faces east, gazing down a street that has recently been given the name Tito Puente Way, as the birthplace of the famous Latin bandleader lies several blocks farther east on East 110th Street (Figure 3.6). Ellington is memorialized on the divide between black and Spanish, with his back to central Harlem and looking outward toward Spanish Harlem, and the symbolism is not lost. As one of the most significant composers and bandleaders in jazz history and a key figure in the Harlem Renaissance but also one of the first African American bandleaders in Harlem to embrace the West Indian roots of African American culture, he is appropriately memorialized facing directly into the heart of Spanish Harlem. His immortalized gaze is directed outward and beyond, with a global perspective for growth and innovation and in tune with the larger circum-Atlantic shared history and tradition. Ellington's "The Peanut Vendor" captured his global perspective and set a precedent for years to come for circum-Atlantic diasporic sonic alchemy. Regardless, Ellington's treatment of "The Peanut Vendor" is rarely mentioned in historical narratives and jazz textbooks, nor is it included in compilations of the composer's works.[32]

FIGURE 3.6 Street signage at the corner across from the Ellington statue. Photo by author.

If we consider "The Peanut Vendor" as "structured by the continuous riff of race," to borrow Ingrid Monson's words, we must address the issues raised by Azpiazú, Armstrong, and Ellington.[33] Azpiazú, as a white Cuban bandleader, appropriated and mediated black street culture to cater to popular white notions of Afro-Cuban blackness, all the while undermining the established and prejudicial racial divides in the milieus in which he performed through his multiracial hiring practices. For Armstrong and Ellington as black jazz musicians, their renditions of "The Peanut Vendor" appropriated Azpiazú's appropriation, all the while negotiating their own positions within confines of white notions of staged blackness. Simultaneously, by pointing to a more othered "otherness" than their own positions as black entertainers within white performance domains, they could (each in his own way) appropriate rather than be the object of appropriation. Armstrong's juxtaposition of novelty (the castanets, for instance) and playful irony, especially with his treatment of the Spanish lyric, typifies a recurrent strategy that he employed throughout his career in which he enabled novelty and the sublime to coexist. Subtly, he lets us know that he is hip to Machín, Azpiazú, *clave*, and misdirected mediation, transcending the triteness of the rendition with truly vintage Armstrong expression and gesture. Ellington, on the other hand, elegantly avoids the novel and instead takes a more creolist approach by navigating innovatively through the blending of seemingly disparate styles, tipping his hat to the diasporic marginalized cultural space that Harlem, Cuba, and Trinidad share in the popular imagination of his day. All three renditions push our generic conceptions of the boundaries of jazz, transcend national boundaries drawing generative agency from outside and inside the United States simultaneously, and push jazz expression into new racial terrain, or what Homi Bhabha labels an "interstitial space" between the binary of black/white.[34] "The Peanut Vendor" transforms any discussion of race from a simplified black/white binary so prominent in jazz writing into a black/brown/tan/mulatto/beige/white universe, a blurred space that more closely resembles where jazz resides.

* * *

In this brief examination of "The Peanut Vendor," I have demonstrated how the multilayered embeddedness of the original Simons composition subtly informs later jazz adaptations and how the dynamic complexity behind popular trends significantly intersects and influences the performance practice and stylistic evolution of jazz. Imbued with contextual inscriptions of race, exoticism, and the logic of transnational appropriation, as well as commercialism, "The Peanut Vendor's" presence and effect on jazz point to the global nature of music's production that fully encompasses intercultural exchange and synthesis. So, perhaps, Borges provides us with an insightful perspective after all about why Azpiazú, Armstrong, and Ellington recorded "that deplorable rumba." Borges recognized that something more profoundly interconnected was at play. Wider acknowledgment of this complexity of interconnectivity, though, has been slow in coming, as advocates struggle for the recognition of how Caribbean and Latin American music and musicians have been tied intrinsically to the development of jazz and popular music for more than a century. For instance, it took more than seventy years after the Azpiazú release for "The Peanut Vendor" to begin receiving a modicum of recognition. In 2001, the Azpiazú recording was inducted into the Latin Grammy Hall of Fame, an award that honors historically significant recordings released more than twenty-five years ago.[35] And in 2005, "The Peanut Vendor" was added to the United States National Recording Registry by the National Recording Preservation Board, with the proclamation: "It is the first American recording of an authentic Latin dance style. This recording launched a decade of 'rumbamania,' introducing U.S. listeners to Cuban percussion instruments and Cuban rhythms."[36] Even with this more recent recognition, the rich contribution of the composition and of the musicians who performed it, which extends way beyond the confines of authenticity and introduction, remains unacknowledged, ignored, and erased.

* * *

In 1931, Azpiazú was fired from the Rainbow Room. The management had hired the Casa Loma Orchestra, a swing band, to alternate sets with Azpiazú. The Casa Loma Orchestra was to play swing, and Azpiazú was to play Caribbean and Latin American music exclusively. Azpiazú, however, refused to just play Caribbean and Latin American music and kept inserting swing numbers into his set. According to the management at the Rainbow Room, no one in New York "wanted to hear a Cuban band playing jazz," and he was eventually fired for doing so. As a pioneer embodying a transnational perspective, Azpiazú saw no reason not to play jazz. In fact, he was willing to lose one of the most prestigious and highly paid gigs in New York to assert his perspective and principles.

When I performed at the Rainbow Room in 1991 with Mauricio Smith's Latin Jazz Orchestra, we were instructed to play only Caribbean and Latin American music, and all jazz and swing arrangements were to be played by the Rainbow Room Dance Band that alternated sets. Smith (1931–2002) was a gifted jazz flutist from Panama who had performed with Mongo Santamaría, Charles Mingus, Dizzy Gillespie, Eartha Kitt, Harry Belafonte, among other jazz luminaries, and was an original member of the Saturday Night Live Band. His résumé and virtuosic jazz soloing abilities were of no consequence, though, and, like Azpiazú, he was banned from playing any "jazz" or music with a swing rhythm at the Rainbow Room. Smith also refused and was eventually fired. Sixty years after Azpiazú, he was still fighting in the same struggle.

As new jazz narratives are constructed, it is time to take inspiration from visionaries like Azpiazú, Armstrong, Ellington, and Smith, and a multilayered perspective within a global framework needs to be developed further to begin to capture the nuanced and intercultural processes involved in the production of jazz and Latin jazz.

NOTES

1. Harris 2000, 118.
2. Walser 1999, 171.
3. Schuller 1958.
4. Schuller 1989.
5. I am a graduate of this program, having received my master's in Third Stream Studies in 1988.
6. For a more in-depth critique, see Lewis 1996.
7. Radano and Bohlman 2001, 40.
8. "Schismogenesis" refers to the recontextualization of music or sound split from its sources. See Feld 1994.
9. See Acosta 2003.

10. See chapter 4 for more details about Cuban music performance in New York.

11. For further information, see Watkins 1995.

12. See Moore 1997.Also see Sublette 2004; and Watkins 1994.

13. Cristóbal Díaz Ayala has pointed out that the authorship of the piece has been disputed, most prominently by Fernando Ortiz in the *Revista Bohemia* (March 14, 1954), who claims that the composer is an anonymous street vendor in Havana from the second part of the nineteenth century. Díaz Ayala 1988, 238.

14. Simons also performed jazz in Paris, playing in a band led by Filiberto Rico, a Cuban expatriate saxophonist. See Fernandez 2003.

15. Sublette 2004, 384.

16. Grenet 1939, xxxii–xxxiii.

17. Moore, 1997, 174.

18. For a comprehensive history of *pregones*, see Díaz Ayala 1988.

19. Díaz Ayala 1988, 241.

20. *Caserita no te acuestes a dormir, sin comerte un cucurrucho de maní. Cuándo la calle sola está casera de mi corazón, el manisero entona su pregón, y si la niña escucha ese cantar, llama desde su balcón. Dame de tu maní!*

21. Quintero Rivera 2007, 85.

22. Díaz Ayala 1988, 238; and also Pérez 1999, 203.

23. In Díaz Ayala's (1999) discography, which is far from complete, he documents 158 recordings of the song from the late 1920s to the 1980s, though most were recorded during the 1930s.

24. Sublette 2004, 393.

25. Ibid., 239.

26. Schuller 1989, 167.

27. Gilroy 1993b, 37.

28. It was so rare for US-based musicians to play Cuban percussion that when it did happen in 1931, it was worthy of writing about in *Time* magazine: " 'The Peanut Vendor' ('El Manisero'), with its hot, catchy rhythm between a jig and a tango, has started an invasion. Don Azpiazu's Havana Orchestra brought the song north last year, played it with other Cuban tunes at RKO's Palace Theatre in Manhattan, afterwards at the smart Central Park Casino. Then Don Azpiazu went back to Cuba to entertain U. S. tourists. He left his tunes behind. Manhattan's Leo Reisman learned to lead them. Reisman's drummer mastered the four complicated beats which Cuban orchestras emphasize with the bongo (a double-headed drum held between the knees and played by the fingers of both hands), the claves (two sticks of a rare Cuban wood, which make a clicking sound when struck together) and the maracas (gourds filled with seeds which make a swishing sound). Vincent Lopez took up Cuban things and so did other jazzmen." "Music: Cuban Invasion," *Time*, February 23,1931, http://content.time.com/time/magazine/article/0,9171,930373,00.html.

29. Schuller 1989, 171.

30. Blesh 1958, 11–12.

31. Guilbault 1993.

32. Even in more recent studies by scholars such as Mark Tucker, Stuart Nicholson, and Terry Teachout, among others, "The Peanut Vendor" is not mentioned and is completely erased.

33. Monson 1999, 58.

34. Bhabha 1994.

35. https://www.grammy.org/recording-academy/awards/latin-hall-of-fame, accessed on November 6, 2016.

36. https://www.loc.gov/today/pr/2006/06-083.html, accessed on November 7, 2016.

4

"EL TEMA DEL APOLLO"

Latin American and Caribbean Music in Harlem

IN 2009, I WAS hired by the Smithsonian's National Museum of African American History and Culture to write a brief history of Latin music at the Apollo Theater in Harlem. The essay was to appear as a chapter in an edited volume, titled *Nothing Like the Real Thing: How the Apollo Theater Shaped American Entertainment*, and was to be published and sold at the traveling exhibit in celebration of the theater's seventy-fifth anniversary. I was given a two-thousand-word limit, access to the theater's archives at the Library of Congress, and one week to complete the assignment. I was told that all of the other chapters had already been completed, most focused on African American performers and a few historical essays on Harlem, and so time was of the essence. From my perspective, this last-minute inclusion of Latin music in a project that celebrated a performance venue most associated with African American culture and sponsored by a museum dedicated to the preservation of that culture seemed to be nothing more than a mere afterthought, perhaps even tokenism. Luckily, however, some enlightened folks on the editorial board realized that possibly something of significance was missing. I had performed at the Apollo a number of times throughout the 1990s and early 2000s with Tito Puente, Celia Cruz, Rubén Blades, Eddie Palmieri, Bobby Sanabria, and Ray Sepulveda, but admittedly, I had never thought much about the significance of performing Latin music on that stage. It was cool to rub the famous stump from the tree of hope for luck, which had been rubbed by everyone from Billie Holiday to Beyoncé. And besides, it usually was a good-paying gig with enthusiastic audiences.

Latin Jazz. Christopher Washburne, Oxford University Press (2020). © Oxford University Press.
DOI: 10.1093/oso/9780195371628.001.0001

I diligently began my hurried study while on tour in Colorado with Bobby Sanabria's Latin jazz nonet, Ascensión. As I furiously combed through the archive while traveling on the band's bus, the musicians inquired about what I was writing. When I told them, Panamanian alto saxophonist Walter Gene Jefferson (see Figure 4.1) said, "You know, Chris, I played in the house band for three years in the late 1960s, while also playing with Tito Rodriguez's band."

This serendipitous information gave me pause. Under the direction of saxophonist Reuben Phillips, the Apollo house band performed daily, backing up almost every major star in black music. What was the significance of having a Panamanian lead alto player performing with everyone from James Brown and Aretha Franklin to Count Basie and Ella Fitzgerald? As Jefferson began sharing his stories about the theater and describing the number of musicians from the Caribbean and Latin America who graced the stage, and as I dug deeper into the archive, I realized that there was no way to complete the writing assignment. I called the editors and said I needed more space and time. They granted it and delayed the publication process. In the end, I wrote two chapters for the book, one titled "Latin Music at the Apollo" and the other "Celia Cruz at the Apollo." After I submitted my

FIGURE 4.1 Gene Jefferson (b. 1930) circa 2010. Photo by Gary Jefferson, courtesy of Gary Jefferson.

chapters, I continued to think about just what it meant when Caribbean and Latin American music resounded from the stage of the Apollo and what relationship this venue had with the development of Latin jazz.[1]

This chapter examines the relationship between African America, Latin America, and the Caribbean through the music and its associated performance practices realized on the stage of the Apollo Theater. Through the lens of race, nation, and ethnicity, I explore the complex and often tenuous relations between the diverse peoples who colluded and collided on the stage of the Apollo to produce some of the most significant and influential contributions to popular cultural expression in the United States throughout the twentieth century. Though the Apollo is closely associated with African American music and performance, I contend that the venue was also one of the most important Caribbean and Latin American stages in the United States during that time. This chapter documents the breadth of Caribbean and Latin American music performance at the Apollo and explores the venue's impact on the development of Latin jazz.

CASE STUDY 6: THE APOLLO THEATER

The Apollo Theater is considered the most significant and influential venue in the twentieth century for African American music, dance, comedy, theater, and film. Ted Fox, chronicler of the venue, contends that "the Apollo probably exerted a greater influence upon popular culture than any other entertainment venue in the world. For blacks it was the most important cultural institution—not just the greatest black theatre, but a special place to come of age emotionally, professionally, socially, and politically."[2] Studying the discourse and historical narratives concerning the theater's history and traditions, one might surmise that Caribbean and Latin American performers rarely graced that hallowed stage. Their presence is almost completely absent in a discourse that is informed by a narrow US-based perspective of blackness. With a few notable exceptions, such as the work of Raul Fernandez, Ruth Glasser, John Storm Roberts, and Ned Sublette, Caribbean and Latin American musicians and their music are silenced in historical accounts and their contributions and participation at the Apollo erased.[3] This is perplexing, especially when considering that between the years 1948 and 1965, Machito and his Afro-Cubans performed fourteen one-week engagements, and Tito Puente's band performed ten. Duke Ellington's band, on the other hand, played nine one-week engagements during that same period.

Since the Apollo is so closely associated with black culture in the United States, acknowledging the diversity of performances complicates matters and could seem to undermine the empowerment of African American culture that the institution provides. I am not arguing for diminishing the contribution of black artists or the importance of the venue for black performance. Rather, in embracing the complicated encounters of intercultural exchange that were part and parcel of the daily routines at the Apollo, a more nuanced and globalized perspective of blackness emerges. And this perspective, I contend, is more empowering in the end, as it expands alliances of shared histories across broad geographical and cultural divides.

To examine the blurred and globalized space of intercultural encounter on the stage of the Apollo, I take direction from Joseph Roach's proposal of a model that focuses on performance and offers an alternative historical narrative of US culture, "one more resistant to the polarizing reductions of manifest destiny and less susceptible to the temptations of amnesia. Such a model emphasizes the truly astonishing multiplicity of cultural encounters in circum-Atlantic America and the adaptive creativity produced by the interactions of many peoples. Such a model requires a performance genealogy in which the borderlands, the perimeters of reciprocity, become the center . . . of multilateral self-definition."[4] I now enter into a historical discussion about how Caribbean and Latin American musicians and their music had a presence at the Apollo with Roach's model in mind. My aim is to counter the omissions, to document some of the significant numbers of Caribbean and Latin American performers who regularly appeared at the Apollo, and to demonstrate that the venue was equally significant for Caribbean and Latin American performance in the United States throughout the twentieth century.

* * *

Situated just blocks from one of the most vibrant Caribbean and Latin American neighborhoods in North America—Spanish Harlem, also known as El Barrio, the Apollo was and continues to be a nexus for intercultural exchange between African American, Latin American, and Caribbean musics. In Harlem, this exchange occurred in a variety of settings, both informal (everyday interactions on the street) and in more established performance venues. The Apollo proved to be one of the main nodes of contact and served as a formalized and prestigiously institutionalized portal through which Caribbean and Latin American culture entered African American consciousness as a viable entertainment option and, later, a viable expression of a related and shared circum-Atlantic colonial past that served as impetus for social commentary and change. Performances at the theater reinvigorated the communal ties of musical expression that emerged in New Orleans in the eighteenth and nineteenth centuries, where Caribbean and Latin American music traditions played an essential role in the emergence of popular music in the United States. As performance venues in New Orleans had been in the past, the Apollo Theater was now a space where racial divides and distinctions in sound were blurred, dismantled, and reconfigured.

Since its opening, the Apollo Theater has served as omphalos—center—for both African American performance and reciprocating intercultural exchange between black and Spanish Harlem.[5] Prior to the Apollo's inaugural show in 1934, the name of the theater had an established association with Caribbean and Latin American performance. As Spanish speaking populations grew in New York City in the mid-1920s, they became large enough to support a performance circuit directed and marketed exclusively to them. A number of Spanish Harlem venues, such as the Golden Casino and the Park Palace Caterer's Hall, began programming daily performances in Spanish. As these productions became more popular, performers sought more lucrative opportunities in established institutions outside of Spanish Harlem. Beginning in 1926, the theater known as the Apollo Burlesque became the first well-established venue outside of Spanish Harlem to feature all-Spanish productions at Sunday matinees. The Apollo Burlesque, owned by Sidney Cohen, was a small theater on West 125th Street located above the foyer of the Harlem Opera House (which happened to be partly owned by Frank Schiffman, future owner of the Apollo Theater) and just next to the theater that is now known as the Apollo Theater.

The matinee shows at the Apollo Burlesque included *zarzuelas, bufos cubanos*, dramas, comedies, revues, musical numbers, and other vaudevillian entertainment. These shows helped launched the careers of many local musicians and showcased a number of highly acclaimed bands from Cuba and Puerto Rico. For instance, the production on September 19, 1926, included the Spanish zarzuela "La Fiesta de San Antón," Vila Martinez, and dancers, along with the highly acclaimed Cuban band Sexteto Occidente, led by Maria Teresa Vera and featuring Ignacio Piñeiro on bass (who would go on to lead the highly influential son group Sexteto Nacional in 1927).

As Glasser has documented, prior to the Spanish programming at the Apollo Burlesque, Caribbean and Latin American performance events in Spanish Harlem tended to be community-sponsored and not associated with a professional network of agents, producers, and promoters. The Sunday shows set a precedent and marked the professionalization of the Caribbean and Latin American performance industry in New York.[6] This shift spawned a number of professional theaters and clubs in Spanish Harlem, such as El Teatro San Jose, and a network of locally based promoters and producers. The epicenter of the burgeoning Latin music industry was Fifth Avenue and East 110th Street, with performance venues and music stores stretching several blocks to the north, south, and east. The music store Casa Hernandez, owned by Puerto Rican composer Rafael Hernandez and his sister Victoria, opened in 1927 and was located on Madison Avenue between East 113th and 114th Streets. Gabriel Oller's Tatay's Spanish Music Center opened in 1934 on the corner of Fifth Avenue and 110th Street. Both businesses served as de facto musicians' union halls (as most Latin musicians were not unionized at the time) and mutual aid societies, where musicians and bandleaders would congregate to obtain work. It was a welcoming first stop for an influx of musicians immigrating from the Caribbean and Latin America. In the late 1920s and early 1930s, performance opportunities greatly increased for locally based groups and for touring bands, especially from Puerto Rico and Cuba. The newly established network of professional promoters and venues in Spanish Harlem was responsible for programming bands such as Don Azpiazú and his Havana Casino Orchestra in New York for their first time, among many other influential acts.

New York became the central location for the Caribbean and Latin American recording industry in the 1920s and 1930s. Numerous groups traveled to the city to record, and often musicians stayed or later returned to take advantage of the burgeoning scene. For instance, Cuban composer Antonio Maria Romeu brought his *charanga* band to record in 1927, bringing a young and impressionable musician named Mario Bauzá, who would later return to the city and transform the history of Latin jazz. The community of Caribbean and Latin American musicians living in New York grew considerably, and their exposure to the music of Harlem spawned much experimentation with jazz and Latin music mixings. At the same time, the immigrating and visiting musicians brought the newest Caribbean and Latin American dance crazes to New York, infusing the local scene with vitality and profoundly transforming popular music in the United States (the same can be said about the impact that US popular music and jazz had on the music in the Caribbean and Latin American as back and forth travel by touring bands became more frequent). The centralized Latin music industry and performance scene in New York facilitated greater access to US record executives looking for the newest trends—they only had to travel uptown to catch the rising stars. This easy access spawned more opportunities for the Spanish Harlem–based promoters, producers, and musicians. This is how RCA Victor Records came to record Don Azpiazú and his "rhumba." In a Borgesian sense, the Spanish programming at the Apollo Burlesque played a key role in these developments, which, in turn, had a profound impact on the development of Latin jazz.

When Sidney Cohen acquired the Apollo Theater, the Apollo Burlesque had just closed, and he subsequently borrowed the name in hopes of capitalizing on the smaller theater's past successes. And as with the Apollo Burlesque, he opened the new venue to black patrons and maintained the programming of Caribbean and

Latin American acts (but in a less segregated way). By the time the new Apollo Theater opened its doors in 1934, the Caribbean and Latin American music that had graced the Apollo Burlesque stage was having a significant impact beyond the confines of Harlem. Due to the success of "The Peanut Vendor," Cuban "rhumba" had become one of the most popular dance crazes of the day. Cohen, and later Frank Schiffman and Leo Brecher (who took over the theater in 1935), opted for a variety-show format at the new theater similar to the ones at the Apollo Burlesque, programming the most popular music, dance, theater, comedic acts, and film on the same show. Newly formed rhumba bands and dance troupes became regular features (almost weekly throughout the '30s), but they were billed as "specialty acts." Cohen and Schiffman had witnessed the success of the Caribbean and Latin American performances at the Apollo Burlesque and enthusiastically included those acts in the new theater's programming. What was new, though, was that the specialty acts shared the same billing as the top black and white performers of the day. This level of racial integration and intercultural mixing onstage was unprecedented in the mid-1930s.

The designation of specialty acts was significant on a number of fronts. "Specialty" in the context of the Apollo meant "other," "separate," and intentionally segregated from black and white performance groups from the United States. These performance traditions were perceived as different, and as such, their "special" characterization clues us in to the divides, tensions, and fraught relations across ethnic and racial divides within Harlem of the 1930s. The "othered" designation demonstrates the precarious positionality of the brown, tan, beige, and mulatto within hegemonic black/white racial categorization in the United States. It reflects a prejudicial legacy that extends back to the Louisiana Purchase, where Anglo-American cultural influence exerted a slow dismantling of the long-established three-caste system of New Orleans (black, creole, and white). This was done systematically through legislation that built on the French Code Noir laws. The newer Black Codes imposed broad segregationist provisions that favored a strict black/white racial binary and culminated in the *Plessy v. Ferguson* court decision in 1896 legalizing racial segregation.[7] As Roach has observed, these decisions artificially collapse culture into simplistic racial categories and then enforce those categories as absolutes.[8] These categories collapse cultural, national, and ethnic difference within both "black" and "white" communities in the United States and leave no space for those who do not self-identify with either of those two racial categories. This erasure still resonates profoundly in a variety of ways. We need look no further than the topic of this book and see how Latin jazz is positioned in relation to jazz and how historical narratives of jazz have been framed as black versus white, repeatedly. Erasure begets erasure.

The position of alterity imposed upon the Caribbean and Latin American performers at the Apollo, like many marginalized positions, yielded some unexpected advantages. In order to keep costs down, all black and white acts were required to perform with the Apollo house band. It was only the biggest stars who could muster enough clout to demand having their regular band members perform. On the other hand, the house band was not allowed to accompany the "specialty acts" and instead "specialists" (i.e., the regularly performing band members of those specialty acts) were brought in to perform the music. Gene Jefferson relates: "Even though I played lead alto in Tito Rodriguez's band, as a member of the house band I was not allowed to play any Latin music at the Apollo. I kind of had to keep quiet about my Latin gigs to keep playing in the house band. In those days, I did not really talk too much about being from Panama."[9] One can only imagine the difficulties that Jefferson and others experienced navigating this racially charged thicket in order to access employment within this African American performance domain. Regardless, the Apollo's performance policy actually provided more opportunities for Caribbean and Latin American musicians than it did for their African American and white counterparts. So even though Caribbean and Latin American performers and their music traditions were segregated discursively, in practice and onstage, there was an unprecedented level of inclusion and integration that foretold many things to come.

Since audiences at the Apollo were primarily African American, the frequent bookings provided high-profile exposure to the newest Caribbean and Latin American music styles, dances, and bands, propelling some groups, such as that of Cuban flutist Alberto Socarrás, to greater popularity and regular appearances in other Harlem clubs, such as the Savoy Ballroom. The increased presence of Caribbean and Latin American musicians in Harlem venues impacted jazz performance practice in a variety of ways. For instance, Socarrás's virtuosic playing established the flute as a viable solo instrument in jazz, something already well established in Cuban music but not in jazz. He recorded the first jazz flute solo in 1927, pioneering the way for generations of flutists.[10] Moreover, like Jefferson, a growing number of musicians from the Caribbean and Latin America began regularly working with the top black bands of the 1930s, whose star leaders could negotiate to have all or at least some of their musicians accompany them on the stage at the Apollo. For instance, Cuban trumpeter Mario Bauzá, who would later direct Machito's band, appeared a number of times at the Apollo as the lead trumpeter for Chick Webb, Noble Sissle, and Cab Calloway; Puerto Rican trombonist Juan Tizol performed with Duke Ellington; Puerto Rican bassist and tubist Rafael "Ralph" Escudero and Puerto Rican trombonist Fernando Arbello played with Fletcher Henderson; and Socarrás and Puerto Rican pianist Nicolas Rodriguez played with Benny Carter at the Apollo. Because of the popularity of Caribbean and Latin American music among dancers in Harlem and the fact that many bands had resident "specialists" performing regularly with the group, these bands expanded their repertoire to include rhumbas, congas, and other Caribbean and Latin American styles. They performed them nightly and occasionally even at the Apollo Theater. The programming at the Apollo was a key factor in maintaining the symbiotic relationship between jazz and Caribbean and Latin American music throughout the 1930s and 1940s.

During the post-WWII years, significant stylistic changes in musics of New York reflected shifts in the social landscape, particularly concerning issues of race, where an emboldened younger generation of innovative musicians began exploring their cultural roots through pan-African explorations. A central figure in these newer trends was trumpeter Dizzy Gillespie, whose fascination with Cuban music spawned a "perceived" new jazz hybrid in 1947, which he coined "Cubop." His interest in Cuban music was rooted in his performances with Socarrás's band and then deepened with his long-term friendship with Bauzá, whom he first met in Chick Webb's band, and they later played together in Cab Calloway's band. As roommates on the road, they spent much time discussing Cuban music. Bauzá's deep knowledge of Afro-Cuban traditions and the philosophical writings of Fernando Ortiz and Nicolás Guillén, along with Bauzá's Caribbean perspective on race, resonated deeply with Gillespie. As one of the collaborative inventors of bebop, a music that sought to disrupt the jazz tradition by infusing issues of race, revolution, high art, intellectualism, and virtuosic individualism to unprecedented higher degrees, Gillespie was deeply invested in exploring his cultural roots through his music. He found the public embrace of their African heritage and lineage by Afro-Cuban musicians inspiring and refreshing, and he felt that Cuban traditions mixed with jazz offered a viable option for sounding out the black archipelago and a shared circum-Atlantic black experience. It was on the stage of the Apollo Theater that he was fully able to realize and sound out the discovery of his cultural roots through his alchemic mix of jazz and Cuban music.

Mario Bauzá (1909–1984) introduced Dizzy Gillespie (1917–1993) to Cuban percussionist Luciano Pozo González, better known as Chano Pozo (1915–1948), when Gillespie expressed an interest in adding a conga drum to his big band for a performance at Carnegie Hall on September 29, 1947. It was a concert billed as "A Program of the New Jazz," featuring Ella Fitzgerald, Dizzy Gillespie and his orchestra, and a guest appearance by Charlie Parker. This was the first time Gillespie was booked at the hall as a headliner, indicating his growing influence and the acceptance of bebop. He wanted to take full advantage of the high-profile opportunity to solidify bebop's place in the jazz tradition and also to introduce a new mixture of jazz and

Cuban music that embraced a wide array of Afro-Cuban traditions while avoiding the trite exotica stagings of the past. In the concert, Pozo was featured as a soloist on George Russell's "Afro-Cuban Drum Suite," an experimentally dissonant modernist piece commissioned by Gillespie specifically for the performance. The suite featured an extended conga solo and an unaccompanied percussion and trumpet duet, both unusual and novel in a 1940s jazz setting.

Reviews of the performance were positive but focused primarily on Gillespie's bebop selections. Pozo's presence was barely mentioned, aside from noting the novelty of the added percussion (one reviewer mislabeled his instrument as "bongos"). Debuting Cubop on one of the world's most prominent classical music stages held much symbolic value, but ultimately, it wasn't the Carnegie Hall performance that had the lasting impact, nor was that where Gillespie was able to realize the full potential and meaning of his collaboration with Pozo. (See Figure 4.2.)

During the following month, the big band toured, and with each performance, Pozo progressively played a more prominent role. The most significant and telling performance occurred on October 31, 1947, when Gillespie brought

FIGURE 4.2 Chano Pozo and Dizzy Gillespie backstage at the Apollo Theater in 1947. Photo by Alan Grant, courtesy of Getty Photos.

his band uptown to perform at the Apollo Theater for a one-week engagement. Critic Dan Morgenstern describes a much different account of the Apollo performance compared to Carnegie Hall, documenting how Pozo served as impetus for a cultural shift in the jazz landscape through his staging of "African traditions." Morgenstern writes: "a powerfully built black man stripped to the waist, bathed in purple light, lit an oil lamp and began to heat the skins of his congas, it was a tableau that created tremendous anticipation. And when he had finished his beautifully timed, unhurried, stately and dramatic preparations and began to play and chant, he gave everything the prelude had promised, and more."[11] Morgenstern's words depict a consummate performer well versed in the staging of primitivism and exotic displays, full of theatrics and highly charged musicality. What is striking about this firsthand account was the speed with which the staging of Pozo's performance changed from the comparatively subdued midtown performance for a primarily white audience, where he was featured on only one number, dressed in a suit and tie, and refrained from singing, to the uptown performance for a black audience, where a ritualized space was created for Pozo to serve as prelude and frame for the performance.

This respectful and informed display of neo-African traditions performed by an expert in Afro-Cuban religious practices drastically diverged from the "exotica" stagings of Cuban music in the 1930s (remember Machín dressed as a street vendor in Havana or the cheesy castanets accompanying Armstrong's version of "The Peanut Vendor") and resonated profoundly with 1940s African American audiences at the Apollo. Moreover, this performance was the first time Harlem audiences heard an African language sung on the Apollo stage with sincerity and deep religious meaning. That was significant in and of itself, but what was more striking was that after hearing Pozo singing on the band's bus shortly after the Carnegie Hall performance, George Russell transcribed the words and melodies and wrote them into a revised version of his arrangement of the "Afro-Cuban Drum Suite." Gillespie's entire band, including both black and white musicians from the United States, were then required to sing in Yoruba as well, becoming the choral response to Pozo's incantations.[12] Such an integrated display of Africanisms in jazz was unprecedented, and it was at the Apollo where such risky innovation was possible in 1947.[13]

Pozo and Gillespie's collaboration was short-lived due to Pozo's untimely death in 1948, but their time together profoundly changed the course of jazz. They toured internationally, reenacting the Apollo performance for audiences across the United States and Europe. The result of their efforts established the conga drum as a viable solo instrument in jazz, they co-composed "Manteca" and "Tin Tin Deo" (both of which became Latin jazz standards), and, by conjuring a shared African heritage, Gillespie and Pozo's Cubop sonically unified the two most prominent communities of Harlem, "black" and "Spanish," and pioneered the way for future generations of innovators looking to explore the "black archipelago." Their more nuanced approach to Afro-Cuban jazz, which diverged from the peanut-tossing staged antics of novelty and "otherness" of the previous generation, served to introduce audiences to a more politically charged and sophisticated take on African American identity. It presented a provocative triangulation of a circum-Atlantic identity by way of New York, Cuba, and Africa, whereby an imagined common African heritage was consciously conjured, sounded, and performed.

Gillespie performed at the Apollo Theater for thirteen one-week engagements between 1947 and 1953, a period during which much of his creative energy was focused on pan-Africanist explorations through Cubop. The Apollo served as platform and portal for Gillespie's explorations, and its stage served as "auditora of cultural self-enunciation," reverberating the musical meldings heard years earlier in Congo Square with its provocative triangulation of a circum-Atlantic identity by way of New Orleans, the Caribbean, and Africa.[14] The first time Gillespie visited Cuba in the 1980s, he remarked, "Being in Cuba is like coming home."[15] The same could be said of the Apollo Theater. Prior to 1947, Gillespie had played there numerous times, both as a sideman and as a leader. Moreover, it is where he met his wife, Lorraine, a dancer who regularly performed at the theater. Performing at the Apollo was like coming home, too, a safe space for experimentation, discovery, self-actualization, and boldly asserting pride in his African heritage. On recordings of the "Afro-Cuban Drum Suite," Gillespie's voice is, tellingly, always the loudest among the chorus.

* * *

Mario Bauzá's impact on Latin jazz reached far beyond his matchmaking of Pozo and Gillespie, and the Apollo Theater played a key role in disseminating his influence and innovative approach to jazz and Cuban music mixings. In 1940, after coaxing his brother-in-law, Cuban bandleader Frank "Machito" Grillo to immigrate to New York City, they formed a band that took full advantage of Bauzá's extensive jazz experience and Machito's Cuban dance-music experience. Machito fronted the band as vocalist and percussionist, and Bauzá served as musical director. Their approach to mixing was unique for 1940, in that it equally balanced Cuban dance-music traditions with jazz big-band performance practices, and their performances were devoid of any notions of novelty and exotica. They employed a combination of well-seasoned Caribbean musicians along with experienced black and white jazz musicians from the United States, sonically unifying Harlem seven years before Gillespie and Pozo. They quickly grew to become the most prominent and influential Latin dance band of the early 1940s, with a repertoire that blurred the lines between traditional Afro-Cuban dance music and Latin jazz (though at the time, their music was referred to as "Afro-Cuban," and specific numbers were generically listed with their associated dances and rhythms, such as *guaracha*, bolero, conga, and mambo). Besides their musical innovations, perhaps the most influential aspect of the band was its name: "Machito and His Afro-Cubans" (see Figure 4.3). This was the first instance in New York where a prominent band's name adopted the "Afro-" prefix, reflecting the influence of Afro-Cubanismo and the writings of Fernando Ortiz and Nicolás Guillén. The name publicly asserted pride in their African heritage and accentuated the African elements that they consciously infused into their performances. For instance, Machito often included short phrases in Yoruba in his vocal improvisations, and their song texts often referenced African lineages of Caribbean culture and Cuban Santeria, a neo-African religion that in the 1940s was secretive and relatively unknown outside of its devotees.[16] Their overt embrace of African themes and practices predates Gillespie and Pozo's collaboration and was certainly a key influence, but it was not

FIGURE 4.3 Machito and His Afro-Cubans in 1947. Photo includes vocalist Graciela Grillo (front left), trumpeter Mario Bauzá (trumpet on back left), and bandleader-vocalist-maracas Frank "Machito" Grillo (front far right). Photo by William Gottlieb, courtesy of the Library of Congress William P. Gottlieb Collection.

until after the debut of the "Afro-Cuban Drum Suite" by Gillespie that Machito began regularly appearing at the Apollo.

Classified as a specialty act by the theater, Machito and all members of his band appeared in fourteen one-week engagements at the Apollo from 1948 through 1962, which was more often than most of the top jazz bands of the time. Their performances promulgated the public assertion of pride in a shared African heritage, something that was set in motion at the Apollo by Pozo and Gillespie. Machito's performances at the theater are also credited, in large part, for the popularization of mambo among African American dancers (a dance craze coming from Cuba that replaced the rhumba and the conga in popularity). This is key to understanding why there was such a uniquely high level of African American participation at the famed Palladium Ballroom (at West Fifty-Third Street and Broadway), the first midtown club (meaning "white") to regularly program Latin music. Catering to an integrated crowd, the Palladium broke down years of audience segregation and established the first truly integrated dance floor in the United States. The audiences at the Palladium crossed racial, class, and ethnic divides in an unprecedented way, surpassing all expectations of promoter Frederico Pagani and owner Max Hyman. They began Latin dance matinee shows on Sundays and Wednesdays in 1948, inspired by the programming traditions stemming from the Apollo Burlesque. The success of the matinees led to nightly Latin music programming, and the Palladium became the most important venue for mambo in New York City. The long history of racially integrated performances on the stage of the Apollo provided a precedent for the Palladium and served as the main conduit for the popularization of Caribbean and Latin American music and dance among African American audiences.

Machito's association with the Apollo Theater was significant in another way. For his debut appearance in 1948, his band was fronted by trumpeter Howard McGee and tenor saxophonist Brew Moore. Regardless of this secondary billing, for all intents and purposes, this was Machito and his Afro-Cubans with two guest soloists. The success of the week's performances secured a recording contract with the Roost record label, propelling his recording career to new heights and solidifying the foundational role of the Afro-Cubans in the emergence of Latin jazz. Their first recording for the label happened just weeks after their Apollo debut and included the repertoire they had played at the theater. The recording, titled "Cubop City Part 1 and Part 2," was released under the name Howard McGee and the Afro-Cuboppers. Roberts has argued that this is the first true Latin jazz recording, with its refined balance between jazz and Cuban music, more so than was ever attained on the Pozo and Gillespie collaborations.[17] For Roberts, Latin jazz was born on the Apollo stage.

In the late 1940s and early 1950s, the programming at the Apollo became even more innovatively progressive in its pairing of seemingly disparate performance traditions and exploration of new formats, both of which continued to popularize Caribbean and Latin American music styles among African American audiences. Much of this change began in March 1949, when prominent radio DJ and Latin music enthusiast Sid "Symphony Sid" Torin (1909–1984) began producing weekly shows at the Apollo, presenting the first "nightclub-style stage show" at the theater, a format that would become a tradition. In the first show, Torin served as the master of ceremonies and programmed the most eclectic and culturally diverse bill to date, which included Machito and His Afro-Cubans, the white bop vocal team of Buddy Stewart and Dave Lambert, Caribbean-American singer Harry Belafonte, and Danish-born trombonist Kai Winding and his All-Stars. The initial success of this genre/culture-mixing variety show format ensured similar performances in the future at the Apollo. Torin also had a penchant for featuring Caribbean and Latin American performers as guest soloists with jazz and popular music groups and jazz soloists with Latin dance bands, thus blurring the "specialty" status and personally engineering novel musical mixings. This practice was what club owner Art D'Lugoff, radio DJ Roger Dawson, and promoter Jack Hook adopted in their long-running and highly successful "Salsa Meets Jazz" series at the Village Gate, a weekly event that lasted from 1977 to 1993.

Throughout the 1950s and 1960s, Torin developed "theme-based" shows that favored Caribbean and Latin American acts. His first venture in this format occurred in 1954, when he booked the first "all-Latin show" at the Apollo, called the "Mambo Rumba Festival."[18] The week's engagement featured the mambo bands of Joe Loco and Tito Puente, Cuban vocalist Miguelito Valdes, Cuban percussionist Cándido, Puerto Rican singer Myrta Silva, Cuban singer Mercedes Valdes, Cuban bandleaders Arsenio Rodriguez and Gilberto Valdes, and the Mambo Aces dancers. Though the show was only moderately successful financially, it set the stage for future all-Latin music presentations and began a theme-style format that replaced the variety shows of the past. Torin later produced an "Afro-Jazz Revue," a "Latin Americana," and an "Afro-Latin Jazz" program (note his very early use of the "Afro-Latin" label, predating O'Farrill and Marsalis by forty years). During the 1950s and 1960s, Torin was responsible for bringing every major Caribbean and Latin American music act to the Apollo, ensuring wide exposure to the latest Latin dances and Latin jazz innovations, and maintaining the theater as New York's preeminent Latin music venue.

Besides Torin's productions, the amateur shows at the Apollo also featured Caribbean and Latin American music acts. A notable example is pianist Eddie Palmieri (Figure 4.4), who first appeared at the Apollo in an amateur contest in

FIGURE 4.4 Trombonist Barry Rogers (1935–1991) with pianist Eddie Palmieri (b. 1936) in 1962 at Kutcher's Resort in the Catskills of New York. Courtesy of Chris Rogers.

1950 as a teenage sideman in a small Latin jazz combo. Palmieri returned in 1964 for a week's engagement with his newly formed band, La Perfecta, which featured the unique instrumentation of two trombones, flute, and rhythm. Their powerful bluesy sound would revolutionize the sound of salsa within the next few years. Frank Schiffman noted the potential of Palmieri's band, writing on one of his now famous notecards: "1st time here & very exciting Latin group. 2 trombones make a big difference in sound" (Figure 4.5).

With so many shows per day, Palmieri started to improvise a riff at the end of each set to serve as an impromptu theme song (which up to that point they did not have). Over the course of the week, trombonist Barry Rogers added melodic phrases, transforming the riff into a number that would later become one of the band's hits, "El Tema del Apollo."[19] Palmieri stated that for him, the song is a tribute to the amazing and supportive audiences at the Apollo.[20]

"El Tema del Apollo" is particularly demonstrative of the sonic cultural mix that was often heard resounding from the stage of the Apollo—an Afro-Cuban cha-cha sung with Spanish lyrics, composed by a Nuyorican bandleader born in Spanish Harlem, cowritten by a Jewish American trombonist whose soloing is infused with bluesy gestures and informed by an African American jazz aesthetic and improvisatory vocabulary, and performed by a band made up of Puerto Rican, Nuyorican, and white musicians. Moreover, the band was booked and produced

EDDIE PALMIERI

7/10/64 - $2500   1st time here & a very exciting Latin group.2 trombones
make a big difference in sound.

FIGURE 4.5 Notecard from Frank Schiffman Archive, documenting the date of the engagement, the fee for the week, and Schiffman's personal observations. Courtesy of the Library of Congress.

by two Jewish entrepreneurs, Schiffman and Torin, reminding us about the back-drop of white mediation, or in this case Jewish mediation, operative in this milieu. As George Lipsitz writes: "All racialized populations suffer from the possessive investment in whiteness in some ways, but the historical and social circumstances confronting each group differ. Consequently, alliances and antagonisms, conflicts and coalitions, characterize the complex dynamics of white supremacy within and across group lines."[21] The Apollo is an example par excellence of the complex dynamics to which Lipsitz refers. Unpacking Torin's personal investment both economically and artistically in asserting a circum-Atlantic black alliance on the stage of the Apollo is complex. For instance, when Torin programmed the themed show "Afro Jazz" in the mid-1960s, he booked jazz drummer Art Blakey, vocalist Arthur Prysock, Cuban percussionist Mongo Santamaría, pianist Palmieri, comedian Flip Wilson, and an African dance troupe. Including Cuban, Puerto Rican, and African American musicians in an "Afro Jazz" show reflects his dedication and advocacy for the legacy of Gillespie, Pozo, Machito, and Bauzá and a progressively inclusive conception of what the prefix "Afro-" asserts, but it is a perspective that was not necessarily shared by all participants in the show. The imposition of such a position by a white producer for African American audiences, who was economically benefiting from such a staging (more so than anyone else on the stage), is fraught in many ways and must be acknowledged and accounted for in any analysis. It is part and parcel of the undergirding of the music business of

Latin jazz and the construction of the problematic historical narratives that this book seeks to address. Possessive investment in whiteness is an operative force in every arena examined in this book, including the sonic intercultural mix heard in "El Tema del Apollo."

With the rising popularity of soul, funk, and rock in the 1970s, less Latin music was programmed at the Apollo. Early salsa stars such as Willie Colon and Hector Lavoe, who performed their hit "Che Che Cole" on a soul revue show in April 1970, did not cross over well to Apollo audiences (though including salsa on a soul show was unprecedented). Schiffman complained in his notes that Colon was "too Latin" and "did not fit."[22] Salsa, a genre that was partly inspired by the civil rights movement, was forged by a young generation of Caribbean and Latin American musicians in New York attempting to assert a Latino cultural pride through music and performance. This culturally introspective musical expression did not easily translate to African American audiences. However, it is surprising that the Colon's and Lavoe's message, song choice, and rhythms did not resonate with the pan-African fervor of the times. They performed their hit "Che Che Kule," a song derived from a South African children's melody that features a mix of Afro–Puerto Rican *bomba* rhythms with West African rhythms that Dominican producer Johnny Pacheco heard while on tour in Africa, lyrics that incite everyone to dance the "African style" with a pan-Latinismo sentiment, and a raw and bluesy New York trombone sound refined by Barry Rogers. Perhaps Colon's and Lavoe's unwillingness to translate or communicate the significance of the song to the Apollo audience contributed to the impression of being "too Latin." Their disregard for reaching non-Spanish-speaking audiences was part of the militant and political stance that Colon and Lavoe were asserting. Unfortunately, their lack of success was a missed opportunity for deeper alliances and marked a hiatus for the Apollo in serving as a central meeting space for African American and Caribbean and Latin American culture in Harlem. Further contributing to this break was that the Apollo closed its doors in 1976, at the height of salsa's popularity and just as the music began appealing to more diverse audiences.

Since the theater reopened in 1983, Caribbean and Latin American music has returned to the Apollo only for special events, although that has not decreased the broad impact of those performances. For instance, in 1987, Tito Puente helped organized a tribute to Machito, which was filmed and later televised. He hired a young dancer, Eddie Torres, to choreograph several numbers. Torres (Figure 4.6) credits the success of the televised show as the seminal moment for launching the international mambo dance revival and for establishing his dance company. The Eddie Torres Dancers arguably have become the most influential Latin dance group in New York over the last thirty years, staging numerous mambo shows

FIGURE 4.6 Dancers Eddie Torres and Melissa Rosado performing at SOBs in New York City. Photo by Hazel Hankin, © Hazel Hankin.

and offering dance instruction throughout the city. His dancers have been central in launching the Salsa Congresses that now thrive internationally.[23] Their careers were launched from the Apollo stage.

Cuban vocalist Celia Cruz (1925–2003; Figure 4.7) provides another example of how Latin music has been incorporated at special events at the theater. Since debuting at the Apollo in 1964, Cruz returned numerous times over the next 40 forty of her career. For Cruz, an artist who was particularly attuned to and proud of her Afro-Cuban heritage and interested in exploring those roots through performance, appearing at the premier venue for African American music was particularly significant. In her autobiography, she made a point to express how honored she felt to perform on "the greatest stage in black America."[24] Her energetic performance style, virtuosic vocal abilities, larger-than-life stage presence, and proud assertions of African pride resonated well with African American audiences, regardless of the fact that many attending could not understand Spanish. Schiffman immediately recognized her talents and potential, noting after her first performance: "First time here. With Symphony Sid. A real star. Looks like Jo Baker and sings and dances with great animation."[25] Her presence always transformed the Apollo into a truly intercultural space, unifying the communities of Harlem through music. In fact, promoters often included her in events that centered on themes of unity. One example occurred on March 23, 1990, when Cruz took

FIGURE 4.7 Celia Cruz press photo from 1957. Courtesy of Photographs and Prints Division, Schomburg Center for Research in Black Culture, New York Public Library, and Omer Pardillo of Celia Cruz Entertainment.

part in a performance staged in celebration of the release from imprisonment of Nelson Mandela. Cruz shared the bill with South African singer Miriam Makeba, the Tito Puente Orchestra, and the Forces of Nature dance troupe. Reminiscent of Pozo's performance forty-three years earlier, Cruz began her performance by singing a tribute to the Santeria deity Chango in Yoruba. Her blend of older West African traditions with contemporary salsa sounds aptly captured the spirit of the emancipative celebration by symbolically sounding out the shared cultural heritage between Africa and Harlem. The Apollo provided a unique and special space for Cruz to realize her greatest potential as a catalyst for bringing diverse communities together in musical celebration.[26] In 2014, she was inducted into the Apollo's Walk of Fame, which honors legendary performers who have built the theater's legacy. She was the first Latin music artist to receive that distinction.

* * *

On June 16, 2011, as we entered the stage at the Apollo with Caribbean, Latin America, African American, and Anglo American performers, Bobby Sanabria turned to me and said, "The concert we are about to play will change Latin jazz history!" (See Figure 4.8.) It was a concert inspired in part by my contribution to the Smithsonian volume in which we "reconstructed" the sounding out of the "multiplicity of cultural encounters in circum-Atlantic America" so central to the Apollo's intercultural history—thus positioning ourselves within an emergent performance genealogy reaffirming a shared historical trajectory and a staged sonic ecology, if you will. Sanabria believed that our performance would reignite the Apollo as a central unifying node of intercultural exchange within the black archipelago. Brent Edwards has written about the emergence of a transnational black diasporic identity, claiming that "certain moves, certain arguments and epiphanies, can only be staged beyond the confines of the United States, and even sometimes in languages other than English."[27] Since its inception, the Apollo Theater has been a space that in many ways transcends the confines of the United States, both racially and ethnically, because it has enabled boundary crossing, conversations, and collaborations that were available nowhere else to the same degree, often enunciated in languages other than English. In 2011, the "New World"

FIGURE 4.8 The Bobby Sanabria Multiverse Big Band at the Apollo Theater on June 16, 2011. Front row, left to right: Nuyorican poet La Bruja, Young Lord member and poet Felipe Luciano, percussionist Cándido Camero, trumpeter Jon Faddis, and composer David Avram. Bobby Sanabria is at the drums in the center, and the author is in the back row at far right. Courtesy of Bobby Sanabria.

along with Latin jazz was being reinvented once again on the stage of the Apollo Theater.

On the mic, Sanabria began the concert by exclaiming, "Welcome to the center of the universe . . . the Apollo Theater in Harlem!" And then every musician onstage joined in singing a collective chant in praise of the Santeria deity Elegua. We all sang in Yoruba, and the significance of that act was clearly understood.

NOTES

1. Washburne 2010a; Washburne 2010b.

2. Fox 1983, 4.

3. Fernandez 2002; Glasser 1995; Roberts 1999; Sublette 2004.

4. Roach 1996, 189.

5. The omphalos was a carved stone located in the temple of Apollo at Delphi, thought to mark the center of the earth.

6. Glasser 1995, 112–113.

7. The *Plessy v. Ferguson* case of 1896 involved Homer Plessy, a New Orleans creole who challenged Jim Crow laws passed by the Louisiana State Legislature in 1892 concerning passengers in rail cars. Plessy had refused to sit in a car reserved for blacks and was arrested. From emancipation until 1877, when Reconstruction began to systematically dismantled the liberty of anyone with African ancestry, both blacks and creoles enjoyed a modicum of liberty and civil rights. For more, see Raeburn 2007.

8. Roach 1996, 191.

9. Personal communication with author, 2009.

10. Clarence Williams, "Shooting the Pistol," Paramount Records (cat. no. 12517), 1927.

11. Liner notes of *The Dizzy Gillespie Orchestra at the Salle Pleyel: Paris, France* (Prestige 7818), 1948.

12. Personal communication with George Russell and author, 1988.

13. Recordings of both versions are available for comparison. The live performance at Carnegie Hall is released on *Dizzy Gillespie and His Legendary Big Band Live at Carnegie Hall, 1947* (Artistry AR110). A recording done just two months later includes the revised vocal version and can be found on *Dizzy Gillespie: The Complete RCA Victor Recordings, 1937–1949* (Bluebird 07863 66528-2).

14. Roach 1996, 28.

15. http://www.carnegiehall.org/BlogPost.aspx?id=4294990480, accessed April 5, 2016.

16. I will return to Machito and a discussion of the coded messages of African culture embedded in his music in greater detail in chapter 5.

17. Roberts 1979, 78. The recording was rereleased in 1993 on *The Original Mambo Kings—An Introduction to Afro-Cubop, 1948–1950* (Verve A 513-876-2).

18. The Mambo Rumba Festival was inspired by a similar and highly successful event at Carnegie Hall and at Brooklyn's Paramount Theatre that same year. Having all-Latin shows at these prominent venues demonstrated the meteoric rise in popularity of mambo.

19. Released on Eddie Palmieri, *Azucar Pa' Ti* (Tico Records SLP 1122), 1965.

20. Personal communication with author, 2012.

21. Lipsitz 1998, 57.

22. Notecard from the Schiffman Archive at the Library of Congress.

23. Salsa Congresses were first established in Puerto Rico in 1997 and are multiday dance festivals that include an array of performances, demonstrations, classes, competitions, and workshops, along with social dancing, which draw thousands of dancers from around the world. Salsa Congresses are now held throughout the Americas, the Caribbean, Asia, Africa, Europe, and Australia. For more information, see McMains 2015.

24. Cruz 2004, 92.

25. Notecard from the Schiffman Archive at the Library of Congress.

26. Another special performance that included a remarkable mix of Caribbean music acts was held on March 19, 1992, for the 2nd Annual Caribbean Music Awards. The artists performing included Tito Puente; the salsa bands of José Alberto, Ray Sepulveda, Conjunto Imagen, and Johnny Ray; the Haitian band Tabou Combo; the calypso stars Lord Kitchner and the Mighty Sparrow. I performed that evening with Sepulveda and was struck by the unusual mix of Caribbean styles on one stage, something that rarely occurred.

27. Edwards 2009, 3–4.

You have to tell it the long way. You have tell about the people who make it, what they have inside them, what they're doing, what they're waiting for. Then you begin to understand.

—CLARINETIST SIDNEY BECHET[1]

5

THE "OTHERING" OF LATIN JAZZ

AS I HAVE DEMONSTRATED in the previous chapters, Caribbean and Latin American music styles shared a common history with jazz and each has played seminal roles in the other's development, intersecting, cross-influencing, at times seeming inseparable. Regardless, in much of the jazz literature, their relationship has been diminished or downright ignored. Discussions of significant innovators with ties to the Caribbean and Latin America, such as Tito Puente, Mario Bauzá, Chico O'Farrill, Frank "Machito" Grillo, Mongo Santamaría, and Hermeto Pascoal, to name just a few, are noticeably absent. This chapter focuses on the conspicuous omission of Latin jazz from the established jazz canon—the seminal collection of jazz history texts and recordings that are used for teaching and researching and the musicians most often programmed and broadcast. I will explore the reasons for these omissions and consider what is at stake when Latin jazz is included. I will demonstrate how the omissions are tied to the economic marginalization of jazz and the push to align the music with high-art traditions.

I first discuss the more recent trends in jazz and then present a historical overview of how the Caribbean and Latin American influence continued throughout the second half of the twentieth century before exploring how omissions manifest in different settings.

* * *

Latin Jazz. Christopher Washburne, Oxford University Press (2020). © Oxford University Press.
DOI: 10.1093/oso/9780195371628.001.0001

Since the mid-1940s, jazz in the United States has been moving away from mainstream popular culture and becoming more aligned with practices associated with Western art-music traditions as well as with alternative and marginalized art scenes.[2] For jazz musicians, this shift from "popular" to "art" status has proved advantageous in some respects, awarding an unprecedented level of "respectability" and increased recognition of artistic merit. This is particularly significant, though bittersweet, for many African American jazz innovators who, after persevering for years through much racial strife, are finally receiving long-overdue accolades. The road from brothels and speakeasies to Lincoln Center was a long and hard-fought one.

From the very beginning, jazz was programmed periodically in concert-hall settings, and musicians, such as Duke Ellington, made efforts to align the music with Western classical music traditions. Ellington wrote a number of long, extended, multimovement works titled "symphony," "concerto," "fantasy," and "suite," and he often performed them in classical-music venues. For instance, starting in 1943, he performed a series of concerts at Carnegie Hall. Predating his performances, James Reese Europe and his Clef Club Orchestra, a 125-piece band that played a variety of pre-jazz and proto-jazz styles, performed at Carnegie Hall in 1912. This was the first concert of African American music performed at the venue since its opening in 1891. Other significant Carnegie Hall performances include John Hammond's "From Spirituals to Swing" programs in 1938 and 1939, Benny Goodman's 1938 performance, and Dizzy Gillespie's historical Cubop performance in 1947. Norman Granz's long-running "Jazz at the Philharmonic" at the Philharmonic Auditorium in Los Angeles, established in 1944, was another important concert series. It was not until the 1990s, when programs with resident ensembles were established at the Kennedy Center in Washington, D.C., and at Carnegie Hall and Lincoln Center in New York, that jazz in the United States obtained substantial and sustainable institutional support and regular productions that were on par with classical music. Doors to institutional funding, concert halls, and universities (i.e., the "privileged white establishment") opened for the jazz world to an unprecedented degree. This certainly can be seen as a victory for musicians and proponents of jazz, such as John Lewis, Milt Jackson, Duke Ellington, Dr. Billy Taylor, Charles Mingus, Leonard Feather, Barry Ulanov, Stanley Crouch, Gunther Schuller, Albert Murray, and others, who for years had been demanding that the music be taken seriously and afforded a respectability absent in much of its history.

These new "art world" opportunities intensified tensions between commercialism and artistic integrity that have fueled debates in jazz for many years. In the 1930s, jazz, often synonymous with popular music, reached the apex of its commercial appeal. At that time, it is estimated that jazz records represented close to 70 percent of the recording industry's market share.[3] Jazz sales have since fallen dramatically (present estimates range from 1.0 to 3.3 percent, depending on what is included under the "jazz" label).[4] Jazz's more recent alignment with art-music traditions has been due, in part, to its economic marginalization. With the dwindling of performance venues and diminished market share in the record industry, like classical music, jazz in the United States was forced to seek other sources of funding and opportunity, such as concert halls, publicly funded venues, public radio and television, college radio stations, jazz festivals abroad, and the ivory tower.

Throughout the music's history, there have been performers who have strategically straddled stylistic lines between popular music and jazz, such as Paul Whiteman, Louis Jordan, Frank Sinatra, Herb Alpert, Quincy Jones, Kenny G, and others. When jazz musicians occasionally cross over and receive considerable popular appeal, such as trumpeter Chris Botti and pianist Diana Krall, in many ways, they are no longer treated as jazz acts within the industry and are instead promoted, marketed, booked, and produced as pop musicians, and their access to "art" venues and funding sources are limited. Producer and bandleader Quincy Jones commented: "What is a jazz record? Any record that sells under 20,000 copies, once it sells over that, it is no longer a jazz record."[5] According to Kevin Gore, who ran the jazz marketing department for Columbia Records, the average jazz album sells around 5,000 copies.[6] Lawrence Levine claims that making distinctions, as Jones does above, is essential for distinguishing art from the popular: "The urge to deprecate popular musical genres is an important element. . . . The process of sacralization endows the music it focuses upon with unique aesthetic and spiritual properties that render it inviolate, exclusive, and eternal."[7]

The economic marginalization of jazz has had a profound impact on younger generations of musicians. For most young musicians, today's jazz education takes place in college classrooms, and school-affiliated ensembles have replaced traditional pedagogical institutions (i.e., professional bandstands and jam sessions).[8] It is a great accomplishment that jazz is considered a serious enough subject to be taught in universities, but this shift is indicative of jazz's financial struggles. Economically, jazz in the United States is barely an independently sustainable entity and frequently must be subsidized to survive. The number of US musicians able to make a living solely through jazz performance is small and keeps dwindling.[9] Many musicians turn to teaching positions, performing other styles of music, and other part-time employment to support their jazz-performance careers. The Senate Concurrent Resolution of 1987 (HR 57) and its renewal in 1997, designating jazz "a rare and valuable national American treasure" worthy of support, was an important acknowledgment of the art form but also further proof that jazz is economically in trouble and in need of governmental support for its survival and preservation.[10]

The alignment of jazz with high and alternative art, the increase in jazz programming in concert halls, and the increase in jazz education opportunities in pre-college programs and in university settings have precipitated a demand for jazz scholarship to determine a canon of "great works" to be preserved through performance, to identify exceptional artists worthy of funding from institutions such as the National Endowment for the Arts and Chamber Music America, and to supply teaching materials. A subject worthy of study is also worthy of rigorous academic analysis and documentation. Accordingly, beginning in the 1990s, numerous monographs, articles in scholarly journals, and doctoral dissertations have been published that focus on jazz—a project that is still well under way. No longer is the construction of jazz historical narratives left primarily to musicians, journalists, and critics. Scholars from a wide range of disciplines, including musicology, ethnomusicology, anthropology, cultural studies, history, English, philosophy, and others, have embarked on the interdisciplinary study of jazz. With the emergence of this new literature, growing institutional support, and the release of influential documentaries and compilations, such as Ken Burns's *Jazz* in 2001 and its spin-off recordings, we are at an important juncture in the construction of the jazz historical narrative. Now is an opportune time, as the canon is being re/constructed, to stop and ask, what history is being written? And what history is being unwritten?

* * *

It was not until the mid-1940s, with the innovative work of Dizzy Gillespie, Chano Pozo, Mario Bauzá, Machito, Stan Kenton, and George Russell, and others, that a separate stylistic label was employed with regularity to differentiate Caribbean and Latin American–inflected jazz from other jazz styles. The jazz climate was ripe for the invention of new labels, as a younger generation of musicians began using "bebop" (and also "rebop") to distance themselves from their swing forefathers and foremothers. These new delineations, motivated by both musical and extramusical factors, proved to be lines of contention drawn by the next generation of jazz musicians who were seen as revolutionary in their musical and social vision.[11] Bebop musicians not only brought structural changes to the music but also initiated shifts in how the music was generally perceived. They self-identified as artists and began making demands that their music be treated as art. In retrospect, this distinction would prove to be a significant step in moving jazz away from the "popular" and closer to its present "art" status. The "bebop" label accentuated this distinction and also served as a marketing tool adopted by record companies to sell the latest musical trend. In some ways, bebop triggered a "label mania" in jazz marketing, where every few years, new names were introduced to an unprecedented degree (e.g., "hard bop," "cool jazz," "free jazz," "West Coast jazz," and "Cubop").

CASE STUDY 7: DIZZY GILLESPIE AND CHANO POZO

Dizzy Gillespie popularized the term "Cubop" as a stylistic label. The combination of his high-profile concerts and recordings featuring Chano Pozo, Gillespie's respected stature in the jazz world, and Pozo's popularity among New York's Hispanic audiences ensured that Afro-Cuban music would continue to have an influential role in jazz for years to come. Yet, as I have demonstrated, this was far from a birth or even a rebirth of a subgenre of jazz—maybe "revitalization" is a more appropriate descriptor. Nonetheless, the impact on subsequent jazz performance practice was significant, though the extent of the impact is rarely recognized.

The influence of the Gillespie-Pozo collaboration on jazz has been profound. Gillespie and Pozo's compositional collaborations yeilded several jazz standards (e.g., "Manteca" and "Tin Tin Deo"), established the conga drum's use in jazz settings (prior to 1946, it was rarely used and mostly just as a novelty item), and paved the way for numerous percussionists to make significant contributions to jazz, such as Mongo Santamaría, Ray Barretto, Sabú Martinez, Willie Bobo, Airto Moreira, Cándido Camero, and Tito Puente. Gillespie's stature in the jazz community legitimized and even demanded the more overt and publicly recognized incorporation of Caribbean and Latin American musical structures and principles into jazz music making and facilitated more collaborative cross-fertilization.

The increased presence of percussionists performing Afro-Cuban music in New York in the wake of Pozo's influence revolutionized the sound of jazz in a variety of ways. Flutist Alberto Socarrás commented that after "Manteca" was released, "a lot of American arrangers or orchestra leaders started having bongos, conga drums, and the same rhythm that Cubans have together with jazz. . . . I credit Dizzy [with the] improvement on the rhythmically poor American music."[12] Exploring more rhythmic options in jazz was a motivating factor in Gillespie's interest in Cuban music. Introduced to the wide variety of rhythms in Afro-Cuban music by his friend and bandmate Mario Bauzá, Gillespie was inspired to infuse jazz with greater rhythmic vitality and possibilities. Drummer Max Roach shared Gillespie's interests and credits watching Tito Puente's band at the Palladium and witnessing the interlocking parts played synchronously by three to four percussionists (typically used in Afro-Cuban rhythm sections) with inspiring his idea of playing with independent limbs (where each hand and foot plays a separate part).[13] Limb independence is the technique that transformed jazz drumming of the 1940s and is one of the most identifiable differences between the swing of the 1930s and the bebop of the 1940s. Reciprocally, Puente credits Roach with transforming his timbale playing, especially in relation to his virtuosic approach to soloing.[14] Their close relationship was on display while I was performing at the Blue Note with Puente's band in 1999. Roach walked into the dressing room unexpectedly, surprising Puente. After a long embrace, they sat close together, enthusiastically exchanging musical anecdotes. Their strong musical and interpersonal connection was very much alive fifty years after their first meeting. The septuagenarians were transformed with youthful exuberance right before our eyes and demonstrated that the interchange between jazz and Caribbean and Latin American traditions was a continual process (see Figure 5.1).

In the mid-1940s, jazz musicians were not well versed in soloing over static chord progressions (repeating vamps) or over nonfunctional harmony, nor were jazz audiences familiar with such performance practice, especially with the ever more complex and fast-changing harmonies of bebop. So when Gillespie cowrote "Manteca" with Pozo, he felt compelled to add a bridge (B section) that included a key change and added harmonic complexity to Pozo's two-chord vamping A section

FIGURE 5.1 Tito Puente (left) and Max Roach (right) backstage at the Blue Note Jazz Club in New York in 1999. Photo by author.

(the overall form is AABA). Gillespie commented: "He had that riff. . . . But Chano wasn't too hip about American music. If I'd let it go like he wanted it, it would've been strictly Afro-Cuban, all the way. There wouldn't have been a bridge. I wrote the bridge."[15] The insinuation in Gillespie's statement is that in 1947, jazz required harmonic complexity in order to maintain its identity. Though there had been other Afro-Cuban songs with simple repeating harmonic movement played by jazz groups for many years, "The Peanut Vendor" being one example, soloing over static harmony was not typical. Armstrong avoided a solo altogether in his version of "The Peanut Vendor," and Ellington added harmonically contrasting sections to the original.[16] Gillespie, the consummate entertainer, wanted to ensure that enough familiarity was presented in his experimental mixings in order to avoid any alienation of his musicians or audiences. He even changed the accompanying rhythm from straight eighths used in Afro-Cuban music to swing eighths used in jazz when he soloed over the form of "Manteca." However, George Russell's "Cubano Be Cubano Bop," featured in the same concert, was different and marked the beginning of a change in jazz performance practice that would be popularized by Miles Davis years later.

Composer Russell commented: "I wrote an introduction to that ['Cubano Be Cubano Bop'] which was, at the time, modal. I mean it wasn't based on any chords. Which was an innovation in jazz because the modal period didn't really begin to happen until Miles popularized it in 1959 . . . the piece was written in 1947."[17] In the late 1940s and early 1950s, Russell was a regular visitor to arranger Gil Evans's apartment, a famous gathering spot for musicians, such as Miles Davis, Gerry Mulligan, John Lewis, and John Carisi. Located behind a Chinese laundry on West Fifty-Fifth Street in midtown Manhattan and just a few blocks from the numerous jazz clubs on Fifty-Second Street, it was a convenient after-hours stop. The late-night salon hangs attracted like-minded innovative musicians interested in developing new directions in jazz. Their exchange of ideas eventually led to the highly influential *Birth of the Cool* recordings by the Miles Davis Nonet, recorded in 1949–1950 for Capitol Records (T-762) and released in 1956. The music of the nonet explored the use of nonfunctional harmony and modal tonalities commonly found in the music of French impressionism but also in Afro-Cuban music. Russell is the key in connecting the modal harmonies of Afro-Cuban music to the music emerging from Evans's salon and to Davis's adoption of a paradigm-shifting new aesthetic in jazz heard on the best-selling record of his career, *Kind of Blue* (1959), as well as other highly successful recordings in which he collaborated with Gil Evans, such as *Miles Ahead* (1957), *Porgy and Bess* (1958), and *Sketches of Spain* (1961).[18] Russell also developed his own modal approach to jazz composition and improvisation which he labeled the "Lydian Chromatic Concept."[19] While I was studying with Russell at New England Conservatory in 1988, he claimed that the modal jazz that emerged in the 1950s was a direct result of his collaborations with Gillespie and Pozo: "Cuban musicians had been playing that way for years; they inherited that from Africa. It came later to jazz. When I brought it to jazz, no one else was doing it."[20] Except for a few scholars, such as Ingrid Monson, the Caribbean connection to modal jazz has rarely been acknowledged.[21]

After the Gillespie and Pozo collaboration, many jazz musicians, such as Art Blakey, Kenny Dorham, Charlie Byrd, and Stan Getz, explored Caribbean and Latin American styles for inspiration and musical mixings. Some US jazz musicians, such as George Shearing and Cal Tjader, dedicated much of their professional energies to performing Latin jazz. For Shearing and Tjader, this was the direct result of bassist Al McKibbon becoming a member of Shearing's band in 1951. McKibbon previously worked with Gillespie and Pozo. He was Pozo's roommate on the road, an experience that transformed his career. He commented: "Dizzy upset the jazz world with the recording of 'Manteca,' but I realize that my entire career in Latin music grew from that date. . . . I began to feel that the Cubans were as close as you could come to African culture because they still practiced the roots of our music."[22] In the 1950s, he encouraged Shearing and Tjader to add Cuban percussionists to their bands. Tjader would go on to lead one of the most influential Latin jazz bands of the 1960s. It is also worthy of note that McKibbon recorded on the famous *Birth of the Cool* sessions with Davis, and he provides yet another link to Afro-Cuban music and the emergence of modal jazz.

For the rest of his career, Gillespie continued to serve as an ambassador for the internationalization of jazz. He visited Cuba, performed on many State Department tours, and for the last ten years of his life directed the United Nations Big Band, which featured mostly musicians from the Caribbean and Latin America. But because of the geographical breadth of the musical mixings, his "Cubop" label proved too limiting (even in his own band) and was quickly replaced by the more inclusive "Latin jazz." Since the time of Gillespie and Pozo's initial collaboration, it has become rare to hear a jazz set without some recognizable form of Caribbean and Latin American influence stemming directly from their mixing. However, as I have argued, having Caribbean and Latin American influence in jazz was nothing new musically, but the public recognition and conscious inclusion of the influence were something new.

With this new level of recognition and conscious incorporation of Caribbean and Latin American music in jazz settings came erasure of the historical legacy I have described above and in chapters 2, 3, and 4 of this book. Once Cubop was marketed and promoted as new, then the innovators of the past that forged the path before Gillespie and Pozo's stylistic change needed to be de-emphasized, as they did not serve the aim of the "newest thing" marketing campaign. What is often overlooked is that the emergence of Cubop was directly related to the performance practice of jazz bands of the 1930s and early 1940s and the growing presence of Caribbean and Latin American musicians participating in jazz.

From the 1920s to the 1940s, Cubans and Puerto Ricans immigrated to Spanish Harlem in significant numbers, bringing a greater demand for musicians from the United States to develop competency in contemporary Cuban and Puerto Rican styles.[23] Cuban bandleader Frank "Machito" Grillo, who first formed his band in 1938, employed and collaborated with many US jazz musicians, including Stan Getz, Stan Kenton, Dexter Gordon, Harry "Sweets" Edison, Zoot Sims, Johnny Griffin, Buddy Rich, and Herbie Mann, just to mention a few. The proliferation of Caribbean and Latin American dance bands in New York caused jazz bandleaders to change their repertoire and performance practice. Kenton credits Puerto Rican bandleader and pianist Noro Morales with inspiring his initial Afro-Cuban experiments, which made up close to 25 percent of the arrangements in his book when he formed his band in 1940.[24] Kenton later collaborated with Machito and the percussionists from the Afro-Cubans on several recordings including a version of "The Peanut Vendor" in 1947.

At the same time, many musicians who had arrived with the migration wave from Cuba and Puerto Rico began to perform regularly with US jazz groups. The interchange of these musicians and the exposure to Caribbean and Latin American music styles they brought leading up to the collaboration of Gillespie and Pozo were integral in the emergence of stylistic change in jazz. After all, it was Bauzá and Gillespie's friendship which developed over several years while sitting next to each other in the trumpet sections of several jazz bands that inspired Gillespie's experimentation with Afro-Cuban music. And it was Bauzá who introduced Pozo to Gillespie. The legacy and historical trajectory that I have described has yet to be fully documented and is rarely taught in university classrooms, included in historical narratives, or related to audiences from bandstands.

Since swing music was connected to dance, jazz bands needed to perform music associated with the dance crazes of the day (as demonstrated by "The Peanut Vendor") to appease their audiences. Along with foxtrots and Lindy hops, a variety of Caribbean and Latin American styles were played whenever their popularity peaked; examples include tango, maxixe, rhumba, samba, merengue, and conga. The extent to which bands incorporated Caribbean and Latin American rhythms and repertoire made demarcating a substyle within jazz seem absurd. The music of the early jazz and swing eras fluidly traversed the Latin jazz continuum (see chapter 1), where bands played music that ranged from swing numbers with little influence, to swing numbers with a certain degree of Caribbean and Latin

American influence, to Latin dance numbers with a certain degree of jazz influence, and to straight-ahead Latin dance numbers with little jazz influence. The terms "Cubop" and "Latin jazz" (and the others I discuss in chapter 1) eventually came to label the middle ground of stylistic mixing that had existed since jazz's beginnings. Gillespie and Pozo's efforts, along with those of others, served to reinvigorate this long-term relationship.

In the wake of Gillespie and Pozo's influence, Caribbean and Latin American–inflected jazz yielded jazz's biggest commercial successes, temporarily realigning the music with popular music. Two examples are *Jazz Samba* (Verve Records V6-8432), recorded by US jazz musicians Charlie Byrd and Stan Getz in 1962 (see Figure 5.2), and Cuban percussionist and bandleader Mongo Santamaría's (see Figure 5.3) 1963 recording of Herbie Hancock's composition "Watermelon Man" (Battle 2 BM 6120).

CASE STUDY 8: CHARLIE BYRD, STAN GETZ, AND *JAZZ SAMBA*

Jazz Samba was the result of the unintended consequences of] cultural diplomacy. In 1961, guitarist Charlie Byrd was sent to Brazil on a State Department tour as a "Jazz Ambassador," a program launched during the Cold War in which

FIGURE 5.2 Guitarist Charlie Byrd and saxophonist Stan Getz circa 1962. Photo by Michael Ochs, courtesy of Getty Images.

FIGURE 5.3 Bandleader and percussionist Mongo Santamaría. Photo by Joe Conzo Jr.

jazz musicians were sent on international tours to regions that were on the verge of embracing communism. Jazz was viewed by the tour organizers at the State Department as the sound of democracy, since every musician is given an equal voice in a jazz ensemble. They typically sent racially mixed groups to present a facade of racial harmony in the United States, as a culture without prejudice and inequality. As I have argued, jazz is not the sound, nor the product, of democracy; rather, its sound encompasses a troubled and fraught colonial past, the resilience of African American culture in spite of prejudice and inequality, and extensive intercultural exchanges fostered through vibrant and long-lasting cross-cultural dialogues. Moreover, the centrality of the jazz aesthetic, with its openness to outside influence that this global music embraces, yeilded some unexpected results. The impact of the jazz performances on prompting democratic reforms in the countries on the tour schedule is difficult to assess; however, the impact on the music is quantifiable. When musicians traveled to other countries, especially those with rich musical traditions, the musical impact tended to be greater on jazz performance practice than the other way around. This was the case when Byrd toured Brazil.

Byrd's tour coincided with the emergence of bossa nova, a highly popular national music that embraced a West Coast jazz-like aesthetic mixed with Brazilian samba traditions. The major proponents were a young generation of Brazilian composers, including Antonio Carlos Jobim, Luis Bonfá, Baden Powell, and others. The rich guitar traditions associated with the music had a transformative impact on the jazz guitarist from the United States. Inspired by recordings he brought back from Brazil, Byrd recorded an album titled *Jazz Samba* with Stan Getz in 1961, which featured US jazz musicians playing the bossa novas and sambas of Brazilian composers Jobim, Powell, Jayme Silva, and Ary Barroso, as well as one Byrd original. Though Getz had not traveled to Brazil prior to the recording, nor was he familiar with bossa nova, he found its rich harmonies and cool jazz aesthetic familiar. The familiarity was due to jazz's far international reach and its long-term interrelationship with Brazilian styles. Brazilian actress and vocalist Carmen Miranda had been central in the international popularization of samba in the 1940s that led to a brief samba craze in the United States, which prompted jazz musicians to include sambas in their repertoire. Brazilian guitarist Laurindo Almeida had collaborated extensively with Stan Kenton and trumpeter Bud Shank in the 1950s, and jazz-inspired ensembles had been commonly heard in Brazil since the 1920s.

The biggest hit from *Jazz Samba* was Jobim's "Desafinado." Translated as "Off Key," it is a nationalist song with an ironic twist aimed at critics of bossa nova in Brazil (though the lyrics were unknown in the United States, and Byrd's recording was purely instrumental). With half a million copies sold within eighteen months of its release, Byrd's recording reached number eleventh on *Billboard*'s Hot 100 and remained on that chart for sixteen weeks, reaching number four on the Adult Contemporary chart as well. This was the highest charting position any jazz record had achieved up to that time.[25] It was the best-selling jazz album in 1962. As with "The Peanut Vendor," the success of "Desafinado" prompted musicians to record their own renditions (Ella Fitzgerald's version reached number thirty-eighth on *Billboard*'s Hot 100 in 1962 as well). Getz went on to collaborate with Brazilian guitarist João Gilberto, vocalist Astrud Gilberto, and composer Jobim. The album *Getz/Gilberto* (Verve Records V6-8545, 1964) won the first Grammy awarded to musicians not from the United States. Due to the popularity of "The Girl from Ipanema" track, it won the Best Album of the Year in 1965, making it the first jazz recording to win this mainstream pop-music award. This would not happen again until 2008 with Herbie Hancock's *River: The Joni Letters* (Verve Records B0009791-02).

The success of Byrd's recording and Getz's subsequent release launched an international bossa nova craze, leading to numerous recordings, especially of Jobim's songs. Songs like his "The Girl From Ipanema," "One Note Samba," and "Wave," among many others, quickly became jazz standards. They opened the way for an influx of Brazilian musicians touring and immigrating to the United States, notably guitarist and vocalist João Gilberto and his vocalist wife, Astrud Gilberto, multi-instrumentalist Hermeto Pascoal, percussionists Airto Moreira and Naná Vasconcelos, pianist Tania Maria, and trumpeter Claudio Roditi. And just as with the Gillespie and Pozo collaboration, the Byrd-Getz project prompted a number of jazz musicians to dedicate significant amounts of their professional energy to performing Brazilian-inflected jazz, such as pianist Chick Corea, guitarist Pat Metheny, and flutist Herbie Mann. Since the 1960s, Brazilian jazz has been regularly included in jazz performances, becoming yet another way that Latin American influence is sounded out from jazz bandstands nightly.

CASE STUDY 9: MONGO SANTAMARÍA AND "WATERMELON MAN"

After its release in 1963, Mongo Santamaría's rendition of "Watermelon Man" quickly rose to number ten on *Billboard*'s Hot 100 (surpassing the peak position of "Desafinado"), number three on the Adult Contemporary chart, and number eight on the R&B charts, making it the best-selling jazz single in 1963. The influence of Santamaría's "Watermelon Man" was far-reaching. Besides being recorded by many other jazz groups and reinvigorating Afro-Cuban influence in jazz, it established a precedent and a successful model for Latin jazz recordings that was employed for many years. When negotiating my first record deal with Jazzheads Records in 1994 for my Latin jazz group SYOTOS (thirty-one years after Santamaría's hit), owner Randy Klein stated, "Just make sure there are several cuts on the record like 'Watermelon Man.' That needs to be our aim. We only need one of them to hit." This was reiterated in the negotiations of my subsequent five releases on Jazzheads. It was their business model for Latin jazz.[26]

The commercial success of "Desafinado" and "Watermelon Man" came at a time when the economic marginalization of jazz was accelerating. In the early 1960s, many influential musicians were experimenting with more esoteric forms of improvisatory expression—Ornette Coleman, John Coltrane, and Miles Davis were exploring freer forms. Soul, funk, and R&B were favored by younger generations. And rock 'n' roll was just on the cusp of sweeping an entire generation away from jazz. But these two recordings, which were primarily instrumental cuts that featured jazz solos (Santamaría's does have a short vocal chorus that repeats the song's title, "Watermelon Man"), defied these trends and pushed jazz expression into the mainstream popular realm once again. The commercial success of these recordings placed the bands and musicians that recorded them at odds with the art-status trajectory of jazz that was well under way. But each recording, in its own way, resulted in a paradigm shift and performance-practice change in jazz. And the fact that they were both Caribbean and Latin American influenced jazz was cause for ambivalence among jazz critics, the recording industry, and some musicians. The ambivalence continues and is made evident by the ambiguous genre labeling that both Byrd's and Santamaría's recordings receive.

Byrd's version of "Desafinado" was inducted into the Grammy Hall of Fame in 2000 and listed under the genre category of bossa nova, reflecting how it was often referred to in the 1960s. But when the entire album *Jazz Samba* was inducted in 2010, it was listed under the genre of jazz. Within ten years, the genre had somehow shifted. Was this in some way indicative of a change in perspective on the position of Latin jazz? When well established jazz musicians from the US perform the music of the "other," is it still then considered jazz? On the other hand, Santamaría's "Watermelon Man" was arranged with a straightforward son montuno rhythm while keeping the funky, soulful quality of Hancock's original version. When it was inducted into the Grammy Hall of Fame in 1998, it was listed under the genre of jazz. Even though Santamaría led a fairly straightforward Afro-Cuban jazz group, due to the success of "Watermelon Man" in the 1960s, the song was rarely referred to as jazz and was most often described as Latin pop, even though it was sonically and aesthetically aligned with the soul jazz of the 1960s. Was this because the group was led by a Cuban musician playing a nontraditional jazz instrument performing with US jazz musicians? Why did the designation change in 1998? The answers to these questions and the others posed above are not clear-cut, but what is certain is that the combination of commercial success and the perception that the success is built on influence coming from outside the jazz tradition created a cognitive dissonance in terms of genre labeling and placement within jazz's historical trajectory. I have discussed the stakes involved in genre labels in chapter 1, so I will not go into more detail here. But it is clear that this cognitive dissonance was, and continues to be, a contributing factor to why both "Desafinado" and "Watermelon Man" are typically not included as part of the jazz canon or in any extensive way in historical narratives of jazz.

The influence of Chano Pozo, Dizzy Gillespie, Charlie Byrd, and Mongo Santamaría continued to reverberate throughout the 1970s and 1980s. Stemming directly from the legacy of Chano Pozo and the popularity of Bossa Nova, Caribbean and Latin American percussionists became mainstays across many genres of music. Having a percussionist added to a band was hardly worthy of note anymore. In jazz, they appeared in a wide array of styles, from Miles Davis's *Bitches Brew* with percussionists Don Alias, Airto Moreira, and Juma Santos (Davis used percussionists in the majority of his subsequent bands), to the fusion band Spyro Gyra with percussionist Gerardo Vélez, and Elvin Jones with *conguero* Cándido Camero, just to name a few. The number of jazz groups playing only Latin jazz grew. A number of Latin dance-music stars of the '50s, '60s, and '70s formed smaller Latin jazz groups as their Latin dance music opportunities waned. Tito Puente, Ray Baretto, Eddie Palmieri, and Larry Harlow are just a few examples. Promoters of jazz festivals and clubs responded by allocating a few spaces for booking, as these high-profile musicians could draw significant audiences. For instance, the Blue Note Jazz Club in New York set aside one month each year for Latin jazz. And a new generation of musicians from the Caribbean and Latin America arrived in the US and began leading influential Latin jazz groups, such as Dominican pianist Michel Camilo, Puerto Rican pianist Hilton Ruiz, Puerto Rican percussionist Giovanni Hidalgo, Cuban clarinetist and saxophonist Paquito D'Rivera, Cuban trumpeter Arturo Sandoval, Brazilian guitarist Romero Lubambo, Brazilian vocalist Flora Purim, and many others. Despite this growing presence of Caribbean and Latin American music and musicians on jazz, the impact still remained mostly unacknowledged.

RECENT DEVELOPMENTS: PRESTIGE AND OMISSION

With the founding of Jazz at Lincoln Center in 1987, the project of aligning jazz with art music was complete, with the jazz presented on that stage remaining exclusive, formal, expensive, and separate from popular music. As Levine writes: "Exoteric or popular music is transformed into esoteric or high art at precisely that time when it becomes esoteric, that is, when it becomes or is rendered inaccessible to the types of people who appreciated it earlier."[27] Though Latin jazz was initially absent from the programming at Lincoln Center, a renewed interest in and resurgence of Caribbean and Latin American influenced jazz that emerged in the 1990s and continued into the 2000s prompted programmatic changes. Indications of the growing popularity of Latin jazz included a massive reissuing of classic recordings (mirroring the jazz recording-industry trends); the release of Latin jazz recordings by well-known jazz artists not previously associated with Caribbean and Latin American styles (e.g., Roy Hargrove, Don Byron, and Charlie Haden); the publication of the *Latin Real Book* and other instructional books; numerous colleges, music schools, conservatories, and pre-college programs offering Latin jazz ensembles as viable options to supplement their students' education; greater presence of Caribbean and Latin American jazz in concert-hall and jazz-festival programming; and increased presence on radio and Internet broadcasts. A growing influx of highly accomplished Cuban musicians arrived, enabled by brief periods of loosening relations with Cuba, allowing for more exchange and exposing audiences to musicians such as the virtuosic pianists Chucho Valdés and Gonzalo Rubalcaba. Musicians such as Panamanian pianist Danilo Pérez and Brazilian trumpeter Claudio Roditi who performed with Gillespie's United Nations Band rose to attain highly coveted (straight-ahead) jazz gigs. Pérez began performing in Wayne Shorter's band in

2000, and Roditi performed with McCoy Tyner, Jimmy Heath, and Horace Silver in the 1990s. Even sixty years after Juan Tizol played with Duke Ellington and Mario Bauzá played with Chick Webb, Pérez and Roditi were exceptions in terms of Caribbean and Latin American participation in straight-ahead US-based jazz groups. They reset a precedent that has only recently influenced change. For instance, it was not until 1998, when Nuyorican bassist Carlos Henríquez joined the Jazz at Lincoln Center band, that Wynton Marsalis hired a musician of Caribbean or Latin American descent in any of his bands.

This renewed interest in Latin jazz has led to a push to construct and record a viable historical narrative, documenting and structuring the complex genealogies of indebtedness and exchange. This has resulted in the publication of a number of historical studies solely dedicated to Latin jazz; notable examples include John Storm Roberts (1999), Luc Delannoy (2001), Raul Fernandez (2002), Leonardo Acosta (2003), and Jason Borge (2018); a number of scholarly articles have been published;[28] the release of *Calle 54* in 2000, a documentary film on Latin jazz; in 2002 the Bravo network produced *The Palladium: Where Mambo Was King*, a two-hour special on mambo in New York; the Smithsonian Institution produced a Latin jazz exhibit that toured the United States throughout 2002–2003; the founding of 3-2music.com in 1994, which publishes Caribbean and Latin American jazz and dance music exclusively; and the Thelonious Monk Institute of Jazz and the John F. Kennedy Center for the Performing Arts implementing an International Jazz Hand Drum Competition in 2000, the first year in the competition's fourteen-year history that hand drums were included (most of the competitors were percussionists from the Afro-Cuban tradition).

As scholars set about formulating the canonical works of Latin jazz, they are confronted with the problematic venture of canon construction that reinforces erasure and encompasses prejudicial limitations—the forces that inspired this book and that I am specifically writing against. Scholar Gary Tomlinson observes the inherent problems of the jazz canon.

> The jazz canon has been forged and maintained according to old strategies - Eurocentric, hierarchical notions behind which the rules of aestheticism, transcendentalism, and formalism are apparent . . . The canon operates . . . with little serious regard for the contexts in which cherished works were created and even less for those in which their meaning and value are continually discovered and revised. The jazz canon is a canon of the same serving a history of the same, and we have already lost sight of the partiality and impermanence of its structure of value.[29]

A brief examination of several influential canonical works—textbooks, scholarship, and music industry practices—demonstrate the pitfalls of the "same serving the same" with one cost being the marginalization or omission of the Caribbean and Latin American influence in jazz.

A monumental step in establishing a jazz canon of great works came by way of scholar Martin Williams' 1973 compilation, the *Smithsonian Collection of Classic Jazz (SCCJ)*. The long-term ramifications of the canonization process set in motion by the *Smithsonian Collection* can be gauged by two of the most frequently used college textbooks on jazz in the 1980s and 1990s, Lewis Porter and Michael Ullman's *Jazz: From Its Origins to the Present* (1993) and by Mark Gridley's *Jazz Styles: History and Analysis* (1978), both of which align their discussions with selections on the *SCCJ*.[30] This alignment was a logical one because of the *SCCJ*'s commercial availability allowed students to purchase their own copies for study at home, easing the logistics of teaching a music course. But Williams' choices reflected his own biases and no Caribbean or Latin American jazz selections or artists, with the exception of Dizzy Gillespie (not playing his Afro-Cuban jazz), are included. Porter and Ullman and Gridley perpetuated his omission. Of their nearly 500-page volume, Porter and Ullman devoted only two paragraphs to Gillespie's work with Chano Pozo and *bossa nova* receives a mere four pages of discussion. Gridley is even more remiss devoting solely one paragraph to the relationship of Afro-Cuban music and jazz. In Gridley's text, names such as Tito Puente and Machito are entirely absent, and Mongo Santamaría is relegated to a mere mention in a footnote. Such dismissive treatment is significant because younger generations rely upon educational institutions for their introduction and exposure to jazz. If the names of Caribbean and Latin American jazz performers and the jazz associated with their cultures are absent from the textbooks, they are most likely not being taught at all, unless instructors are aware of and willing to introduce supplementary texts and recordings. Since most jazz educators teaching today received their training in university settings, there is a tendency to adopt the familiar approaches and textbooks of their professors thus perpetuating the same serving the same—a jazz history without the Caribbean and Latin America. My own jazz history professor Richard Davis, despite his extensive performance career in New York City, used the Gridley textbook and omitted any discussion of the Caribbean and Latin America. When I began teaching jazz history in 2000 I was surprised to find that more recently published textbooks that are accompanied by their own listening compilations continue in a similar vein and have not added significant Caribbean and Latin American content. I eventually decided to forego using a textbook altogether and with significant effort and expense built a website that was aligned with the *SCCJ*, but included extensive supplementary materials on the Caribbean and Latin American influence in jazz.

Some of the most innovative jazz scholarship in recent years has questioned old paradigms of jazz historical writing and offers valuable new approaches; however, most forgo consideration of Latin jazz or the musicians who play it. For instance, Paul Berliner's paradigm-shifting ethnomusicological study of jazz, *Thinking in Jazz* (1994), offers an unprecedented and comprehensive examination of how jazz is played, conceived, and thought about from the perspective of its practitioners.[31] Berliner's list of "Interviewed Artists" whom he consulted for his research is impressive in its breadth and scope, stretching across generations and styles; however, he does not include a single musician from the Caribbean or Latin America or any musician who has dedicated much energy to playing any form of Latin jazz, with the exception of trumpeter Doc Cheatham, who performed with Machito and Pérez Prado. Another example is Scott DeVeaux's highly insightful study of bebop, *The Birth of Bebop: A Social and Musical History* (1997).[32] This impressively well-researched and attentive study neglects the innovative work by Machito, Bauzá, or any other musician playing Afro-Cuban jazz during the formative years of bebop. This omission is perplexing considering that Gillespie was one of the founding fathers of bebop and that he was collaborating with Bauzá throughout its formative years. And in Thomas Brothers's 2006 monograph, *Louis Armstrong's New Orleans*, after meticulously researching the influence of plantation culture on the emergence of early jazz and the relationship between creoles and African Americans in New Orleans jazz, he adopts a stance that is in opposition to acknowledging the role of the Caribbean and Latin America. He writes: "The arguments for a substantial contribution from the Creoles in the creation of jazz are based partly on mistaken notions about the role of Latin dance rhythms that found their way into Creole circles and partly on the role that many Creoles did play in jazz."[33] He does not expound further or stipulate what he means by Latin rhythms, but when discussing the wide range of styles that trumpeter Buddy Bolden performed, he conspicuously omits Caribbean and Latin American popular genres such as the habanera and the tango from his list. Brothers writes: "Bolden played all types of dances, including the quadrille, schottische, waltz, polka, and mazurka."[34] In spite of the brilliant value and innovation of these important contributions to jazz scholarship, they, too, perpetuate the exclusion of the Caribbean and Latin America.

In the most widely disseminated and heavily promoted documentary in jazz history, Ken Burns's *Jazz,* first broadcast in 2001, there is almost a total absence of discussions of the Caribbean, Latin America, Latin jazz, or any Latin jazz musician. Peter Watrous, jazz critic for the *New York Times*, said: "I can't help but think how jazz writing is so provincial, the fact that Ken Burns's first segment says nothing about the Caribbean demonstrates that and how big a role nationalism plays in the jazz scene."[35] Historian Robin Kelley also has discussed the nationalistic forces at work in Burns's project. He writes that Caribbean music and even African-infused jazz are omitted from Burns's *Jazz* because they "counter [one of] the film's burning assumptions: that jazz is exclusively American to be exported to the rest of the world as an advance guard in the struggle for democracy. . . . According to Burns, jazz is not only the exclusive property of the United States, but it has been a premiere manifestation of this nation's democratic ethos."[36] Both Watrous and Kelley are correct in identifying nationalism as an exclusionary force at play. But what I find more problematic is the particular notion of nation that is being purported in the documentary and in so many other avenues concerning jazz. It is a myopic and exclusionary perspective that selectively erases the complexity of our shared colonial past and in the process erases a significant portion of the people living in and contributing to the "nation." The brown, tan, beige, and mulatto are absent, along with much of the history I have presented in this book. Regardless, the Burns documentary and accompanying recording compilation proved impactful, with an expansive reach of more than 40 million viewers. The Burns compilation became the most extensive set of jazz recordings available for purchase, replacing the *Smithsonian Collection of Classic Jazz (SCCJ)* (which temporarily went out of print in 2000) in educational settings. Of its ninety-four tracks in the five-CD set of *Ken Burns Jazz: The Story of America's Music*, only one could be considered Latin jazz: Chano Pozo and Dizzy Gillespie's "Manteca."[37] Since 1973, when the *SCCJ* was first made commercially available, through 2001, little progress was made, and the omission was perpetuated.

The popular media, radio, and other record-industry structures have historically demonstrated a reluctance to embrace Caribbean and Latin American contributions to jazz and Latin jazz in general, a practice somewhat still in place. For instance, it was not until 1972, twenty years after Pozo arrived in New York, that *Down Beat* magazine added a percussion category to its annual awards. One writer for that publication (who wished to remain anonymous) commented: "Throughout the 1980s and 1990s, for some reason, if the record wasn't straight-ahead jazz, they would penalize it. For instance, every time I would review an Eddie Palmieri record and give it five stars, they would publish the review with only four stars. They would only occasionally let me write articles on Latin jazz players. But I could never figure out why they did that with the star rating."[38] According to Awilda Rivera, DJ at New York's main jazz radio station, WBGO, the station's long-standing policy was that no more than one Latin jazz cut could be played per hour. It was not until 1999, when she took over the nightly jazz show, that she was able to influence a programming change—reflecting, in part, a personal interest in her own Puerto Rican heritage. Now two or three cuts could be played per hour. She proudly stated: "They listened to me, and the programming department has now changed its policy. Now I can interview you and others that play Latin jazz on nights that were always reserved for straight-ahead styles. It broadens the audience for Latin jazz musicians."[39] And it was not until the 1990s that the Best Latin Jazz Album category was instituted at the Grammy Awards. This was a very significant development, as it marked recognition from the mainstream music industry, and award recipients enjoyed significant boosts in professional opportunities.

Despite these gains, however, musicians and advocates of Latin jazz must continue to be vigilant, as they experience constant attempts at marginalization and erasure that continue to plague jazz associated with the Caribbean and Latin America. A prime example of such an attempt occurred in 2011 when the trustees overseeing the Grammys unexpectedly reduced the awards categories from 109 to 78. They claimed that by eliminating categories that received fewer submissions, the competition across genres would be more equitable. They wanted to ensure that all Grammy Awards held the same competitive value. The Best Latin Jazz Album category was one of the eliminated awards. This was a particularly bitter pill for musicians such as Eddie Palmieri, Ray Barretto, and Larry Harlow, who had lobbied for years to establish the award category, a hard-fought battle against the prejudice that I have describe. They wanted to sculpt out a place for the recognition of Latin jazz musicians (especially Hispanic musicians and those from the Caribbean and Latin America), who had been excluded from winning and being nominated for Grammy Awards in the past. Until the Latin jazz category was established, no musician from the Caribbean or Latin America had won in the Best Jazz Performance category. Charlie Byrd's "Desafinado" was the only Latin jazz group to win in that category, but Byrd's group did not include any musicians from the Caribbean or Latin America. These types of exclusionary practices have not been reciprocal. Since the Latin jazz category was established, five of the twenty-two awards have gone to non-Hispanic musicians without any Caribbean or Latin American cultural ties (trumpeter Roy Hargrove, bassist Charlie Haden, vibraphonist Dave Samuels, trumpeter Brian Lynch, and composer Clare Fischer).

In 2011, Latin jazz musicians did not accept the explanation from the trustees concerning the changes, which impacted mostly music with ethnic-minority affiliations. Racist undertones were perceived, and Latin jazz musicians collectively protested with town-hall-style meetings, many resigned from the Recording Academy, and some returned previous Grammy Awards. When examining the number of submissions in 2010 more closely, it became apparent that the numbers had actually increased, but the judging committee had surreptitiously orchestrated the decrease by denying a number of submissions on the grounds that they were not Latin jazz and moved them over to jazz categories without notifying the bands. This happened to my own 2010 release of my Latin jazz group SYOTOS's recording *Fields of Moons* (Jazzheads Records JH1159, 2010). Our previous five recordings had all made the first round of Grammy voting in the Latin jazz category. My SYOTOS band was started in 1992, and we had been leading a well-known and longest-running weekly Latin jazz jam session in New York's history. We were an established Latin jazz band that *Time Out New York* had labeled "a New York Latin jazz institution," and our recordings were squarely within the traditional confines of what was widely considered Latin jazz. We were marketed that way, appeared in numerous articles in *Latin Beat* (the most important trade magazine for Caribbean and Latin American music), were regularly booked in Latin jazz festivals, played on Latin jazz radio programs, and self-identified as a Latin jazz band. The band members all performed regularly with Ray Barretto, Tito Puente, Mongo Santamaría, Arturo O'Farrill, and the like. *Fields of Moons* was a collection of boleros, ballads, *guajiras*, and son montunos played in a typical Latin jazz format. Despite all of this, in 2010, the Grammys no longer considered our music Latin jazz. When I contacted the Recording Academy to protest, I received the following one-line email explanation: "Your recording was examined by a panel of experts and they determined that your recording is a jazz recording, not a Latin jazz recording." When I inquired about who the experts were and what criteria were used to determine if a recording is jazz or Latin jazz, they declined to respond. I could only conclude that I was moved out of the Latin jazz category, along with a number of other musicians, in order to lower the number of submissions and bolster claims for the elimination of the category. Once again, Caribbean and Latin American jazz was erased and omitted. The real motivations for the elimination of so many marginalized musics has never come to light, though the marginalization process is a familiar one to musicians, and many attributed the decision to the inherent racism of the music industry.

In response, percussionist Bobby Sanabria led a group of New York Latin jazz musicians in a well-publicized lawsuit that alleged that the trustees had not followed proper procedures by not keeping its members abreast of the decision process, nor did they include the membership for comment during the process. The suit was later thrown out, but the accompanying media campaign had applied significant pressure. As a member of the board of governors of the New York chapter of the Recording Academy, Arturo O'Farrill lobbied from his inside position, and in 2012, the category was reinstated. According to Neil Portnow, the president and chief executive of the Recording Academy, strong advocacy from academy members and a sharp rise in Latin jazz submissions caused the reversal of the decision.[40]

I have identified marketing forces, ambiguous genre affiliation, nationalism, racism, and the dynamics of canon construction as forces involved in the omission of Latin jazz. I will now turn to other components involved in the canonization process of this systemic marginalization.

SO WHY IS LATIN JAZZ OMITTED FROM THE CANON?

Caribbean and Latin American songs have been incorporated into the repertoire of most jazz bands throughout history. For instance, in the 1930s, the Savoy Ballroom and other New York venues advertised dances featuring rumba bands, swing bands, and groups that played both. Both swing bands and Latin dance bands included both swing and Caribbean and Latin American numbers in their sets. The ease with which jazz musicians fluidly traversed these culturally diverse dances and rhythms is telling and reveals their close historical interrelationship. But the recorded history of jazz is deceptive when it comes to reflecting this cross-stylistic performance practice. With few exceptions, swing bands tended not to record many Caribbean and Latin American numbers, and Latin dance bands tended not to record swing numbers due to industry standard practices fueled by inherent racist and protectionist attitudes. The recorded jazz repertory thus appears more segregated than what was actually being played on the bandstand. This points to one cause of the Caribbean and Latin America's diminished role in jazz histories. Since many historical narratives are constructed primarily through the study of the music's recorded history, the role of the Caribbean and Latin America is typically diminished or missed.

Even when Latin-influenced jazz recordings are examined, historians of recorded jazz are disadvantaged by past prejudices held by the jazz industry. Due to the exoticism associated with Caribbean and Latin American music in the United States in the 1930s and 1940s, promulgated by the media and through performers such as Desi Arnaz and Carmen Miranda, Caribbean and Latin American influenced jazz was often viewed more as a novelty than as a serious musical venture. As such, Latin percussionists, viewed as ancillary, were seldom given credit in liner notes throughout the 1930s and the early part of the 1940s. For instance, on Louis Armstrong's version of "The Peanut Vendor," all musicians are listed except those playing percussion. Likewise, on Cab Calloway's 1940 recording of "Goin' Conga" (Okeh 5911), despite being the first jazz recording that features an extended percussion solo, no credit is given to the soloist or accompanying percussionist. The fact that an established jazz musician, Mario Bauzá, was playing maracas and Alejandro Rodriguez soloed on the bongos pointedly illustrates the record industry's disdainful views. When Bauzá played trumpet, on the other hand, he was rarely omitted from liner credits. In the context of these prevailing attitudes, it becomes evident how important the efforts of Gillespie, Kenton, and others were in calling for proper recognition of Caribbean and Latin American musicians whose participation and musical traditions were integral to the making of the music. By the late 1940s, percussionists were indeed credited equally and with more frequency.

Gillespie's advocacy had a profound and positive impact; however, his insistence on the "Cubop" label had some unintended negative consequences, as it began a formalized move that distanced the music from jazz, if only by way of name, and relegated it to status as a substyle. This built a barrier to the music's prospects for incorporation into the canon and has proven divisive when musicians, for exclusionary purposes, were pejoratively characterized as "Latin jazzers." Latin jazz has been systematically segregated ever since evidenced by its separate Grammy category and radio programming. As I pointed out in chapter 1, this stylistic pigeonholing has little to do with what jazz musicians actually play, but it still persists in the press, in the recording industry, and even among musicians. Was Gillespie a bebopper or a Latin jazzer? The answer to this question is obvious: he was a great musician, and jazz is a style of music that has, since its inception, incorporated a wide range of influences. As Jerome Harris writes: "The history of jazz supplies an openness, for jazz has been a syncretic art from the beginning . . . the incorporation of influences from non-jazz musics by jazz is quite substantial and it's likely to continue to be significant."[41] Regardless of jazz's openness to new sources of influence and its long interrelationship with Caribbean and Latin American styles, the marginalization of Latin jazz and Latin jazz artists persists.

The canonization process itself, which privileges preservation and requires the delineation of a tradition in which to preserve, is fraught with inherent difficulties. Since all historical texts are economies of truth, what gets economized is motivated by a complex of factors. Canonization presents a wholesale transference of non-jazz concepts to the study of the music. What it often does not allow space for is the internationalization of the jazz scene and the multiplicities that jazz encompasses. In fact, the "canon" resists or attempts to expel ambivalences in the definitorial field in order to create a unified narrative, which will not allow for heterogeneous trails of origin. In this context, canon building undermines the global nature of jazz to avoid the disempowerment of the African American jazz legacy—or an American jazz legacy.

Harris deftly identifies two positions taken by writers and musicians. The first he labels the "canon position," where jazz is seen as a music defined by a specific African American–originated canon and socially constituted guild. The second, the "process position," views jazz as the result of certain African American–originated processes and aesthetics manifested in the music.[42] The former treats jazz as an object or noun, the latter as an action, a way of music making, or verb. Both are slightly problematic in their essentialism, although the latter constitutes a more porous, open-ended approach to the tradition, providing room for a wide array of contributors and influences. The canon position is strategic, because it defines jazz as a sort of endangered species and elevates it to a high-art status, which as a result brings higher visibility and even a small but significant economic boost (e.g., Burns's *Jazz*). When the jazz tradition is viewed more as a process, individual musicians are empowered to innovate through a much broader spectrum of media forces than is the case within the strictly canon-based conception of jazz as an "establishment." In reality, most musicians operate somewhere between these two positions.

Latin jazz necessarily straddles the "canon" and "process" positions because of its constitutive role in early jazz and its use as a continual source for experimentation in the internationalization of the jazz scene. And it is this duality of positions that prevents and postpones its acceptance into the canon. For many in the jazz establishment (i.e., the community of musicians, promoters, educators, writers, DJs, industry professionals, and consumers), Latin jazz represents something alien, a continual disruption, which is paradoxical exactly because it shares a common origin with mainstream jazz yet has undergone several stages of disassociation along the road. Borrowing a physics metaphor from the trans-linguistic science of Mikhail Bakhtin (1986), one could define the impact of the Caribbean and Latin America on the jazz tradition as one of centripetal (unifying) and centrifugal (dispersing or disseminating) forces, respectively, constantly replaying this theme of participation without belonging. Every time it comes back to knock on the door, it unsettles the tradition and creates ambivalence.

Most visibly, the centrifugal dynamics inherent in Latin jazz serve to promote a heterogeneous texture in the music, allowing for individual musicians to explore a wide variety of styles that resist the singular aesthetics of the canon and promote globalization and internationalization. Latin jazz explicitly invites the participation of other non–African American cultures in jazz, as such possessing a transformational engine feeding off an ambivalence regarding musical and cultural affiliations. In other words, the Caribbean and Latin American presence in jazz history complicates the black/white dichotomy of racial politics in the US jazz scene.

Conversely, an occasion when Latin music served as a centripetal force on jazz was the emergence of Cubop. Cubans coming to New York in the 1930s and 1940s were steeped in the philosophies and sentiments associated with the Negritude movement. This was an intellectual movement that was promulgated in Cuba by the writings of Fernando Ortiz and Nicolás Guillén, which encouraged the exploration of the African roots in their culture, taking pride in their African heritage, and accentuating African elements in their arts and religion. The influence of these ideas is evident in the name that Machito chose for his New York band, the Afro Cubans. Chano Pozo was also a key figure in introducing this Afro-centric sensibility to the New York jazz world. A consummate performer who possessed a comprehensive knowledge of both sacred and secular Afro-Cuban styles, Pozo introduced the North American jazz scene to the deep spirituality essential to so many Afro-Cuban music styles without the novelty of the Latin jazz of previous eras. Pozo's vocal interjections in African languages, his use of Afro-Cuban religious musics tied to his Abakwa beliefs (an Africa-derived spiritual practice in Cuba), and his playing of an African-derived instrument (the conga drum) gave African American jazz musicians a direct connection, by way of Cuba, to an African homeland that resonated with the burgeoning civil rights movement of the mid-1940s.

The fact that Cubop's emergence coincided with political interest in the African diaspora in New York is not coincidental. Gillespie's explorations into Afro-Cuban musics were explorations into his own roots: "I found the connections between Afro-Cuban and African music and discovered the identity of our music in theirs."[43] Monson observes that as an African diasporic consciousness grew in the 1940s and '50s among jazz musicians, an urge to articulate that consciousness in the music grew, and Afro-Cuban music traditions became central to the process of triangulating between Africa and African America.[44] Drummer Art Blakey provides a prime example. Throughout his career, Blakey used Afro-Caribbean rhythms as referential expressions of Africa, and many of his recordings, such as *The African Beat* (Blue Note Records BLP 4097, 1962), *Holiday for Skins* (Blue Note Records BLP 4004, 1958), and *Orgy in Rhythm* (Blue Note Records BLP 1554 and BLP 1555, 1957), have African themes, express that "Africanness" through the incorporation of Afro-Cuban rhythms, and include collaborations with Afro-Cuban percussionists Sabú Martínez and Carlos "Patato" Valdés.

Not all musicians, though, have embraced Cuba in the articulation of an African consciousness and, by extension, an added racial dimension in jazz. Saxophonist David Murray, speaking of his work with Senegalese musicians, stated: "I'm not interested in going to Cuba and mixing, I mean that's been done. I'm not from Cuba; I'm from somewhere in Africa. I'd just like to find that place and know that I've touched home."[45] It seems clear that part of Cuba's appeal in Gillespie's search for African roots was access. In the 1940s, it was much easier to interact with Cuba than with African nations (most of which still remained under colonial rule), especially since many Cuban musicians were living and working in New York. In recent times, Senegalese musicians have become more accessible, and for Murray, they represent a more "authentic" homeland. Cuban musicians are no longer needed as mediators for that purpose and in some ways have been discarded for a "closer to the roots" connection. How does acknowledging a Caribbean or Latin American influence in jazz affect those who wish to accentuate the African and/ or African American origins of the music? How does it affect those who adopt a nationalist stance and focus on American essentialism? Without the acknowledgment of their centripetal possibilities, the Caribbean and Latin America can be seen as a disrupting force and a threat to the African American jazz legacy. Those wishing to promote that legacy will ensure that Latin jazz remains outside of the canon.

Harris discusses the anger that African Americans feel concerning their underrepresentation in the jazz industry, arguing, "It is not surprising that some African Americans have become vested in a definition of jazz (also held by some whites) as a cultural form in which no non–African American can validly participate." And as jazz becomes less relevant in everyday African American life, with more nonblack performers and foreigners in the industry, "the pangs of dislocation that [these trends] engender could well increase for some of the jazz community, putting more pressure on their narrow definitions of jazz and their exclusionist sense of cultural identity."[46] Those associated with Jazz at Lincoln Center, for example, have discovered that the canon position, which endows jazz with high-art status, also provides access to large portions of public and private funds previously reserved for Western art-music traditions. Narrowing their definition of jazz allows them to claim it as their own, and in some ways, this exclusionist approach plays into predetermined structures in the US public and private funding infrastructure. Since funds are scarce and the jazz economy is dwindling, a protectionist atmosphere is encouraged by those who are presently funded. A growing interest in Latin jazz presents a threat to this fragile balance of the jazz economy, creating an even greater need to continue the marginalization of Latin jazz.

Latin jazz presents another clash with the canon position, because, unlike other newer jazz styles, it has maintained a close connection with dance, and performances frequently include audience dance participation. Jazz's newly attained high-art status, which brings with it European-derived listening practices, is somewhat at odds with this dance component. They typically are not dancing in the aisles of Lincoln Center or Carnegie Hall. In fact, Tito Puente's contract for his last performance at Carnegie Hall specifically stated that dancing in the aisles was strictly forbidden, due to a fire regulation. In protest, Puente made sure to announce from the stage the presence of this clause while rolling his eyes. This compelled several members of the audience to rebelliously stand up and dance to his music. They were expeditiously berated by ushers with threats of expulsion. Since dancing has been divorced from most jazz performance for so long, this dance connection can create confusion among Latin jazz outsiders, pushing some to ask if the music can be classified as jazz at all and at times conflating popular Latin dance musics, such as salsa and mambo, with Latin jazz. There have been a number of times when my own Latin jazz band, SYOTOS, will arrive at a gig to find out that we have been advertised as a salsa band. Though they are related, like most Caribbean and Latin American musics and jazz, the stylistic differences between salsa and Latin jazz are quite distinct, as salsa tends to feature vocalists, infrequent and shorter idiomatic instrumental improvisations, and an aesthetic that is more in line with popular dance music. Latin jazz, on the other hand, fully embraces a jazz aesthetic and features extensive instrumental improvisation. Nevertheless, this genre confusion distances the music from jazz.

CONCLUDING REMARKS

Robert O'Meally observes that the ideology driving Jazz at Lincoln Center is that "jazz is a black yet distinctly American art form," and this "is taken directly from the [Ralph] Ellison canon."[47] In light of the thriving European, Asian, Latin American, and Caribbean jazz scenes, it is obvious that jazz has long ago broken out of US borders and that it is time to reconsider the Ellison canon. The beauty of jazz expression is that it can be adapted in so many contexts. That has been its nature from the beginning, inheriting the flexibility and openness of the African American culture from which it blossomed. I take inspiration from the views of DeVeaux concerning jazz historical narratives:

> I am increasingly aware of this narrative's limitations, especially its tendency to impose a kind of deadening uniformity of cultural meaning on the music, and jazz history's patent inability to explain current trends in any cogent form. . . . The narratives we have inherited to describe the history of jazz retain the patterns of outmoded forms of thought, especially the assumption that the progress of jazz as art necessitates increased distance from the popular. If we, as historians, critics, and educators, are to adapt to these new realities, we must be willing to construct new narratives to explain them.[48]

Yet years after DeVeaux's publication in 1991, we are still struggling to construct an inclusive narrative that attends to the rich and nuanced complexities that make jazz so compelling in the first place.

Promoter George Wein once stated, "No Europe, no Jazz," when commenting on jazz's economic reliance on overseas markets for survival.[49] He was making a reference to Blakey's well-known comment that he frequently repeated from the bandstand, "No America, no jazz," which Blakey followed with "We are a multiracial society."[50] This begs the question of what "America" and what "races" will be included in our conceptions of jazz? Might "No Caribbean and Latin America, no jazz" be warranted?

NOTES

1. Bechet 1960, 209.

2. Portions of this chapter were previously published in Washburne 2001–2002.

3. There is some debate concerning this 70 percent estimate, since opinions differ when determining which recordings and musicians should be defined as jazz. Moreover, in the 1930s, there was no clear way to verify sales in any uniform manner.

4. According to the Recording Industry Association of America, jazz sales fluctuate between 1.9 and 3.3 percent of all music sales. For instance, for the period 1993–2002, the statistics based on Nielsen SoundScans were as follows: 1993, 3.1 percent; 1994, 3.0 percent; 1995, 3.0 percent; 1996, 3.3 percent; 1997, 2.8 percent; 1998, 1.9 percent; 1999, 3.0 percent; 2000, 2.9 percent; 2001, 2.4 percent; 2002, 3.2 percent (www.riaa.com).

5. "Quincy Jones: In the Pocket," *American Masters*, PBS, aired November 18, 2001.

6. Watrous 1997.

7. Levine 1988, 132, 136.

8. The first jazz education program in a college was founded by Gene Hall at North Texas State University in 1947. Although this program served as a model for others, similar programs did not proliferate until much later.

9. For further demographic and financial information, see the study of jazz musicians conducted by Joan Jeffri in 2002, "Changing the Beat: A Study of the Worklife of Jazz Musicians," supported by the Research Center for Arts and Culture under a cooperative agreement with the National Endowment for the Arts and the San Francisco Study Center, https://www.arts.gov/sites/default/files/JazzExecSummary.pdf, accessed March 11, 2017.

10. *Congressional Record—House*, September 23, 1987, H7825–27.

11. For more information, see DeVeaux 1997.

12. Gillespie 1979, 323.

13. Personal communication with author, 2000.

14. Personal communication with author, 2000.

15. Gillespie 1979, 321.

16. See chapter 3 for further comment.

17. Gillespie 1979, 324.

18. *Kind of Blue* (Columbia Records CL 1355); *Miles Ahead* (Columbia Records CL 1041); *Porgy and Bess* (Columbia Records CL 8085); *Sketches of Spain* (Columbia Records CL 8271).

19. For more information about the Lydian Chromatic Concept, see http://www.lydianchromaticconcept.com/main.html; Boothroyd 2010.

20. Personal communication with author, 1988.

21. Monson 1998.

22. http://www.independent.co.uk/news/obituaries/al-mckibbon-302918.html, accessed April 4, 2017.

23. For further information, see Glasser 1995.

24. See Roberts 1999.

25. http://www.officialcharts.com/search/singles/desafinado.

26. Personal communication, 1994.

27. Levine 1988, 234.

28. See my discussion of recent scholarly work in chapter 2.

29. Tomlinson 1992.

30. Porter and Ullman, 1993; Gridley, 1978.

31. Berliner 1994.

32. DeVeaux 1997.

33. Brothers 2006, 187.

34. Ibid., 141.

35. Personal communication, 2001.

36. Kelley 2001, 10.

37. *Ken Burns Jazz: The Story of America's Music* (Columbia Records C5K 61432, 2000).

38. Personal communication, 2004.

39. Personal communication, 2000.

40. McKinley Jr. 2012.

41. Harris 2000, 116.

42. Ibid., 121.

43. Gillespie 1979, 290.

44. Monson 2000, 17.

45. Unpublished interview with Tim Mangin, 2000.

46. Harris 2000, 118–120.

47. O'Meally 2001.

48. DeVeaux 1991, 553.

49. Nicholson 2001, 28.

50. Taylor 1993, 242.

To tell a story is to *relate*, in narrative, the occurrences of the past, bringing them to life in the vivid present of listeners as if they were going on here and now. Here the meaning of the "relation" has to be understood quite literally, not as a connection between predetermined entities, but as the retracing of a path through the terrain of lived experience. Making their way from place to place in the company of others more knowledgeable than themselves, and hearing their stories, novices learn to connect the events and experiences of their own lives to the lives of predecessors, recursively picking up the strands of these past lives in the process of spinning out their own. . . . And in the story as in life, it is in the movement from place to place–or from topic to topic–that knowledge is integrated.

—TIM INGOLD[1]

6

"MORE COWBELL"

Latin Jazz in the Twenty-First Century

IN FEBRUARY 2009, Bobby Sanabria and his Afro-Cuban jazz nonet, Ascensión, were hired to perform at Yale University for an event in honor of Wynton Marsalis, a recipient of the prestigious Chubb Fellowship. As a highlight in the festivities, Sanabria had invited Marsalis to perform one song with his band. Staying true to the improvisatory nature of the jazz tradition, there was no rehearsal, and Sanabria did not tell Marsalis which song he would play or any of the particulars about his featured moment. Staying true to the competitive nature of the jazz tradition (and accentuating the long-term contentious relationship between jazz and Latin jazz), Sanabria chose Ronald Muldrow's "Soleshia," an obscure song with a particularly complex arrangement of shifting rhythmic feels and challenging harmonic changes. This ensured that Marsalis would not be familiar with the song or be able to easily predict the arranging shifts. This was a direct and adversarial challenge cloaked in the spirit of celebratory music making.

Sanabria's arrangement opened with all of the band members playing hand percussion over a 6/8 *bembé* groove and singing traditional chants in Yoruba. Shortly after the band began the introduction, Marsalis entered the stage and took his place next to me in the horn section. Noticing that all band members were playing percussion, he set his trumpet down and grabbed an extra cowbell and stick with the intention of joining in. However, once he started striking the bell, he realized something was amiss, as he was rhythmically out of sync and clashing with the rest

Latin Jazz. Christopher Washburne, Oxford University Press (2020). © Oxford University Press.
DOI: 10.1093/oso/9780195371628.001.0001

of the band. He turned to me with a confused look and urgently asked, "Where's the one [the downbeat and start of the musical phrase]?" Rhythmic disorientation in Afro-Cuban music is not uncommon among novices to the tradition. It had happened to me many times when I first began playing the music. So, sympathetically, I pointed out where the measure began by stomping my foot and yelling out "One!" I had to repeat this several times before he was finally able to reorient his hearing and begin to play in sync with us. My first thought was, "My God! I just gave one of the most gifted jazz musicians of our time a very rudimentary lesson in Afro-Cuban music . . . maybe a high point in my musical career!"

After the introduction, we set the hand percussion aside and played the melody once through before launching into solos. Marsalis played along with the band's trumpeter John Walsh, doubling his written melodic parts. At the conclusion of the melody, Sanabria pointed to Marsalis to take the first solo. This was another direct challenge, as it denied Marsalis time to ascertain the formal structure of the solos and to hear the chords he was expected to solo over. Marsalis embraced the challenge by skating gingerly through the first full chorus, straining to hear the structure and chords. This resulted in one of the most mediocre solos I had ever heard coming out of his bell. However, he proved his deep musicality by using only the first chorus to learn the complex structure before launching into three more choruses of some of the most profound and inspired soloing I had ever heard. And he never lost where the "one" was throughout (I take partial credit). He not only rose to the challenge but musically transcended the composition. A great musician indeed. (See Figure 6.1.)

This experience clearly illustrated Marsalis's relationship to Latin jazz which often is positioned in opposition to "his jazz." It was apparent he had never seriously studied or obtained the experience necessary to understand the interlocking complex of rhythms rooted in the West African traditions that undergird Afro-Cuban music and, by extension, much of Latin jazz (and, as I have argued in this book, much of jazz). This is particularly surprising considering that ever since Marsalis first met Cuban pianist and bandleader Chucho Valdés in 1996, they have maintained a close friendship. Marsalis claims that "he has been like another father ever since." When Valdés first visited Marsalis's home in that year, he brought two pages of transcriptions of *tumbaos*, melodic and rhythmic vamps that undergird Afro-Cuban music, and told the trumpeter, "Learn these!"[2] Did Marsalis ignored this fatherly advice? moreover, the audacity of Marsalis choosing the loudest percussion instrument onstage and attempting to play it despite his unfamiliarity was viewed by the musicians as disrespectful to the rich Afro-Cuban music traditions that are foundational to the jazz tradition that he espouses. In particular, the cowbell and its associative rhythms embody the legacy of slavery and its

FIGURE 6.1 Wynton Marsalis and the author at Yale University, taken just after his guest appearance with Bobby Sanabria's Ascensión in February 2009. Photo by John Walsh.

associated traditions of resilience that emerged in places like Congo Square—a legacy that Marsalis celebrates and posits at the center of "American" culture in his 1994 Pulitzer-winning jazz oratorio, *Blood on the Fields*.

Cowbells were transformed from farming tools to musical instruments by Africans seeking to emulate the sounds of their motherland while enslaved on plantations throughout the Caribbean and the Americas. Emerging from the metallurgical developments of early African civilizations, the penetrating sounds of struck metal objects (a variety of bells) easily projected over large drum ensembles and deftly served to rhythmically organize and align dancing and music making (especially in large open-air spaces with many participants). Bells playing rhythmic time lines became essential components in music traditions throughout West Africa. Lacking traditional bells in the colonial Caribbean and Americas, inventive African musicians adapted metallic farming tools to serve similar percussive functions in emergent neo-African music and dance traditions. Marsalis's apparent disregard for the instrument's significance in the tradition he bears—not worthy of practice and serious study before playing it onstage with musicians who have undertaken serious study—reflects a common lackadaisical attitude that has pervaded jazz for years (think of the castanets on Louis Armstrong's "The Peanut Vendor"). After the Sanabria performance one musician commented: "Jazz musicians are going to ruin Latin jazz for us. Everyone thinks that all you have to do is just hire a Latin rhythm section and play over them instead of dedicating years to playing the music."[3] These attitudes extend beyond jazz and into popular culture as well.

In the early 2000s, "More Cowbell" became an omnipresent pop-culture meme, adorning T-shirts, posters, coffee mugs, and various other paraphernalia. This popular phrase did not originate in historical studies of Congo Square but rather from a soft cowbell played in the background of the 1976 rock hit "(Don't Fear) The Reaper" by Blue Oyster Cult. As a mainstay in the sonic palette of many musical styles throughout the last half of the twentieth century, due to the popularity of Afro-Cuban dance styles such as mambo, conga, cha-cha, and salsa and their mass production and commercial availability in the United States by Latin Percussion (LP), a company founded by engineer and Latin jazz promoter Martin Cohen in 1964, cowbells were often added for various sonic effects in a wide array of musical settings. When comedian Will Ferrell noticed the cowbell being played in the background of "The Reaper," it inspired a short comedy sketch that he wrote for TV's *Saturday Night Live*. The sketch, first aired on April 8, 2000, reenacted the original recording session of the song and featured Chris Kattan, Chris Parnell, Horatio Sanz, and Jimmy Fallon as the Blue Oyster Cult band, with Christopher Walken as record producer Bruce Dickinson and Ferrell as a fictional cowbell player, Gene Frenkle. Ferrell's character appears to sabotage the recording by playing the cowbell loudly, but to the dismay of the band members, Walken's character keeps asking for "more cowbell," insisting that it is the key to making the song a hit. The sketch was later aired on VH1's *Behind the Music*. The inventive wit and performance of Ferrell had remarkable popular appeal, and the sketch is now considered one of the best in the history of *Saturday Night Live.* The result of its broad appeal and dissemination was the adoption of the phrase "More Cowbell" in multiple contexts.

As someone who has studied the organological history of percussion used in Latin jazz, I have always celebrated expressions of "More Cowbell" as they signify, albeit mostly unconsciously, an acknowledgment of our shared and troubled colonial past. When cowbells are played, reverberations of resilience of the enslaved Africans prevailing in the face of adversity resound. However, those celebratory reverberations are undermined when traditions are treated with disregard, especially by prominent figures in influential positions. The insult on the bandstand with Sanabria was amplified by the fact that the concert took place in the home of Robert Farris Thompson, one of the foremost scholars of West African music and

Afro-Latin dance traditions. That night at Yale, "More Cowbell" was not needed. We already had plenty played by seasoned veterans who had dedicated much of their professional lives to studying and performing Afro-Latin jazz.

If the situation were turned around, how would Marsalis or other "jazz traditionalists" respond? What if New York jazz musicians joined a New Orleans band and attempted to play traditional New Orleans music? Would we be allowed to join in? Well, I already knew. In 2006 and in the aftermath of Hurricane Katrina, Columbia University's Center for Jazz Studies and the Institute for African American Studies hosted a conference, "New Orleans: Rebuilding a Musical City." A number of displaced jazz luminaries from the Crescent City, including composer and pianist Allen Toussaint, vocalist Juanita Brooks, drummer Herlin Riley, and clarinetists Michael White and Evan Christopher, were invited to play an opening concert. As the director of Columbia's Louis Armstrong Jazz Performance Program, I, along with a number of other New York–based musicians, were asked to perform with the New Orleans musicians in a show of solidarity and support for their devastated city. Riley, Marsalis's longtime drummer and a renowned expert in New Orleans music, served as the musical director for the concert. All musicians were to be featured on one song and then perform all together on the closing number. Knowing my experience with Latin jazz, Riley chose "The Peanut Vendor" for my feature. A rousing rendition of "When the Saints Go Marching In" was appropriately chosen for the finale. In the rehearsal for the "Saints," Riley wanted all of the horn players to play a traditional brass call that typically precedes the well-known melody. This is not a practice that is common outside of New Orleans, and so during the rehearsal, Riley had to teach the short musical phrase to the New York musicians. He sang the phrase to us, and we immediately played it back to him. Though it was note perfect, he objected to our rhythmic feel. He continued to sing the phrase with the inflection he wanted, and we continued to attempt to match his feel, but each time, he objected to our efforts. This went on for close to ten minutes for just two measures of music. In frustration, he told us that we would never get it, as we were playing it like New York jazz musicians, and that he would scat sing it instead. None of us could hear the subtleties that we were missing. We had not taken the time to study the tradition or acquired the necessary experience, and as a result, we were silenced by the traditionalists of New Orleans. We respected his request, though it seemed strange in the performance when the drummer of the band sang a phrase that was obviously meant to be played by the horn players. For Riley, that was a better option than a "sacrilegious" rendition.

The inequities of the anecdotes above reflect a repeating dynamic between musicians who dedicate themselves to Latin jazz and musicians who consider themselves firmly in the "jazz tradition" (and in the case with Riley, the regional tensions that pervade jazz in general). In the years since the 2009 incident, Marsalis has begun to slowly embrace the Cuban traditions he dismissed in the past. In 2010, the year after the incident at Yale described above, Marsalis proactively embarked on delving more deeply into the Cuban sacred tradition by touring to Cuba with his Lincoln Center Jazz Orchestra to perform and collaborate with Chucho Valdés. The impact of that experience was profound, as he witnessed firsthand the similarities between traditions of his hometown New Orleans and Cuba. In 2014, Marsalis assembled a team of Latin music experts, including Valdés, Cuban percussionist Pedrito Martinez, and Puerto Rican bassist Carlos Henríquez to collaborate with and to compose *Ochas*, an extended three-part suite that combined the ritual rhythms and chants of Santería, the Yoruba-derived religion that developed in Cuba, with big-band jazz. Commenting on his collaborative process, Marsalis stated that Valdés was his spiritual guide, Martinez was his teacher of rhythms and chants, and Henríquez served as musical translator. Marsalis's aim was to express "the meaning of the religion as it passes through the sound of the batá drums and to capture a spiritual essence that has long coursed through jazz. . . . This is all personal. . . . It's about sharing, like you do in a family."[4] Significantly demonstrating a shift in his perspective, the premiere of *Ochas* opened Jazz at Lincoln Center's 2014 season.

I now turn to several case studies of prominent musicians—Eddie Palmieri, Michele Rosewoman, Carlos Henríquez, Miguel Zenón, and Bobby Sanabria— who are shaping Latin jazz in the twenty-first century, exploring their voices and perspectives and how they navigate this terrain of inequity and adversity.[5] This is not meant to be a comprehensive list of the innovators shaping Latin jazz—that list is extensive and much too long to include in this book—but each of these musicians adopts unique strategies that represent significant trends that will assert much influence on generations of musicians to come.

CASE STUDY 10: EDDIE PALMIERI—HARLEM RIVER DRIVE WITH THE PATRIARCH OF LATIN MUSIC

Pianist and bandleader Eddie Palmieri (Figure 6.2) was born on East 112th Street between Madison and Park Avenues in New York City (now known as Charlie Palmieri Way as a tribute to his musician brother), right on the edge of where Spanish Harlem meets Central Harlem, the meeting point of Latin American, Caribbean, and African American culture, and just blocks above the Upper East Side, the most affluent white neighborhood in the city. Growing up, he

FIGURE 6.2 Pianist and bandleader Eddie Palmieri. Photo by Enid Farber.

experienced firsthand the discrepancies and differences between these segregated neighborhoods. However, he also learned that music was something that could not be segregated or contained by racial prejudice, rent regulations, or economic inequality. Sound penetrates walls and social barriers and can travel across deep cultural divides. The young Palmieri listened intently across those divides. He learned early of the power of music as a unifying force and of its potential for promoting positive social change. These early lessons were the foundations of his illustrious musical career which would sonically capture the rich cultural tapestry of his youth. In 1936, the year of his birth, his neighborhood was the epicenter of a thriving Latin music scene, where the best acts from Latin America and the Spanish Caribbean could be heard nightly. Just a few blocks to the west, the best African America artists performed. This is where Palmieri came from—the edge between cultures, between races, between ethnicities. This is key to understanding the complexity of his music, his true artistic contributions, and his place in the twenty-first century as the elder statesman of Latin jazz.[6]

After he moved to the Bronx as a child, the diversity of sounds continued to penetrate his life through the jukebox in his father's luncheonette, which was aptly called El Mambo. He spent hours in the shop listening to all of the current Latin, jazz, and pop-music hits. At the insistence of his mother, music education played a large part in the lives of Eddie and his brother, Charlie. Both began piano lessons at an early age. Charlie was nine years older and a natural talent and began performing professionally in his teens. He set the bar high for his younger brother, who, as a left-handed pianist, had to work extra hard to catch up. Charlie introduced Eddie to the great jazz pianists of the day, such as Thelonious Monk, Bud Powell, Bill Evans, and McCoy Tyner, all of whom, along with Charlie, became musical influences in Eddie's life. Success in music came early. At age eleven, he won an audition to play in a youth concert of classical music at Carnegie Hall, quite an auspicious debut in a venue that he would return to as a headliner much later in his career. Rebellious in spirit and against the wishes of his mother, Eddie quit playing piano at thirteen to play percussion, his "true love." His first professional gig was on timbales with his uncle's Latin dance band. But that was short-lived, and by age fifteen, he was back on piano and resigned himself to be "a frustrated drummer" the rest of his life. He often claims that he takes out those frustrations on the piano. He plays the piano as though it is a drum, pushing its capabilities to the edge of its limits and often just past them. He has been known to abandon his fingers and pound on the keys with his forearms, using the full force of his weight. Pianos explode in sharp rhythmic bursts like slaps on the congas and rim shots on the timbales.

Charlie began sending Eddie on gigs throughout the city with various Latin dance bands, launching his career as a pianist. He played with Eddie Forrester, Johnny Segui's band, and the popular Tito Rodriguez Orchestra. He played all of the main venues in Harlem, including the famed Apollo Theater, making his debut in an amateur contest in 1951, at the age of fifteen, with a small Latin jazz combo. They did not win that evening (they won second place, and each band member received the prize of a new wallet), but he would later return with his own bands performing numerous times at the most important venue in the United States for black music.[7]

Working for other bandleaders proved too musically limiting. So in 1961, Palmieri launched his own band in order to pursue the full potential of his musical vision. His first band was audaciously called La Perfecta (The Perfect) and featured the unique instrumentation of two trombones, flute, and an Afro-Cuban rhythm section, unprecedented for its time. La Perfecta's sound remained true to Eddie's Nuyorican roots, embracing both his Puerto Rican heritage and his New York experience. Its sound captured the ethnic, racial, and cultural mix of his youth and the grit and intensity of the city. The band featured young and virtuosic Puerto Rican, Nuyorican, Brazilian, and white musicians, and their sonic mix, with its powerful bluesy expression deeply rooted in Afro-Cuban dance music, soul, and jazz, revolutionized the sound of Latin music. They quickly rose to compete with the top dance bands of the day and became the most popular Latin band among African American audiences. Palmieri observed, "We were the favorite of blacks because they were dancers, and no one swung like La Perfecta."

His reputation grew as a pioneering and uncompromising artist. His 1963 hit "El Molestoso" ("The Bothersome One") said it all. It was an autobiographical composition that referred to his reputation as a person unwilling to compromise in order to fulfill his artistic vision. He was militant in this venture. Last Poet and former Young Lord member Felipe Luciano observed, "Eddie is a guerrilla fighter, a slash and burn pianist who takes no prisoners and asks no one for approval of his Puerto Rican dreams and melodies."[8]

In 1968, Palmieri broke up La Perfecta and entered his most artistically experimental period. The late '60s was an intensely turbulent time in the inner city of New York and a period of crisis and transition for Latin music. The cessation of diplomatic relations between the United States and Cuba in 1962 and the subsequent economic and travel restrictions greatly reduced the influence of Cuban music, opening new opportunities for Puerto Rican and Nuyorican musicians to assert their influence. At the same time, the dominance of rock 'n' roll led to a decline in Latin music's popularity, prompting a new wave of experimentation as musicians sought to develop a new sound that would capture the next generation of audiences. The civil rights movement and the black power movement profoundly changed the political climate, and many Latinx adopted similar modes of protest and organization. Harlem became a cauldron of militant assertiveness and artistic creativity. Palmieri was one of the first Nuyorican musicians to react to these developments, forging a new sound that would capture the sentiments of "the street" and speak to the youth living in the inner cities. Inspired by writings of the nineteenth-century economist Henry George, he sought to represent the unheard and disenfranchised people through his music. Themes of social justice became the focus of his music, and he began performing in prisons and local neighborhood concerts to directly reach the people for whom he was advocating. His 1969 release *Justicia* (*Justice*),[9] which featured the one and only track where Eddie sings lead vocals, singing in English about social disparity, was the first step and foreshadowed the shape of things to come.

Driven by a deep political and social consciousness, he co-led with his brother Charlie the revolutionary group called Harlem River Drive. The band was named after a highway that allows cars to bypass the local streets of Harlem, allowing the rich to circumvent the inner city and avoid confronting harsh social realities. For Palmieri, this highway was a symbol of the inequalities of modern society. This group consciously combined Latin, soul, and free jazz to an unprecedented degree that sought to unify all of Harlem in the face of adversity. The band employed members of Aretha Franklin's band and some of the most important Latin musicians and jazz soloists of the day—quite a potent cocktail which broke down stylistic and cultural divides.

Soul singer Jimmy Norman was featured as the lead vocalist, singing in English so that everyone could understand the messages that addressed poverty and the social ills experienced in the daily life of the inner city. The project not only sonically unified both black and Spanish Harlem, aligning and empowering two communities that were suffering similar inequities, but also reflected the everyday integrated lives of Harlemites. As Norman observed, "When I came to New York, it was like every corner, almost, had congas and timbales and cats singing rumba and stuff on it. So I grew accustomed to that just by being a part of the ambience."[10] Harlem River Drive stylistically cut a broad swath through Harlem, zigzagging between the popular grooves and mashing them up in novel ways—from the *guajira* funk mix of the title track, to the straight-ahead soul of "If We Had Peace Today," to a funk *guaracha* mix of "Idle Hands," to the Miles Davis's *Bitches Brew*–inspired free-jazz jam of "Broken Home," and to the funk mambo mix of "Seeds of Life." The breadth of the music was large, and so were the aspirations of the project.[11]

In the end, the project was short-lived and not economically successful, and other than a live recording done at Sing Sing prison,[12] the band did not continue to perform. In many ways, the project was way before its time but also of its time, a condition of being on the edge of innovation. Regardless, its impact was long-lasting, inspiring many other bands to explore unique cultural mixes in music that could serve as a unified voice for the people. Groups such as War and Carlos Santana took inspiration from the Palmieris' cutting-edged band. In 2017, Eddie Palmieri resurrected the music for a concert and documentary for Red Bull Music Academy. The music sounded fresh and as though it had just been written.

After Harlem River Drive, Palmieri continued to pioneer in both salsa and Latin jazz, recording more than forty albums that set the standards in both genres. He remained a fierce advocate for the recognition of Latin music within the United States. In 1975, he began to reap the benefits of his efforts. That year, his album *The Sun of Latin Music* won the first Grammy awarded in Latin music. The establishment of the Best Latin Recording category came decades after Latin music first began playing a large role in the popular music of the United States. This demonstrates the adversarial arena in which Palmieri worked and innovated. His music had been persistently ignored by the mainstream music industry. He fought hard for its acceptance and finally won:

It took us seventeen years to put Latin music into the Grammys. Musicians like Tito Rodriguez and my brother never had a chance to win in their lifetimes. But then there was only one Grammy for all of Latin music. I won the first two. . . . Several years ago, they tried to destroy our progress overnight and take away our Latin jazz Grammy. The fight is never over. You see, jazz has had their category, but we [Latin jazz musicians] would never win. But things are still not equal, because now when we have our category, we have jazz artists in our category like Charlie Haden. Having them in our category takes away the essence of what it stood for, and that is another scar tissue."

Even Kenny G, who never recorded Latin jazz until 2015, was nominated in the Latin jazz category in that year (though he didn't win). Despite the competition, Palmieri has received nine Grammys throughout his career.

In the wake of the Grammys awarded, Palmieri finally began receiving the wider recognition he deserved. In 1988, he was designated an American icon by the Smithsonian's National Museum of American History. In 2002, he received Yale University's Chubb Fellowship, a prize usually reserved for international heads of state but given to Palmieri in recognition of his work building communities through music (the same fellowship Marsalis won). In 2009, the Library of Congress added his composition "Azucar Pa' Ti" to the National Recording Registry, which at the time included only three hundred compositions documenting the history of all recorded music in the United States. "Azucar Pa' Ti" was chosen because of its unprecedented length and commercial success. In 1965, this eight-and-a-half-minute track dismantled the standard three-and-a-half-minute format favored by radio for popular music, pioneering the way for many artists to experiment with the long-playing songs and subsequently revolutionizing the rock-music recordings of the 1970s. In 2013, Palmieri received a Lifetime Achievement Award from the Latin Academy of Recording Arts and Sciences, and he also received the National Endowment for the Arts Jazz Master Award, the highest honor an American jazz artist can receive.

The achievements listed above are even more remarkable when considering the racial prejudice, exploitation, and hardships Palmieri faced as a Nuyorican musician working in New York. Palmieri recalls:

For years, as Puerto Ricans and Cubans, we were denied access to venues because, like so many African Americans, we could not get cabaret cards, and so we could not work where they served alcohol. The Palladium changed that, and we finally had a midtown club where we could play. But to break into the business, I had no choice but to sign with agent Morris Levy in 1963. He was backed by the Gambino and Colombo families, which made it possible for

him to own the Birdland Night Club at age twenty-one. He had a tapestry behind his desk that read, "Oh, Lord, bring me a basket with talent." And when
I signed, I was looking at that and knew he would take everything. Once you
signed with him, nothing came to you. No royalties, nothing, nothing, and
you couldn't argue with him; otherwise, you would end up in the foundation
of the Verrazano Bridge . . . and that's when he was in a good mood!

As a young Nuyorican musician, Palmieri did not have many opportunities to
work with jazz groups, and so instead, he worked only with Latin dance and Latin
jazz bands. Because of this, he did not develop as a jazz player at a young age. He
comments:

I did not really understand jazz until trombonist Barry Rogers took me
to Birdland one Sunday to see the John Coltrane Quartet. McCoy Tyner
was playing piano, and he played twenty-minute solos that kept growing
and swelling. It was the same thing Afro-Cuban bands were doing. That
is when I figured out that every composition must have sex and danger.
That puts the human organism in a state of instability. The resistance is
what gives the climax in music. After that, McCoy became my mentor. And
that got me into jazz and led me more to Latin jazz. But I am not a jazz
player, because I do not know the repertoire of jazz. What I do know is that
I follow the harmonic structure of jazz, and I'm a Latin jazz player because
of the Latin rhythmical patterns that I comprehend. That is the underlying principle that makes Latin jazz, when well played, very exciting. And
it goes beyond any of the jazz musicians who have tried to record Latin
jazz. To me, it is a disaster. Even the great McCoy Tyner. . . . It is beyond
their comprehension because of our rhythmical patterns. The drum was
never allowed in the US, only allowed in the Caribbean. The African and
Spanish mixed, the mulatto came out, and that mulatto put the world to
dance with their drum. Latin jazz, to me, is the fusion of the twenty-first
century. But I prefer to call my music Afro-Caribbean jazz. You see, first
we had Afro-Cuban, then Afro-Caribbean when it came to NYC, now "Afro-
World" is really what we play.

As an octogenarian, Palmieri continues to play at the edge of possibilities,
pushing the limits of sound, and his infectious and relentless grooves build and
intensify beyond imaginable limits in the Afro-World music he commandeers.

CASE STUDY 11: MICHELE ROSEWOMAN—NEW YOR-UBA AND
THE SPIRITUAL SIDE OF LATIN JAZZ

Pianist, composer, and bandleader Michele Rosewoman was born in 1953 in
Oakland, California. In her youth, she studied both piano and percussion. She
credits being raised in a household full of music, from jazz to R&B to spiritu-
ally based musical forms from around the world, as the path to serious study of
Cuban and Haitian folkloric and sacred traditions. Those studies profoundly set
the course of Rosewoman's musical career and are the roots of her pioneering fusion of Afro-Cuban folkloric and sacred traditions with jazz, most fully realized
and embodied in her New Yor-Uba project. Despite the large role Afro-Cuban
traditions play in her compositions, however, she prefers to not label her music
"Latin jazz." Rosewoman states:

> I don't use Latin jazz to describe the music, but it's OK that others do. It is
> helpful in the industry if your music fits into some acknowledged category.
> I cannot describe my music with a label, only with sentences. . . . I would de-
> scribe myself as presenting original music that is rooted in more than one
> tradition, far-reaching contemporary jazz which is steeped in spirituality and
> based on Cuban folkloric musical influences. The result is expanded forms
> and an expanded musical language.

She first performed with various R&B groups in the Bay Area. In the mid-'70s,
she began leading ensembles while also working with trumpeter and composer
Baikida Carroll and trombonist Julian Priester. She says: "The phone was not
ringing off the hook, and I saw no need to wait. So I formed my own bands and
began to manifest my musical ideas and further develop a voice. I did not have too
many models of other women leading bands, but Carla Bley and Joanne Brackeen
were both inspiring." After coming to New York in 1978, she formed new ensembles
and continued presenting her music with New York–based musicians, while also
establishing a freelance career as a pianist working with jazz luminaries such as
Jimmy Heath, Freddie Waits, Billy Hart, Reggie Workman, Oliver Lake, Julius
Hemphill, James Spaulding, Gary Bartz, John Stubblefield, Rufus Reid, Howard
Johnson, Billy Bang, and Carlos Ward, and many others. She also performed with
a number of Latin musicians, including Celia Cruz, Los Kimy, Paquito D'Rivera,
Alfredo "Chocolate" Almenteros, Daniel Ponce, Andy Gonzales, and others.
Meanwhile, her interest in Afro-Cuban traditions fully blossomed into a lifelong
spiritual quest that culminated in her own initiation in 2007 into the sacred Yoruba-
by-way-of-Cuba belief systems associated with the music she was so bound to.

In the 1980s, Rosewoman formed two groups, Quintessence and New Yor-Uba (Figure 6.3). Both of her bands received critical acclaim and firmly established her as a prominent bandleader. Quintessence was her main vehicle for showcasing her evolution as a jazz quintet pianist and composer with the instrumentation of two horns, piano, bass, and drums. Rosewoman chose young, creative jazz musicians to work with, such as saxophonists Greg Osby, Gary Thomas, and Steve Coleman and drummer Terri Lyne Carrington, most of whom were not associated with Latin jazz but were kindred and adventurous spirits who were aligned artistically and conceptually. Quintessence began as a group without any pronounced Afro-Cuban influence; however, as Rosewoman delved deeper into Cuban's folkloric and sacred traditions, that influence began to permeate all of her music making. She says, "Everything is intrinsically connected because of how steeped I am in certain rhythmic traditions that shape both my writing and playing." The group evolved, and its repertoire often incorporated Cuban rhythms and performance practices typically associated with Latin jazz.

Debuting in 1983, New Yor-Uba evolved out of her close musical collaboration with master folkloric musician Orlando "Puntilla" Rios. Later, percussionists Pedro Martinez and Roman Díaz became foundational ensemble members. In this band, Rosewoman consciously unites accomplished jazz musicians with musicians

FIGURE 6.3 Michele Rosewoman and New Yor-Uba performing at the Painted Bride in Philadelphia in 2016. From left to right: Michele Rosewoman, Yunior Terry, Amma McKen, Rafael Monteagudo, Robby Ameen, Roman Diaz, Mauricio Herrera, Alex Norris, Roman Filiu, Stacy Dillard, and the author. Photo by Tom Erlich.

specializing in Afro-Cuban folkloric traditions in a large group setting (New Yor-Uba's most recent iteration includes a three-member *batá* drum ensemble, a folkloric vocalist, piano, bass, drum set, trumpet, alto saxophone, tenor saxophone, and tuba/bass trombone). Unlike other bandleaders who have blended these forms, she takes advantage of her comprehensive knowledge of the traditions and, by collaboratively working with experts, namely, Rios and Díaz, adheres closely to traditional practices while maintaining an innovative compositional approach that is interlaced with inventive spaces that allow for both traditional folkloric and jazz improvisation. Rosewoman coined the group's name to reflect how traditions traveled with the Yoruba people of Nigeria to Cuba through the slave trade and eventually came to New York. The music of the group sonically captures the influence of each location to produce an unprecedented blend. The ensemble's repertoire includes Rosewoman's original compositions that utilize rhythmic folkloric elements, as well as challenging jazz arrangements of traditional Yoruba and Arara (from Dahomey) sacred chants that pay tribute to the Orishas, deities from Yoruba spiritual practices. She was among the first musicians to present undiluted forms of Afro-Cuban folkloric traditions in jazz clubs and festivals throughout the United States and Europe. The balance of such a wide musical spectrum, with music coming from each end of the Latin jazz continuum (introduced in chapter 1), is what makes her music so unique. Her innovative approach of combining the traditions has earned her major support through grants from the National Endowment for the Arts, Chamber Music America, and ASCAP.

What makes her deep explorations into Afro-Cuban sacred drumming traditions even more remarkable is that women are typically not allowed to play percussion in those traditions. Rosewoman remarks:

I faced some adversity because women were not allowed to play *batá* here, although they were playing in both Africa and Cuba. But I was lucky, as I had some open-minded teachers, the first being Marcus Gordon, in Oakland. He had grown up in New York with percussionist Gene Golden, and they were among the first to play *batá* in public in New York City. I remember the first class I showed up to—there were about twelve men and three congas. I was the only woman and wondered if I would even get a chance to play, but I sure did. Marcus was beautiful; he brought me all the way in. It helped that I could play. I have chosen to view the world not through the eyes of an oppressed woman but rather to align myself with all oppressed people. In Puntilla's world, women did not touch the *batá*. I felt no need to challenge that, because I was right where I wanted to be. He saw where I was headed and invited me to his *batá* classes so that I could learn. It was hard to learn without touching the drum. Until I did, my knowledge was very scattered. Meanwhile, he often invited me as a guest to perform with his group, Nueva Generación. I played piano and sang in the chorus. He used to show me off on congas now and then—he was proud of me and very supportive. I had to stop performing publicly on percussion, though, as it was not good for my hands and piano playing. But I have never stopped studying and playing.

In spite of the exclusionary traditional practices, Rosewoman has persevered and developed an impressively comprehensive knowledge of the traditions and performance practices. A grant from Chamber Music America in 2015 enabled her to realize the full potential of her compositional prowess, her ambition of composing with a greatly extended form in a jazz setting, sonically exploring her great wealth of knowledge of the folkloric traditions. A few recent years of hands-on study prepared and enabled her to compose this new work which closely follows a liturgical set of rhythms from a sacred musical sequence of a Santería ceremony known as Oru de Igbodu or Oru Seco. The Oru Seco is a sequence of rhythms played by the *batá* without vocal accompaniment at the beginning of a ceremony called Tambor del Santo (Drums of the Saint). It consists of multiple rhythms and rhythmic sequences played for twenty-three Orisha spirits. She utilized a recording of a live ceremony played by Díaz and his drummers and composed on top of it. Adhering to and leaving room for the conversation that takes place between the three *batá* drums, at times she pianistically joins the *batá* in specific conversations, while individual solos and thoroughly original orchestrations weave in and out. Played by an accompanying jazz septet, the compositional elements are intrinsically connected to the *batá* patterns, at times abstractly referencing the traditional *cantos* (hymns or songs). Her pioneering work is entitled *Oru de Oro* and was premiered in New York in 2016, recorded in 2017, and commercially released in 2019.

In many ways, *Oru de Oro* is a continuation of what Chano Pozo began seventy years before with his introduction of Cuban folkloric and sacred traditions on the Carnegie Hall and Apollo Theater stages. However, the depth, openness, and full embrace of the sacred practices are what makes Rosewoman's approach unique. She credits how deeply tied *Oru de Oro* is with her spiritual beliefs:

Though I rarely talk publicly about my personal spiritual relationship to the traditions, my initiation added another level of meaning, a deeper spiritual understanding of the music. This allowed me to deepen my experimentation with the tradition. I have gotten much support bringing this sacred music out in public, because I always aim to present the traditions in a respectful way and stay true to the sacred ways. I realized one day that nobody can do what I do, because they are not hearing it the way I do and cannot fully integrate in the way or to the extent to which I do.

In Rosewoman's mind, the journey continues as she plans to delve deeper into the tradition by returning to Cuba soon to study the folklore for more inspiration.

CASE STUDY 12: CARLOS HENRÍQUEZ—LATIN JAZZ FROM THE INNER SANCTUM

While playing with salsa singer Pete "El Conde" Rodriguez in 1994 at a small club in the Bronx called Sidestreet, a fifteen-year-old bass player named Carlos Henríquez was escorted to the stage by his mother. As we prepared to begin the set, the band of veteran musicians looked at the kid skeptically, that is, until he began to play. At such an early age, he had remarkably mastered salsa's difficult *tumbaos* (bass lines) and had developed a comprehensive understanding of the *clave*'s function in Afro-Cuban traditions. Henríquez relates: "I was blessed, because when I was in high school, four of the best Latin bass players—Victor Venegas, Ruben Rodríguez, Bobby Rodríguez, and Andy Gonzalez—took me under their wings and taught me a lot. They gave me my first breaks." After that first successful night, the bass prodigy became a fixture on the salsa scene and was accepted as one of the cats at an unusually young age. Until he was twenty-one, he always was chaperoned in the nightclubs by a family member. He went on to perform with many of Latin music's greatest musicians, including Tito Puente, Eddie Palmieri, Celia Cruz, Rubén Blades, Marc Anthony, and Chucho Valdés. However, his intensive work in the salsa scene lasted only until 1998, when he became the first Puerto Rican ever to be hired by Wynton Marsalis and to play in the Lincoln Center Jazz Orchestra. As of the writing of this book, he is still the only Latinx musician to be a regular member in any of Marsalis's bands.

Born in the Bronx in 1979, Henríquez (Figure 6.4) is a second-generation Nuyorican. Recognizing his talent early, his mother enrolled him in Juilliard's Music Advancement Program, a program targeted to children from "backgrounds underrepresented in American performing arts."[13] This program prepared him for acceptance into the highly competitive LaGuardia High School of Music and Art (the New York City public school portrayed in the 1980 film *Fame*). When the school's concert jazz band won the Jazz at Lincoln Center's Essentially Ellington High School Jazz Band Competition and Festival in 1996, adjudicator Wynton Marsalis took notice of the young bassist's prowess. According to Henríquez,

FIGURE 6.4 Bassist Carlos Henríquez at Hostos Community College in the Bronx in 2018. Photo by Joe Conzo Jr.

Marsalis began mentoring him at jam sessions, at hangouts, and sometimes even on the basketball court in after-school pickup games. In 1998, shortly after Henríquez graduated from high school, Marsalis asked him to join his septet and the jazz orchestra. For close to twenty years, he has held one of the most coveted bass gigs in jazz. He says: "I got the gig with Wynton before I had a chance to pay dues playing jazz. So I had to learn on the job, and it was a lot of work learning the tradition. I had to learn how to play like all of the great jazz bass players." Marsalis also helped him develop his pedagogical skills by conducting workshops for the Jazz at Lincoln Center educational programs and eventually assisted in securing a faculty position at Northwestern University in 2008 for the bass player. Securing teaching positions for alumni and current members of his band at universities across the United States, a strategy Marsalis has employed for many years, ensures his influence on future generations of jazz musicians. Henríquez is just one of numerous musicians to enjoy this perk of working for Marsalis.

For the first ten years of his employment at Jazz at Lincoln Center, Henríquez played exclusively with the septet and the jazz orchestra, rarely playing Latin jazz at Lincoln Center. However, several years after the demise of the Afro-Latin Jazz Orchestra in 2007 that was led by Arturo O'Farrill, Henríquez would be thrust into the forefront of Latin jazz due to his extensive knowledge of Afro-Cuban traditions, his Nuyorican heritage, and his Spanish-speaking skills. Marsalis seized the opportunity to enlist one of his own band members to lead the Afro-Latin programming that O'Farrill had established. Henríquez was appointed musical director for the Jazz at Lincoln Center Orchestra's cultural exchange with the Cuban Institute of Music and pianist Chucho Valdés in 2010 and once again in 2014, when salsa singer Rubén Blades debuted as a guest artist with the Jazz at Lincoln Center Orchestra. In 2017, Henríquez headlined and was musical director of a concert titled "The Latin Side of Dizzy with Carlos Henríquez." What was unique about this concert was that Henríquez was given more artistic control over the music and was allowed to hire "specialists" in Afro-Cuban music, and no musicians from Marsalis's current bands performed (much like the case with O'Farrill). Henríquez took the opportunity to assert his Puerto Rican roots in a number of ways. His arrangements included Puerto Rican *bomba* and *plena* rhythms, something that Gillespie's originals did not include. On several arrangements, he played his electric Ampeg baby bass, an upright electric instrument that is a mainstay in salsa bands but is rarely played in Jazz at Lincoln Center programs. For the arrangements in which he played acoustic bass, he brought an instrument previous owned by Bobby Rodriguez (a Puerto Rican musician who is one of the most important bassists in Latin music) and which was played by Rodriguez while recording with Gillespie.[14] Henríquez's influence could also be witnessed in the promotional announcements about the concert: "The concert explores how Dizzy Gillespie brought Cuban rhythm back to the forefront of jazz in the 1940s."[15] This is a most remarkable assertion from the inner sanctum of jazz which publicly acknowledges that Cuban rhythm had been at the forefront of jazz prior to 1940. This was a new and important development and no doubt directly tied to the presence of Henríquez.

In 2015, Henríquez released his first recording as a leader, titled *The Bronx Pyramid*, on Jazz at Lincoln Center's own label, Blue Engine Records. Once more, he took the opportunity to make a statement by releasing an album firmly centered in the Latin jazz realm. With the exception of drummer Ali Jackson, no musicians are included from the Marsalis bands, and instead, he chose mainly Nuyorican and Cuban musicians who specialize in Latin jazz, such as trumpeter Michael Rodriguez, pianist Robert Rodriguez, saxophonist Felipe Lamoglia, percussionists Pedrito Martinez and Bobby Allende, and a special guest appearance by vocalist Rubén Blades. For Henríquez, there is no cognitive dissonance between his work with Marsalis and his own Latin jazz. "The habanera rhythm plays an important role in the roots of jazz, and for aspiring bass players, that is the most important thing to understand. You can hear this in jazz, because there is a 'big four' beat that falls on every other measure [where the fourth beat in the measure is accented]. You need to learn that as a jazz bass player. It is just like Latin music, except that in Latin music, it falls on the fourth beat of every measure. There are so many connections between the musics."

When Henríquez put together a mambo orchestra for a tribute to Tito Puente in 2017 on a Jazz at Lincoln Center program, he was touted in the press materials as "the most important Latin Jazz artist in New York City today, the heir to the legacy of Tito Puente."[16] This raised many eyebrows among veterans of Puente's band, but it is indicative of the gravitas that comes from Henríquez's association with Marsalis. Henríquez has been firmly indoctrinated by Marsalis and his associated discourse that asserts jazz as art and American. And Henríquez has greatly benefited from that assertion, having obtained and maintained one of the best-paying gigs in jazz for many years. However, what is significant is how he has begun to use his powerful position to incite change from within by acknowledging the contribution of the Caribbean and Latin America and thus raising the profile of brown, beige, tan, and mulatto in jazz. Henríquez comments: "Jazz encompasses all races. Jazz has a lot of DNA in it. Everyone is a part of it. Jazz is a symbol of what America is. And America is so much more than the United States." With Henríquez, Marsalis's America is expanding.

CASE STUDY 13: MIGUEL ZENÓN—CENTERING PUERTO RICO

In 2008, at the age of thirty-one, saxophonist, composer, and bandleader Miguel Zenón (Figure 6.5) became the second Puerto Rican and the first jazz musician associated with Latin jazz to receive a prestigious and highly coveted MacArthur Fellowship, more commonly known as the "Genius Grant."[17] In the description of the young musician's contributions that led to the award, the MacArthur Foundation's biographical narrative states:

> Miguel Zenón is a young jazz musician who is expanding the boundaries of Latin and jazz music through his elegant and innovative musical collages. . . . His third album, *Jíbaro* (2005), illuminates his intense engagement with the indigenous music of his native Puerto Rico. Forgoing the Afro-Caribbean sound that characterizes most Latin jazz . . . in Zenón's hands the essential elements of *Jíbaro* serve as the compositional and rhythmic underpinning of his contemporary jazz arrangements. This young musician and composer is at once reestablishing the artistic, cultural, and social tradition of jazz while creating an entirely new jazz language for the 21st century.[18]

FIGURE 6.5 Saxophonist and bandleader Miguel Zenón. Photo by Jimmy Katz, courtesy of Miguel Zenón.

Couched in this tribute are the notions that the tradition of jazz is in need of "reestablishing," that the future of the "jazz language" is rooted in the incorporation of the music of the "other" (as I have shown in previous chapters, this is nothing new in jazz, though Zenón's source material and approach are new), and that forgoing the stereotypical Latin jazz sound (read: the hegemony of Afro-Cuban influence discussed throughout this book) was essential to his winning the award. Putting aside these questionable notions, Zenón has forgone much of what is considered typical in jazz and Latin jazz by resisting established performance practice conventions and by forging a career that emplaces his "Puerto Rican jazz" firmly in the center of jazz, thereby expanding the vistas of where jazz resides.

Zenón was born in 1976 in Puerto Rico. Raised in the Residencial Luis Llorens Torres housing projects in San Juan, he qualified for a musical program for "disadvantaged youth" and began lessons at the age of ten. That experience prepared him for acceptance to the Escuela Libre de Música, a performing-arts middle school and high school, where he studied classical saxophone. At sixteen, he was introduced to the music of Charlie Parker and other jazz greats and quickly became enchanted by improvisation and decided to pursue a career in music. After graduation, it took much perseverance and nearly two years to secure enough funds through gigs, scholarships, and financial aid to be able to attend Berklee College of

Music in Boston in 1996. Zenón recalls: "It took me a while to get there . . . because I come from a working-class family. My family didn't have any money to help me with; I basically had to save everything from the [plane] ticket to tuition . . . by playing gigs and pop gigs and all this stuff."[19] The faculty at Berklee, and later at Manhattan School of Music, where he received a master's in 2001, profoundly changed the course of his career.

In particular, Berklee faculty member and Panamanian pianist Danilo Pérez became a significant mentor and served as a model for Zenón's career. Zenón says: "I discovered Danilo's music and a lot of other Latin Americans who were making jazz music, while still maintaining their identities as Latin Americans. When I got to Boston, I sought him out. He was really open and very welcoming and really supportive."[20] He also says: "People like Danilo Pérez, David Sánchez, the Fort Apache Band, Edward Simon, I felt that these were musicians that were honoring their roots and the music of their upbringing, but at the same time were able to play within a traditional jazz context, convincingly. Like, hearing Danilo play with Dizzy Gillespie, playing in a pure Bud Powell style. And then hearing his record and hearing all this stuff from Panama . . . and also hearing some Herbie Hancock and Keith Jarrett in the mix."[21] Zenón sought to emulate that global approach in his own music.

After he arrived in New York in 1999, his talents were recognized quickly, and he was shepherded up to the highest echelons of jazz. He became one of the founding members of the SFJazz Collective and performed with Charlie Haden, Fred Hersch, Kenny Werner, the Village Vanguard Jazz Orchestra, the Mingus Big Band, Bobby Hutchison, and Steve Coleman. He also performed in the Latin jazz bands of Ray Barretto, Jerry Gonzalez and the Fort Apache Band, and Guillermo Klein and Los Guachos. But it was only after living in the United States for several years and playing and composing in his own quartet that he was able to formulate a way to honor his own Puerto Rican roots while "convincingly" playing in a traditional jazz context. Zenón relates: "Some of the recent attempts that I have made of filtering Puerto Rican and Caribbean music through jazz, come directly from my experiences growing up in the island. After living in the States for a while, I was able to relate to these experiences from a different perspective and find an organic and personal way to connect to them through my music."[22]

In 1999, he formed his highly acclaimed quartet, with a global membership including Venezuelan pianist Luis Perdomo, Austrian bassist Hans Glawischnig, and Mexican drummer Antonio Sanchez (later replaced by Puerto Rican drummer Henry Cole). All of these musicians are virtuosic and well versed in jazz and Latin jazz styles, which has enabled Zenón to realize his diverse and broad musical vision that finely balances his love for the jazz tradition and his deep commitment to his Puerto Rican cultural roots. The group's ten recordings embrace a broad stylistic swath; however, several are of particular interest, as they explore aspects of Puerto Rican music and culture in ways that were hitherto not a central focus in jazz, and as a result, Zenón has expanded the stylistic realm of Latin jazz and jazz in innovative ways.

The quartet's third recording, *Jíbaro*, released in 2005, features music that is rooted in the Puerto Rican folk music known as *la música jíbara*.[23] *Jíbaros* are rural peasant farmers and are often used to symbolize truly authentic Puerto Rican culture. Though it was not the first time this body of music was used in a jazz setting (groups such as Viento de Agua had been mixing this music with jazz and popular musics since 1999), Zenón's explorations approach the music with a modern jazz sensibility that subtly draws on the traditions with integrity and nuance. The improvisations and harmonic structures on the recording are firmly rooted in the language of jazz, but the melodic gestures, song forms, and underlying rhythms stay firmly rooted in *la música jíbara*. This project was released on Marsalis Music, a record label created by saxophonist Branford Marsalis and coming from within the highest circles of jazz. This was something very new for a project located within the purview of Latin jazz and demonstrates an important contribution by Zenón, using his gravitas acquired from performing with famous jazz artists to facilitate his efforts to firmly place Puerto Rican traditions in the center of jazz to an unprecedented degree. The recording received two Grammy nominations for Best Improvised Jazz Solo and Best Latin Jazz Recording, as well as a Latin Grammy nomination for Best Latin Jazz Recording. Being nominated in both jazz and Latin categories attests to Zenón's unique position bridging both musical worlds. *Jíbaro*'s success led to subsequent releases on Marsalis Music, support from a Guggenheim Foundation Fellowship that Zenón used to expand his explorations in other aspects of Puerto Rican musical culture, and wider recognition and accolades that eventually led to his MacArthur Fellowship.

Projects followed that explored other Puerto Rican music. In 2009, he augmented his quartet by adding folkloric percussionists and vocalists on *Esta Plena*, which incorporates the rich traditions of *plena*, an Afro–Puerto Rican music associated with urban street culture.[24] His 2011 release, *Alma Adentro: The Puerto Rican Songbook*, expanded his quartet with a ten-piece woodwind ensemble and features the compositions of five prolific Puerto Rican composers: Rafael Hernández, Bobby Capó, Tite Curet Alonso, Pedro Flores, and Sylvia Rexach.[25] Zenón's intention in recording this body of work was to introduce the Puerto Rican songbook to a larger audience and to demonstrate that these composers are on par with the composers who constitute the "American songbook," such as Irving Berlin, George Gershwin, Cole Porter, Jerome Kern, and the like. In the process, he introduces new potential jazz standards to the repertoire, much as Charlie Byrd and João Gilberto did with Brazilian music in the 1960s. *Alma Adentro* was widely recognized as one of the best jazz recordings released in 2011 and was nominated for the Grammy for Best Large Jazz Ensemble Album and the Latin Grammy for Best Instrumental Album. And his 2014 recording, *Identities Are Changeable*, released on Miel Music, is an ambitious large-group and multimedia project that explores how national identity is experienced by the Puerto Rican community in New York.[26] Zenón describes the album: "The whole project is inspired [by] a series of interviews I conducted with New Yorkers of Puerto Rican descent. I asked them questions related to their national identity and about how they felt being both from New York and Puerto Rico. I then edited the content and wrote a series [of] compositions around the audio and video from the interviews."[27] Excerpts of the interviews are interwoven throughout the recording, giving voice to a wide range of Puerto Rican perspectives within the musical context. The album was released with an accompanying video by David Dempewolf. *Identities Are Changeable* received a Grammy nomination for Best Latin Jazz Album.

This collection of recordings has raised awareness of Puerto Rican music culture among jazz audiences to an unprecedented degree and has widened the possibilities of source material for jazz. However, despite his accomplishments as a jazz musician working with the best musicians in the world, Zenón's recordings that draw on Puerto Rican traditions are often posited as Latin jazz recordings, evidenced by their Grammy nominations in the Latin jazz category, along with some nominations in the jazz categories. Not surprisingly, Zenón resists this relegation. He comments:

> With other examples of when Latin American music and jazz mixed, what I heard was almost like instrumental dance music with some improvisation based in the jazz language. Or putting this idea of jazz on top of a rhythmic structure that was from Cuba or wherever. I wasn't as attracted to that. And with the term "Latin jazz," when that term was born, it was born out of this collaboration of musicians coming out of the bebop school specifically. I'm talking about Dizzy and Chano Pozo and Bird and Machito and all that stuff—specifically their collaboration with Afro-Cuban music. A very specific genre of Cuban music that was coming out of rumba and had this very percussive element. And for the longest time, that became sort of like a seal. It's like you were marked by that very amazing accomplishment they made.

But, you know, if you were from anywhere in Latin-America, and you were trying to play jazz, you *must* be playing that way. You must be coming out of that specific thing. For the longest time it was very hard for Latin-American musicians to say "Yes, I'm a Latin-American musician, but I'm coming at it from a different place." Now, it's kind of happening, in a way. I hear all these musicians from all these different countries, and they're finding their own identity. That's why I feel that the term "Latin jazz" itself is almost dated. You're referring to music from 60 years ago.[28]

Regardless, as a Puerto Rican musician playing jazz that is informed by Puerto Rican music, Zenón remains mostly relegated to Latin jazz by the industry, critics, audiences, and other musicians.

However, his deep commitment to his cultural roots extends far beyond his recordings and genre contestations. In 2011, using the MacArthur Fellowship for support, Zenón launched the program "Caravana Cultural" ("Cultural Caravan"). The main goal of the program is to present jazz concerts in communities throughout Puerto Rico and to support jazz education for young Puerto Rican musicians by hosting local jam sessions:

> The idea is to organize a series of concerts, free concerts of course, but spe-
> cifically we're going into the rural areas of Puerto Rico where they don't get
> a lot of culture activity at all—not only concerts but anything else. The idea
> is to try to bring the music to places where usually it doesn't go, but also to
> try and eliminate preconceived ideas of what jazz is and the kind of people
> that should listen to jazz and should be exposed to jazz. So in that sense it's
> more like cultural investment in my country. And the more time that I spend
> out of Puerto Rico, I've been more and more involved in things that have to
> do with Puerto Rico—not only my home music but also trying to do things
> there I felt that are necessary and are not there and weren't there when I was
> young.[29]

The concerts tend to feature the music of jazz greats, such as Charlie Parker and Duke Ellington, and not Latin jazz artists.

Zenón has proved a tireless advocate for creating a space for Caribbean and Latin American musicians in jazz, one free of constraints colored by racist, nation-alist, and ethnocentric agendas. He continues to strive for the acknowledgment of the vitality of local music cultures in the Caribbean and Latin America to infuse jazz with new possibilities. His fight, though, is far from over.

CASE STUDY 14: BOBBY SANABRIA—CUBAN MUSIC WITH A
NEW YORK ATTITUDE

In 1999, bandleader and drummer Bobby Sanabria recorded a live album at the
Birdland in New York with his newly formed nineteen-piece big band. When
Sanabria asked me to contribute an arrangement for the session, I suggested
"Nuyorican Son."[30] I had written the piece to commemorate the fourth anniversary of my weekly Latin jazz gig at the Nuyorican Poets Café in the East Village
in Manhattan. In the composition, I tried to sonically capture the essence of my
café experience, with its wide array of cultural and ethnic mixing, as a way to
express my deep gratitude to both the club and the Nuyorican musicians who
graciously invited me to participate in their rich musical culture. Sanabria was
always forthcoming and generous with sharing his knowledge of the music's history. The song's title is a play on the word "son," referring to both the Cuban
genre that the composition is based on and the filial relationship I felt toward
the musicians (*mis hermanos*) who were mentors in my musical development,
such as Tito Puente, Eddie Palmieri, Ray Barretto, and Sanabria. "Nuyorican
Son" mashes up Cuban son montuno and mambo with the blues, jazz, funk, adventurous harmonies, and an occasional odd meter to sonically sound out the
rich tapestry of intersecting cultures at the café, and it also happens to sonically
capture Sanabria's musical tastes. Sanabria comments: "You know, I am into everything, all kinds of music, not just Latin music. I was influenced by Machito and
Puente but also Frank Zappa. And my biggest influence is Don Ellis [jazz exper-
imentalist and trumpeter known for his pioneering and virtuosic arrangements
in odd meters]. He was the most forward-thinking musician of our time. That is
what my big band is about."

For the recording, Sanabria assembled a mix of seasoned veterans of Afro-
Cuban jazz and young recent grads who had played in the college bands he directs.
He commissioned arrangements of the iconic Latin jazz piece ("Manteca"), jazz
standards ("Donna Lee" and "Angel Eyes"), chants from the Yoruba and Abakua
traditions ("The Opening," "Olokun/Yemaya"), and new compositions ("Mosscode,"
"Adios Mario," "Troubadours," and "Nuyorican Son"). In the liner notes, Sanabria
writes: "I've always had one foot in the past, one in the present, and my head toward the future. The Afro-Cuban jazz tradition was born in New York City in the
1940s; there is no other place in the world where it could have happened." From his
repertoire choices and his vocal interjections throughout the performance, it is apparent that he conceives of the "Afro-Cuban jazz tradition" with a broad historical
and futuristic reach and his hometown as nexus for its emergence.

One revealing example of how Sanabria's views manifest occurs when he verbally frames the performance of "Nuyorican Son." In the first few measures of the introduction, he shouts over the band, "¡Oye mi son cubano! Ahi na' ma'!" ("Listen to my Cuban son! Here it is!"), and then, just after the final chord, declares, "Yeah, yeah! Cuban music with a New York attitude!" The bilingual declarations embody his Nuyorican experience of straddling a bicultural world that is both a part of and apart from the city he calls home. At the same time, his choice to use Spanish on a recording destined for jazz radio across the United States serves as a shout-out to Latinx and Hispanics (who would surely understand both statements), overtly asserting his own cultural pride and reminding all of the presence of the brown, tan, beige, and mulatto in this music. His opening declaration specifically recognizes the central role of Cuba's music traditions in his music. But by recognizing only Cuba, the overt roles of other places and traditions, such as Puerto Rico, New York, blues, jazz, and funk, to which my composition is indebted, remain unacknowledged. In his closing statement, Cuba is once more recognized but with the caveat of the special role of his hometown's attitude (meaning a streetwise and hard-driving aesthetic). Moreover, the word "jazz" is conspicuously omitted, despite the fact that the band was performing in one of New York's premier jazz clubs; the arrangement featured extended jazz solos by saxophonist John Stubblefield, trumpeter John Walsh, and myself; and we were recording for a jazz label. When asked about the omission, Sanabria commented: "The jazz community is supposed to be hip, but they view the Latin and Brazilian scene as mere novelty and never view the players as legitimate jazz improvisers. It is really frustrating to always have to deal with that." Circumventing this was a subtle political strategy that discursively reversed the erasure Sanabria has been contending with throughout his career. Released on Arabesque Records (AJOI49), *Afro-Cuban Dream . . . Live & in Clave* received critical acclaim and was nominated for a Grammy for Best Latin Jazz Recording (Sanabria's first of several nominations). The album's release marked a pivotal moment in Sanabria's career that launched his pioneering work as spokesperson, activist, and arbiter of Latin jazz.

Born in 1957 in the projects of the South Bronx and of Puerto Rican parentage, Sanabria is a first-generation Nuyorican whose identity is firmly rooted in New York but has strong ties to the island. He came of age hearing a broad range of music emanating from streets of his youth—salsa, soul, R&B, rock, and jazz. His parents instilled a deep pride in his Puerto Rican heritage and for the Fort Apache section of the South Bronx where he grew up. He has spent much of his professional life asserting that pride and working tirelessly to acknowledge and promote the South Bronx's rich cultural history. He attended the Berklee College of Music in Boston and in 1979 became the first Puerto Rican to graduate. Long after completing his formal education, he remained a serious student of Latin music history and has dedicated his career to sharing his knowledge in various educational settings.

Upon returning to New York, he began performing with many of the Latin jazz luminaries, including Dizzy Gillespie, Tito Puente, Paquito D'Rivera, Mongo Santamaría, Chico O'Farrill, Ray Barretto, Marco Rizo, Arturo Sandoval, Cándido Camero, Yomo Toro, Francisco Aguabella, Larry Harlow, and Mario Bauzá. In the early 1990s, he formed his own Latin jazz nonet, Ascensión. Its debut recording, *¡NYC Aché!* released in 1993 on Flying Fish Records, reflected his deep commitment to researching the historical roots of the music, and the tracks sonically trace the West African roots of Latin jazz in New York. The band's multigenerational and multicultural membership (currently, it has octogenarians sharing the stage with musicians in their thirties, forties, fifties, and sixties and musicians from Colombia, Panama, Mexico, Puerto Rico, and the United States), a rarity in jazz, is made up of musicians who share an expertise in Afro-Cuban traditions. The generational and geographical diversity is also found in his big band and in his ¡Quarteto Aché! (formed in 2001) and reflects Sanabria's insistence on passing traditions from older to younger generations and his vision of the cultural breadth that is so central to the music he plays.

In the 1990s, he obtained several teaching positions in New York schools—the Drummer's Collective, New School University, and Manhattan School of Music. He began Afro-Cuban big bands in the latter two, making them the first universities in the United States (and probably in the world) to have big bands dedicated solely to that tradition. This trendsetting move launched a number of Latin jazz ensembles of various sizes in schools across the United States. It was a strategic move by someone dedicated to firmly establishing Afro-Cuban and Latin jazz traditions as worthy of serious study and preservation, the same fight that Gunther Schuller had led for jazz decades before. And this was when Sanabria's self-proclaimed labels of "activist and multicultural warrior" began to take shape. He astutely identified the dearth in advocacy for Latin jazz in a number of realms and positioned himself as the articulate musician-scholar spokesperson for *la tradición*.

In addition to traveling in the United States and conducting educational workshops, masterclasses, and lectures, he has produced a number of films and documentaries on Latin jazz, which include a three-part video instructional series, *Getting Started on Congas*, released by DCI; a DVD of Ascensión's appearance at the 2006 Modern Drummer Festival; a PBS documentary *From Mambo to Hip Hop: A South Bronx Tale*, produced with City Lore; and the Bravo Network's *The Palladium: Where the Mambo Was King*, which received the Imagen Foundation Award for Best Documentary for Cable TV in 2003. And he served as a consultant for the Smithsonian's traveling exhibit, "Latin Jazz: La Combinación Perfecta." Sanabria has written articles on Latin jazz in the popular press for *NY Latino, Highlights in Percussion, Modern Drummer, Descarga Newsletter, Allegro*, and *DownBeat*.

As an activist, he has been relentless in his advocacy of Latin jazz matters, more so than any other musician. In 2006, he, along with Ray Barretto and DJ Awilda Rivera, successfully spearheaded a campaign to restore the Latin jazz programming at WBGO, the only all-jazz station in the New York area. Their efforts resulted in Latin jazz becoming an integral part of the station's programming to an unprecedented extent (with two to three cuts per hour). In 2019, he took over as host of the weekly *Latin Jazz Cruise* radio show on WBGO from Rivera. And in 2011, Sanabria filed a lawsuit with fellow plaintiffs Eugene Marlow, Ben Lapidus, and Mark Levine in New York State Supreme Court to pressure the Recording Academy into reinstating the Latin jazz category in the Grammys, which it did the following year. In an effort to extend his sphere of influence, he serves as the chair of the International Association of Jazz Education's Afro-Cuban Jazz Resource Team, is a board member of the Duke Ellington Foundation, is on the advisory board of Women's Health and Economic Development Corporation (a leading builder in the revitalization of the South Bronx), and has cofounded and codirects the Bronx Music Heritage Center, an artist-curated facility that provides work-space for local artists and hosts performances, discussions, art exhibits, and film screenings, promoting and celebrating the borough's music traditions and cultural contributions.

For his efforts, Sanabria received recognition and a number of awards, including a National Endowment of the Arts grant, Meet the Composer grants, two INTAR Off-Broadway Composer awards, and several Mid-Atlantic Foundation Arts Connect grants. In 2003, he received the Outstanding Lifetime Achievement Award from Ivan Acosta, producer and director of Latin Jazz USA, in recognition of Sanabria's "extraordinary creative contributions to Latin jazz." In 2006, he was inducted into the Bronx Walk of Fame, having a section of the Grand Concourse (the main thoroughfare in the South Bronx) named after him in recognition of his contributions to music and the arts.

The cover art and inside tray art for *Afro-Cuban Dream . . . Live & in Clave* (Figures 6.6 and 6.7) encapsulate how Sanabria views his position in Latin jazz and his aim to push the music in futuristic directions while remaining firmly rooted in the music's past. Sanabria describes his design:

> The cover was inspired by my favorite TV show, *The Twilight Zone*. It is about entering a new dimension, and that is what I do with my music. I wanted the design to hold many hidden messages. That is why the door is there. Go through it to the new dimension. I am dressed in black and holding the black

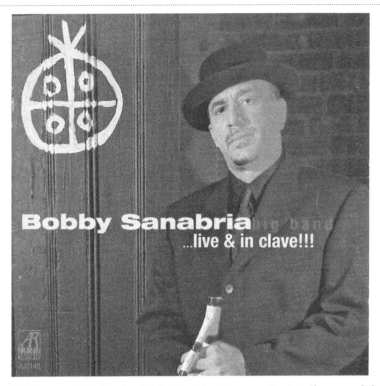

FIGURE 6.6 Cover art for Bobby Sanabria's *Afro-Cuban Dream . . . Live & in Clave*, recorded at the Birdland jazz club in New York in 1999. Courtesy of Bobby Sanabria.

and white staff to represent Elegua. He is the Yoruba god of the crossroads and is the avatar of justice. That is my role in the band. The drawing on the door is the *mokongo* from the Abakua tradition in Cuba, a secret all-male mutual aid society stemming from the colonial period. It is the sign of the high priest, and that is my role in the music. The circle represents infinity, the circles represent eyes on the front and back of our heads, the cross is the crossroads, and the three lines on top signify the three original Abakua tribes of the Calabar region in Africa.

Sanabria's coded messages rooted in neo-African spiritual practice are in line with a long tradition in jazz stemming from its beginnings; two of the numerous examples are "Eh Lá Bas," a creole folk song recorded by Kid Ory in 1946, which signifies Elegua, and Machito's vocal interjection of "Iboru-iboya" on his 1965 recording of "Tanga."[31] "Tanga," written in 1943 by Mario Bauzá, is an Abakua term meaning "spiritual power" and also slang for "marijuana," and "Iboru-iboya" is a standard greeting to a *babalawo*, a priest in Santeria.[32]

On the inside tray of the CD package is a picture depicting a family altar like those commonly found in the homes of Santería practitioners. Altars pay tribute to ancestors but can also include heroes or inspirational figures. It is an honor for a deceased spirit who is not in the immediate family to be included on a family altar, and by including them, it is believed that the spirit will help guide the family through their daily lives. On this altar, Sanabria pays tribute to the pantheon of jazz and Latin jazz greats, enlisting Chano Pozo, Mario Bauzá, Charlie Parker, Dizzy Gillespie, and Arsenio Rodríguez for spiritual guidance.

Sanabria comments: "In 1999, I finally felt ready to take on the responsibility of running a big band. I formed it to realize my musical vision. And it is the highest form of our art. It is jazz's symphony orchestra. But I do not have a Latin jazz big band. Some people call it that. I don't have a jazz big band. Some people call it that. What I have is a futuristic big band. I call it the 'Multi-verse.' It's bigger than any one universe." As in his proclamation after "Nuyorican Son," he strategically avoids the use of "Latin," "Afro-Cuban," and "jazz" or any other generic descriptor in an attempt to transcend the limitations, confines, and loaded baggage that can

FIGURE 6.7 Inside tray art from CD package of *Afro-Cuban Dream . . . Live & in Clave*, depicting an altar from the Santería tradition paying tribute to (clockwise from bottom left) Charlie Parker, Chano Pozo, Mario Bauzá, Arsenio Rodríguez, and Dizzy Gillespie. Courtesy of Bobby Sanabria.

pigeonhole, bog down, exclude, and erase. But for Sanabria, this is not avoidance. Just like his challenge to Marsalis in the opening vignette of this chapter, it is a direct challenge to the legacy of prejudice, exclusion, and the silencing of the brown, tan, beige, and mulatto in jazz.

* * *

What Eddie Palmieri, Michele Rosewoman, Carlos Henríquez, Miguel Zenón, and Bobby Sanabria have in common is a deep respect for and understanding of the history of Latin jazz; they comprehend their place within the tradition, have a strong commitment to education, and view their advocacy work as cultural warriors as essential and integral to their role as bandleaders. Each pushes for the acknowledgment of the diversity that has always been a part of jazz but has been continually silenced and erased. Each pushes the limits of possibilities of what Latin jazz can encompass, while amplifying the resonances and reverberations of the music's past. Saxophonist Bill Easley defined jazz as "a beautiful response to adversity." Through their unique approaches to music making, Palmieri, Rosewoman, Henríquez, Zenón, and Sanabria all seem to embrace this definition of jazz and choose to navigate the terrain of inequity and adversity that they face daily by creating beautiful expressions of Latin jazz.

NOTES

1. Ingold 2009, 200.
2. Blumenfeld 2014.
3. Personal communication with author, 2009.
4. Ibid.
5. Unless otherwise noted, all quotes from this chapter are from personal communications with the author.
6. Portions of the Palmieri case study were originally published in Washburne 2016.
7. See chapter 4 for a discussion of the Apollo Theater and Latin jazz.
8. http://www.imdb.com/name/nm0658573/bio, accessed June 1, 2017.
9. *Justicia*, Tico Records SLP 1188 (1969).
10. Yglesias 2016.
11. *Harlem River Drive*, Roulette Records (SR 3004, 1971).
12. *Live at Sing Sing*, Tico Records (CLP 1303, 1972).
13. https://www.juilliard.edu/youth-adult-programs/music-advancement-program, accessed June 25, 2017.
14. Rodriguez played bass on Dizzy Gillespie and His Orchestra, "Manteca" (Verve Records MG V-8208, 1956).
15. http://www.jazz.org/blog/playlist-carlos-henriquez-on-dizzy-gillespies-latin-side, accessed July 1, 2017.
16. https://www.newyorklatinculture.com/events/carlos-henriquez, accessed July 1, 2017.

17. Cuban drummer and composer Dafnis Prieto is the only other Latin jazz musician awarded a MacArthur Fellowship. He received his award in 2011.

18. https://www.macfound.org/fellows/815, accessed July 6, 2017.

19. https://www.allaboutjazz.com/miguel-zenon-jazz-sherpa-miguel-zenon-by-lawrence-peryer. php, accessed July 6, 2017.

20. Ibid.

21. http://wbgo.org/post/miguel-zen-n-speaks-about-his-new-album-t-pico-and-power-steady-band#stream/0, accessed July 7, 2017.

22. https://www.allaboutjazz.com/miguel-zenon-celebrating-the-music-of-la-isla-miguel-zenon-by-steve-bryant.php?pg=3, accessed July 7, 2017.

23. Miguel Zenón, *Jíbaro*, Marsalis Music (11661312, 2005).

24. Miguel Zenón, *Esta Plena*, Marsalis Music (0874946001205, 2009).

25. Miguel Zenón, *Alma Adentro: The Puerto Rican Songbook*, Marsalis Music (2011).

26. Miguel Zenón, *Identities Are Changeable*, Miel Music (2014).

27. https://www.allaboutjazz.com/miguel-zenon-celebrating-the-music-of-la-isla-miguel-zenon-by-steve-bryant.php?pg=3, accessed July 7, 2017.

28. http://wbgo.org/post/miguel-zen-n-speaks-about-his-new-album-t-pico-and-power-steady-band#stream/0, accessed July 7, 2017.

29. https://www.allaboutjazz.com/miguel-zenon-jazz-sherpa-miguel-zenon-by-lawrence-peryer. php, accessed July 7, 2017.

30. For more about this composition, see Washburne 2001.

31. Kid Ory's Creole Orchestra, "Eh La Bas," Columbia Records (37275, 1946); Machito and His Afro-Cubans, *Mucho Mucho Machito*, Palladium Latin Jazz & Dance Records (PCD 119, 1965).

32. Miller 2009, 93.

EPILOGUE

MASSIVE DIVERSITY IS always key to the healthiest ecologies. This is true for nature and human expressivity. The diversity of the rich social and cultural fabric of
jazz's past is precisely why the music has been able to thrive in so many places and
in so many unique ways. Not embracing that diversity prevents us from hearing
the multitude of voices that collectively make the music so compelling. Jazz's
sound reverberates Borgesian entangled histories that encompass a tapestry of
racial distinctions and blurred lines between geographical divides. It is a product
of the black, brown, tan, mulatto, beige, and white experience throughout the
Americas and the Caribbean. To deny this is to deny the resilience and fortitude
of our foremothers and forefathers of jazz. It denies the music's open aesthetic
that we have inherited from African American culture. And it denies what truly
reverberates in every jazz solo heard from stages across the globe.

This book acknowledges, pays tribute to, and celebrates the diversity of culture,
experience, and perspectives that are foundational to jazz. Thus, the music's legacy
is shown to transcend far beyond stylistic distinction, national borders, and the
imposition of the black/white racial divide that has only served to maintain the
status quo in the United States. The reality of jazz is much more nuanced and
multivalent.

By expanding the discussion of race, ethnicity, nation, and place and recognizing
the myriad diverse artistic spaces that were essential in the emergence and continued development of jazz, the richness of the music's past and present can be
fully embraced. The true entanglement of culture, of people and events, and the
global nature of human experience that is intrinsically connected through colonial
encounters of the past and present are finally exposed. Jazz is a product of the confluence of slavery, colonialism, plantation life, postcolonialism, emancipation, and

Latin Jazz. Christopher Washburne, Oxford University Press (2020). © Oxford University Press.
DOI: 10.1093/oso/9780195371628.001.0001

the tensions associated with processes connected to the indigenization of subjects with unequal power relations. Jazz resounds a new creolized space, marked by a fusion of cultural elements drawn from Caribbean, American, African, and European cultures, which is permanently translated and indelibly marked upon every iteration of the music. Jazz and Latin jazz are the expressive outcomes of such encounters and processes.

Music traditions are often portrayed by means of the metaphor of a tree. It is constructed like a family tree, and the roots, trunk, and branches demonstrate kinship relationships of influence and indebtedness. Figure E.1 was conceived by flutist Herbie Mann—a white jazz musician from the United States who dedicated much of his professional career to playing Latin jazz. In typical fashion, Africa is centered in the root system along with the colonizing cultures of the New World. Cuba, Puerto Rico, and Brazil serve as the trunk and lowest branches in this Latin jazz tree. The outer branches encompass specific genres and major innovators (many of whom are discussed in this book). Various branches are then interconnected by musicians who are represented like vines that fluidly

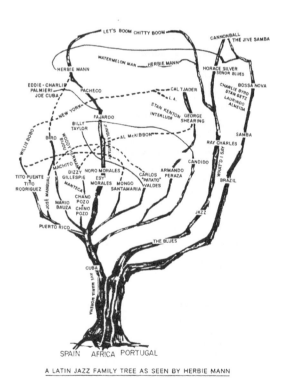

A LATIN JAZZ FAMILY TREE AS SEEN BY HERBIE MANN

FIGURE E.1 Flutist Herbie Mann's representation of the Latin jazz family tree, from the liner notes of his 1966 release *Latin Mann* (Columbia Records CL2388).

traverse the tree from style to style and place to place (Mann himself is depicted in that role, and he appears in two spaces in the canopy of the tree connecting jazz, Brazil, and Cuba). Conceiving of Latin jazz this way has some benefits, as it acknowledges the shared past in a validly metaphorical way that represents the kinship relations among innovative musicians. However, once again, it relegates Latin jazz to being a separate singular tree, not necessarily connected to other conifers growing in the same forest. As a separate entity, the Latin jazz tree does not capture the full extent of the cross-pollination, the intercultural exchange, the intrinsic interconnectivity, and the truly global breadth of the music. If we must conceive of jazz or Latin jazz in this way, what must be clarified is which species of tree.

I suggest that a better model would be the metaphor of an aspen tree. Aspen forests are not collections of individual trees but rather all one organism sharing the same root system. The forest is a singular tree. Aspens are considered the second-largest living organism on earth, second only to the Great Barrier Reef. Within each sprout, the same DNA and past history are embodied. In jazz, each iteration, substyle, and performance resonates the music's past, its roots, and its social history reaching back to the mid-1700s.

The rhizomic connections that Jorge Luis Borges constructs in the short story that opens this book, with its seeming haphazardness and unpredictability that intertwine and blur delineation of the histories of the Caribbean and the Americas (North and South), and the transcendence of past and present that demonstrate how past colonial encounters throughout history ensnare our present, become visible within an aspen metaphor. In an aspen forest, each manifestation of the organism looks like a distinctive tree with unique features, but just beneath the trees' outward appearance, they are fundamentally the same. The same can be said of the musicians and their respective distinctive styles of jazz—all sharing the same DNA. Conceived of in this way, Duke Ellington, Louis Armstrong, Tito Puente, Machito, Mario Bauzá, Dizzy Gillespie, Chano Pozo, and every other musician discussed in this book are unified and interconnected on the most fundamental and foundational level. All manifestations of jazz are intercultural, transnational, and multivocal at their core.

The silencing of Latin jazz and the erasure of the brown, tan, beige, and mulatto deny jazz's rich polychromatic and global character and must no longer be perpetuated. This book embraces and celebrates jazz's rich global nature and heralds the significant and undeniable Caribbean and Latin American contributions to this beautiful expressive form. Whether it's jazz or "other jazz," the Latin jazz discussed in this book can no longer be silenced or erased. All jazz deserves to be singularly embraced.

Bibliography

Acosta, Leonardo. 2000. *Descarga cubana*. Havana: Ediciones Unión.

Acosta, Leonardo. 2003. *Cubano Be, Cubano Bop: One Hundred Years of Jazz in Cuba*. Washington D.C: Smithsonian Books.

Ake, David. 2002. *Jazz Cultures*. Berkeley: University of California Press.

Alen, Olavo. 1986. *La musica de las sociedades de tumba francesca en Cuba*. Havana: Casa de las Americas.

Armstrong, Louis. 1955. *Satchmo*. New York: Signet.

Atkins, E. Taylor, ed. 2003. *Jazz Planet*. Jackson: University Press of Mississippi.

Austerlitz, Paul. 2005. *Jazz Consciousness: Music, Race, and Humanity*. Middletown, Conn.: Wesleyan University Press.

Bakhtin, Mikhail. 1986. *Speech Genres and Other Late Essays*, edited by Caryl Emerson and Michael Holquist. Austin: University of Texas Press.

Barbé-Marbois, François. 1830. *The History of Louisiana, Particularly of the Cession of That Colony to the United States of America*. Philadelphia: Carey & Lea.

Bhabha, Homi. 1994. *The Location of Culture*. New York: Routledge.

Bechet, Sidney. 1960. *Treat It Gentle: An Autobiography*. London: Cassell.

Benítez-Rojo, Antonio. 1996. *The Repeating Island: The Caribbean and the Postmodern Perspective*, translated by James E. Maraniss. Durham: Duke University Press.

Berliner, Paul. 1994. *Thinking in Jazz*. Chicago: University of Chicago Press.

Bernabé, Jean, Patrick Chamoiseau, and Raphaël Confiant. 1990. "In Praise of Creoleness," translated by Mohamed B. Taleb Khyar. *Callaloo* 13, no. 4: 866–909.

Blesh, Rudi. 1958. *Shining Trumpets: History of Jazz*, 2nd ed. New York: Alfred A. Knopf.

Blumenfeld, Larry. 2008. "Cultural Conversation: Arturo O'Farrill, the Son Also Rises—And Embraces His Musical Roots." *Wall Street Journal*, April 29, D7.

Blumenfeld, Larry. 2014. "Jazz at Lincoln Center Opens with Cuban Beats: Wynton Marsalis Brings in Cuban Musicians Chucho Valdés and Pedrito Martinez." *Wall Street Journal*, September 14. http://online.wsj.com/articles/jazz-at-lincoln-center-opens-with-cuban-beats-1410746046, accessed July 1 2018.

Bohlman, Philip. 2007. "Becoming Ethnomusicologists: On War, Peace, and Reconciliation." *SEM Newsletter* 41, no. 4 (September): 1, 4.

Boothroyd, Miles. 2010. "Modal Jazz and Miles Davis: George Russell's Influence and the Melodic Inspiration behind Modal Jazz." *Nota Bene: Canadian Undergraduate Journal of Musicology* 3, no. 1, article 5.

Borge, Jason. 2018. *Tropical Riffs: Latin America and the Politics of Jazz*. Durham: Duke University Press.

Borges, Jorge Luis. (1935) 1998. "The Cruel Redeemer Lazarus Morell." In *Collected Fictions*, translated by Andrew Hurley, 6–12. New York: Penguin Books.

Born, Georgina, and David Hesmondhalgh, eds. 2000. *Western Music and Its Others: Difference, Representation, and Appropriation in Music*. Berkeley: University of California Press.

Borneman, Ernest. 1959a. "Creole Echoes." *Jazz Review* 2, no. 8 (September): 13–15.

Borneman, Ernest. 1959b. "Creole Echoes: Part II." *Jazz Review* 2, no. 10 (November): 26–27.

Borneman, Ernest. 1969. "Jazz and the Creole Tradition." *Jazzforschung* 1: 99–112.

Brasseaux, Carl A., and Glenn R. Conrad, eds. 1992. *The Road to Louisiana: The Saint-Domingue Refugees, 1792–1809*. Lafayette: Center for Louisiana Studies, University of Southwestern Louisiana.

Briggs, Charles, and Richard Bauman. (1992) 2009. "Genre, Intertextuality, and Social Power." In *Linguistic Anthropology: A Reader*, edited by Alessandro Duranti, 214–244. Chichester: Wiley Blackwell.

Brothers, Thomas David. 2006. *Louis Armstrong's New Orleans*. New York: W. W. Norton.

Brubaker, Rogers. 2005. "The 'Diaspora' Diaspora." *Ethnic and Racial Studies* 28, no. 1 (January): 1–19.

Burton, Richard. 1993. "Ki Moun Nou Yé: The Idea of Difference in Contemporary French West Indian Thought." *New West Indian Guide* 67, nos. 1–2: 5–32.

Cale, John G. 1971. "French Secular Music in Saint-Domingue (1750–1795) Viewed as a Factor in America's Musical Growth. Ph.D. diss., Louisiana State University and Agricultural and Mechanical College.

Carpentier, Alejo. 1988. *El reino de este mundo*. Barcelona: Seix Barral.

Chediak, Nat, Carlos Galilea, and Fernando Trueba. 1998. *Diccionario de jazz latino*. Madrid: Fundación Autor.

Chilton, John. 1987. *Sidney Bechet: The Wizard of Jazz*. New York: Oxford University Press.

Clifford, James. 1986. "Introduction: Partial Truths." In *Writing Culture: The Poetics and Politics of Ethnography*, edited by James Clifford and George Marcus, 1–26. Berkeley: University of California Press.

Clifford, James. 1988. *The Predicament of Culture: Twentieth-Century Ethnography, Literature, and Art*. Cambridge, Mass.: Harvard University Press.

Collier, James Lincoln. 1993. *Jazz: The American Theme Song*. New York: Oxford University Press.

Cornelius, Steve, with John Amira. 1991. *The Music of Santeria: Traditional Rhythms of the Batá Drum*. Crown Point, Ind.: White Cliffs Media.

Cruz, Celia, with Ana Cristina Reymundo. 2004. *Celia My Life: An Autobiography*. New York: HarperCollins.

Debien, Gabriel. 1992. "The Saint-Domingue Refugees in Cuba, 1793–1815," translated by David Cheramie. In *The Road to Louisiana: The Saint-Domingue Refugees, 1792–1809*, edited by Carl Brasseaux and Glenn R. Conrad, 31–112. Lafayette: Center for Louisiana Studies, University of Southwestern Louisiana.

Debien, Gabriel, and René Le Gardeur. 1992. "The Saint-Domingue Refugees in Louisiana," translated by David Cheramie. In *The Road to Louisiana: The Saint-Domingue Refugees, 1792–1809*, edited by Carl Brasseaux and Glenn R. Conrad, 113–243. Lafayette: Center for Louisiana Studies, University of Southwestern Louisiana.

Delannoy, Luc. 2001. *Caliente: Una historia del jazz latino*. Mexico: Fondo de Cultura Economica.

Dessens, Natalie. 2007. *From Saint-Domingue to New Orleans: Migration and Influences*. Gainesville: University Press of Florida.

DeVeaux, Scott. 1991. "Constructing the Jazz Tradition: Jazz Historiography." *Black American Literature Forum* 25, no. 3: 525–560.

DeVeaux, Scott. 1997. *The Birth of Bebop: A Social and Musical History*. Berkeley: University of California Press.

Díaz Ayala, Cristóbal. 1988. *Si te quieres por el pico divertir . . .: Historia del pregón musical latinoamericano*. San Juan: Editorial Cubanacán.

Díaz Ayala, Cristóbal. 1999. *Cuando sali de la habana 1898–1997: Cien años de musica cubana por el mundo*. San Juan: Fundación Musicalia, 1999.

Díaz Ayala, Cristóbal. 2006. *Los contrapuntos de la música cubana*. San Juan: Editorial Callejón.

Domínguez, Virginia R. 1986. *White by Definition: Social Classification in Creole Louisiana*. New Brunswick: Rutgers University Press.

Dreyfus, Hubert, and Paul Rabinow. 1982. *Michel Foucault: Beyond Structuralism and Hermeneutics*. Chicago: University of Chicago Press.

Ecklund, Peter. 2001. "'Louis Licks' and Nineteenth-Century Cornet Etudes: The Roots of Melodic Improvisations as Seen in the Jazz Style of Louis Armstrong." *Historic Brass Society Journal* 13: 90–101.

Edwards, Brent. 2009. *The Practice of Diaspora: Literature, Translation, and the Rise of Black Internationalism*. Cambridge, Mass.: Harvard University Press.

Elkins, Stanley M. 1976. *Slavery: A Problem in American Institutional and Intellectual Life*, 3rd ed. Chicago: University of Chicago Press.

Ellington, Edward Kennedy. 1938. "Music Is 'Tops' to You and Me . . . And Swing Is a Part of It." *Tops*: 14–18.

Epstein, Dena. 1977. *Sinful Tunes and Spirituals: Black Folk Music to the Civil War*. Urbana: University of Illinois Press.

Erin, Ronald. 1984. "Cuban Elements in the Music of Aurelio de la Vega." *Latin American Music Review* 5, no. 1: 1–32.

Ewing, Katherine Pratt. 1997. *Arguing Sainthood: Modernity, Psychoanalysis, and Islam*. Durham: Duke University Press.

Feather, Leonard. 1957. *The Book of Jazz: A Guide to the Entire Field*. London: Horizon.

Feld, Steven. 1994. "From Schizophonia to Schismogenesis: On the Discourses and Commodification Practices of 'World Music' and 'World Beat.'" In *Music Grooves*, edited by Steven Feld and Charlie Keil, 257–289. Chicago: University of Chicago Press.

Fellezs, Kevin. 2011. *Birds of Fire: Jazz, Rock, Funk, and the Creation of Fusion*. Durham: Duke University Press.

Fernandez, Raul A. 2002. *Latin Jazz: La Combinación Perfecta*. San Francisco: Chronicle Books.

Fernandez, Raul A. 2003. *"Si No Tiene Swing No Vaya' a la Rumba": Cuban Musicians and Jazz*. In *Jazz Planet*, edited by E. Taylor Atkins, 3–18. Jackson: University of Mississippi.

Fiehrer, Thomas. 1989. "Saint-Domingue/Haiti Louisiana's Caribbean Connection." *Louisiana History* 30: 419–437.

Fiehrer, Thomas. 1991. "From Quadrille to Stomp: The Creole Origins of Jazz." *Popular Music* 10, no. 1 (January): 21–38.

Fiehrer, Thomas. 1992. "From La Tortue to La Louisiane: An Unfathomed Legacy." In *The Road to Louisiana: The Saint-Domingue Refugees, 1792–1809*, edited by Carl Brasseaux and Glenn R. Conrad, 1–30. Lafayette: Center for Louisiana Studies, University of Southwestern Louisiana.

Flaes, Rob Boonzajer. 2000. *Brass Unbound: Secret Children of the Colonial Brass Band*. Netherlands: Royal Tropical Institute.

Flores, Juan. 1997. "The Latino Imaginary: Dimensions of Community and Identity." In *Tropicalizations: Transcultural Representations of Latinidad*, edited by Aparicio and Susana Chavez-Silverman. Lebanon, N.H.: University Press of New England.

Flores, Juan. 2000. *From Bomba to Hip Hop: Puerto Rican Culture and Latino Identity*. New York: Columbia University Press.

Foucault, Michel. 1977. "Nietzche, Genealogy, History." In *Language, Counter-Memory, Practice: Selected Essays and Interviews*, edited by Donald F. Bouchard, 139–164. Ithaca: Cornell.

Fox, Ted. 1983. *Showtime at the Apollo: 50 Years of Great Entertainment from Harlem's World-Famous Theater*. New York: Holt, Rinehart and Winston.

Franklin, John Hope. 1948. *From Slavery to Freedom*. New York: Alfred A. Knopf.

Friedland, Will. 2002. *The Future of Jazz*. Chicago: A Cappella Books.

Gabbard, Krin. 1995. "The Jazz Canon and Its Consequences." In *Jazz among the Discourses*, edited by Krin Gabbard, 1–28. Durham: Duke University Press.

Gara, Larry. 1992. *The Baby Dodds Story as Told to Larry Gara*. Baton Rouge: Louisiana State University Press.

Garcia, David. 2007. "'We Both Speak African': Gillespie, Pozo, and the Making of Afro-Cuban Jazz." *Institute for Studies In American Music Newsletter* 37, no. 1 (Fall): 1, 2, 13, 14.

Garrett, Charles Hiroshi. 2008. *Struggling to Define a Nation: American Music and the Twentieth Century*. Berkeley: University of California Press.

Gates, Henry Louis, Jr. 1992. "African American Criticism." In *Redrawing the Boundaries*, edited by Stephen Greenblatt and Giles Gunn, 303–319. New York: Modern Language Association of America.

Gehman, Mary. 2001–2002. "The Mexico-Louisiana Creole Connection: A Scholar Researches Descendants of Creole Émigrés Who Fled Racial Prejudice." *Louisiana Cultural Vistas* (Winter): 68–75.

Gennari, John. 2006. *Blowin' Hot and Cool: Jazz and Its Critics*. Chicago: University of Chicago Press.

Getz, Stan. (1990) 2000. Interview by Terry Gross. *Fresh Air*, National Public Radio, December 27.

Giddens, Anthony. 1990. *The Consequences of Modernity*. Cambridge: Polity Press.

Gillespie, Dizzy. 1979. *To Be or Not to Bop: Memoirs of Dizzy Gillespie with Al Fraser*. New York: Da Capo.

Gilroy, Paul. 1993a. *The Black Atlantic: Modernity and Double Consciousness*. Cambridge, MA: Harvard University Press.

Gilroy, Paul. 1993b. *Small Acts: Thoughts on the Politics of Black Culture*. London: Serpent's Tail.

Giroux, Henry. 1992. *Border Crossings: Cultural Workers and the Politics of Education*. New York: Routledge.

Glasser, Ruth. 1995. *My Music Is My Flag: Puerto Rican Musicians and Their New York Communities, 1917–1940*. Berkeley: University of California Press.

Glenny, Misha. 2010. "The Gift of Information." *New York Times Style Magazine*, December 4. http://tmagazine.blogs.nytimes.com/2010/12/04/the-gift-of-information/?ref=holiday-issue, accessed December 6, 2010.

Glissant, Edouard. 1976. "Free and Forced Poetics." *Alcheringa* 2, no. 2: 95–101.

Glissant, Edouard. (1990) 1997. *Poetics of Relation*. Ann Arbor: University of Michigan Press.

Gonzalez Alcantud, José. 2002. *Lo moro: Las lógicas de la derrota y la formación del estereotipo Islámico*. Barcelona: Anthropos.

Gottlieb, Bill. 1947. "Rhumba Bands May Cut Hot Orks: Latin America's Rhythm Heralds New Kind of Jazz." *DownBeat* 14 (July): 10.

Grenet, Emilio. 1939. *Popular Cuban Music: 80 Revised and Corrected Compositions*, translated by R. Phillips. Havana: Carasa.

Gridley, Mark C. 1978. *Jazz Styles: History and Analysis*, 2nd ed. Englewood Cliffs, N.J.: Prentice-Hall.

Guilbault, Jocelyne. 1993. *Zouk: World Music in the West Indies*. Chicago: University of Chicago Press.

Guilbault, Jocelyne. 1994. "Créolité and the New Cultural Politics of Difference in Popular Music of the French West Indies." *Black Music Research Journal* 14, no. 2 (Autumn): 161–178.

Gushee, Lawrence. 1988. "How the Creole Band Came to Be." *Black Music Research Journal*, 8, no. 1: 83–100.

Gushee, Lawrence. 1994. "The Nineteenth-Century Origins of Jazz." *Black Music Research Journal* 14, no. 1: 151–174.

Hall, Gwendolyn Midlo. 1992a. *Africans in Colonial Louisiana: The Development of Afro-Creole Culture in the Eighteenth Century*. Baton Rouge: Louisiana State University Press.

Hall, Gwendolyn Midlo. 1992b. "The Formation of Afro-Creole Culture." In *Creole New Orleans: Race and Americanization*, edited by Arnold Hirsch and Joseph Logsdon, 58–90. Baton Rouge: Louisiana State University Press.

Hall, Stuart. 2003a. "Créolité and the Process of Creolization." In *Créolité and Creolization: Documenta 11, Platform 3*, edited by Okwui Enwezor et al., 27–41. Ostfildern-Ruit, Germany: Hatje Cantz.

Hall, Stuart. 2003b. "Creolization, Diaspora, and Hybridity in the Context of Globalization." In *Créolité and Creolization: Documenta 11, Platform 3*, edited by Okwui Enwezor et al., 185–198. Ostfildern-Ruit, Germany: Hatje Cantz.

Handy, D. Antoinette. 1981. *Black Women in American Bands and Orchestras*. Metuchen, N.J.: Scarecrow Press.

Handy, W. C. 1941. *Father of the Blues: An Autobiography*. New York: MacMillan.

Hannerz, Ulf. "The World of Creolisation." *Africa* 57, 4 (1987): 546–559.

Harris, Jerome. 2000. "Jazz on the Global Stage." In *The African Diaspora: A Musical Perspective*, edited by Ingrid Monson, 103–134. New York: Garland Publishing.

Hirsch, Arnold. 1992. "Simply a Matter of Black and White: The Transformation of Race and Politics in Twentieth-Century New Orleans." In *Creole New Orleans: Race and Americanization*, edited by Arnold Hirsch and Joseph Logsdon, 262–319. Baton Rouge: Louisiana State University Press.

Hirsch, Arnold, and Joseph Logsdon, eds. 1992. *Creole New Orleans: Race and Americanization.* Baton Rouge: Louisiana State University Press.

Holt, Fabian. 2007. *Genre in Popular Music.* Chicago: University of Chicago Press.

Hunt, Alfred. 1988. *Haiti's Influence on Antebellum America.* Baton Rouge: Louisiana State University Press.

Hurston, Zora Neal. 1935. *Mules and Men.* Philadelphia: Lippincott.

Hutnyk, John. 2000. *Critique of Exotica: Music, Politics and the Culture Industry.* London: Pluto.

Ingold, Tim. 2009. "Stories against Classification: Transport, Wayfaring and the Integration of Knowledge." In *Kinship and Beyond: The Genealogical Model Reconsidered*, edited by Sandra Bamford and James Leach, 193–213. New York: Berghahn Books.

Jackson, Joy J. 1969. *New Orleans in the Gilded Age: Politics and Urban Progress, 1880–1896.* Baton Rouge: Louisiana State University Press.

Jackson, Travis. 2001. "Jazz Performance as Ritual: The Blues Aesthetic and the African Diaspora." In *The African Diaspora: A Musical Perspective*, edited by Ingrid Monson, 23–82. New York: Garland Publishing.

Jacques, Geoffrey. 1998. "CuBop! Afro-Cuban Music and Mid-Twentieth-Century American Culture." In *Between Race and Empire: African-Americans and Cubans before the Cuban Revolution*, edited by Lisa Brock and Digna Casteñeda Fuertes, 249–265. Philadelphia: Temple University Press.

Jeffri, Joan. 2002. "Changing the Beat: A Study of the Worklife of Jazz Musicians." https://www.arts.gov/sites/default/files/JazzExecSummary.pdf, accessed March 11, 2017.

Johnson, Jerah. 1991. "New Orleans's Congo Square: An Urban Setting for Early Afro-American Culture Formation." *Louisiana History* 32, no. 2: 117–157.

Johnson, Jerah. 1992. "Colonial New Orleans: A Fragment of the Eighteenth-Century French Ethos." In *Creole New Orleans: Race and Americanization*, edited by Arnold Hirsch and Joseph Logsdon. Baton Rouge: Louisiana State University Press.

Johnson, Jerah. 2000. "Jim Crow Laws of the 1890s and the Origins of New Orleans Jazz: Correction of an Error." *Popular Music* 19, no. 2: 243–251.

Jones, LeRoi. 1963. *Blues People.* Westport, Conn.: Greenwood Press.

Kelley, Robin. 2001. "In a Mist: Thoughts on Ken Burns's Jazz." *ISAM Newsletter* 30, no. 2 (Spring): 8–15.

Kendall, John Smith. 1922. *History of New Orleans*, 3 vols. Chicago: Lewis Publishing.

Kinzer, Charles E. 1996. "The Tios of New Orleans and Their Pedagogical Influence on the Early Jazz Clarinet Style." *Black Music Research Journal* 16, no. 2: 279–302.

Kmen, Henry A. 1966. *Music in New Orleans: The Formative Years, 1791–1841.* Baton Rouge: Louisiana State University Press.

Knowles, Richard. 1996. *Fallen Heroes: A History of New Orleans Brass Bands.* New Orleans: Jazzology Press.

La Chance, Paul. 1992. "The 1809 Immigration of Saint-Domingue Refugees." In *The Road to Louisiana: The Saint-Domingue Refugees, 1792-1809*, edited by Carl Brasseaux and Glenn R. Conrad, 245–284. Lafayette: Center for Louisiana Studies, University of Southwestern Louisiana.

Lapique, Zoila. 1998. "Aportes franco-haitanos a la contradanza cubana: Mitos y realidades." In *Panorama de la música popular cubana*, edited by Radamés Giro, 140–149. Havana: Editorial Letras Cubanas.

Largey, Michael. 2006. *Vodou Nation: Haitian Art Music and Cultural Nationalism.* Chicago: University of Chicago Press.

León, Argeliers. 1974. *Del canto y el tiempo*. Havana: Instituto Cubana de Libro.

Levine, Lawrence. 1988. *The Emergence of Cultural Hierarchy in America*. Cambridge, Mass.: Harvard University Press.

Levy, Louis Herman. 1976. "The Formalization of New Orleans Jazz Musicians: A Case Study of Organizational Change." Ph.D. diss., Virginia Polytechnic Institute and State University.

Lewis, George E. 1996. "Improvised Music after 1950: Afrological and Eurological Perspectives." *Black Music Research Journal* 16, no. 1: 91–122.

Lionnet, Françoise. 1993. "Creolite in the Indian Ocean: Two Models of Cultural Diversity." *Yale French Studies* 82, no. 1: 101–114.

Lipsitz, George. 1990. *Time Passages: Collective Memory and American Popular Culture*. Minneapolis: University of Minnesota Press.

Lipsitz, George. 1998. *The Possessive Investment in Whiteness: How White People Benefit from Identity Politics*. Philadelphia: Temple University Press.

Lomax, Alan. (1950) 1973. *Mister Jelly Roll: The Fortunes of Jelly Roll Morton, New Orleans Creole and "Inventor of Jazz."* 2nd ed. Berkeley: University of California Press.

Lomax, Alan. (1950) 2001. *Mister Jelly Roll: The Fortunes of Jelly Roll Morton, New Orleans Creole and "Inventor of Jazz."* Berkeley: University of California Press.

Logsdon, Joseph, and Carolyn Cossé Bell. 1992. "The Americanization of Black New Orleans." In *Creole New Orleans: Race and Americanization*, edited by Arnold R. Hirsch and Joseph Logsdon, 201–261. Baton Rouge: Louisiana State University Press.

Lopez, Ana M. 1993. "Are All Latins from Manhattan? Hollywood, Ethnography, and Cultural Colonialism." In *Mediating Two Worlds: Cinematic Encounters in the Americas*, edited by John King, Ana Lopez, and Manual Alvarado, 67–80. Bloomington: Indiana University Press.

Mandel, Howard. 1993. "Remembering Dizzy: All Dizzy's Children." *DownBeat* 60 (April): 25–26.

Manuel, Peter. 1994. "Puerto Rican Music and Cultural Identity: Creative Appropriation of Cuban Sources from Danza to Salsa." *Ethnomusicology* 38, no. 2: 249–280.

Marquis, Donald M. 1978. *In Search of Buddy Bolden, First Man of Jazz*. Baton Rouge: Louisiana State University Press.

Martínez, Raymond, ed. 1971. *Portraits in New Orleans Jazz: its peoples and places*. New Orleans: Hope Publications.

Matory, J. Lorand. 1999. "Afro-Atlantic Culture: On the Live Dialogue between Africa and the Americas." In *Africana*, edited by Henry Louis Gates Jr. and Kwane Appiah, 36–44. New York: Basic Civitas.

McCusker, John. 1998–1999. "The Onward Band and the Spanish American War." *Jazz Archivist* 13: 24–35.

McKay, George. 2005. *Circular Breathing: The Cultural Politics of Jazz in Britain*. Durham: Duke University Press.

McKinley Jr., James C. 2012. "Grammys Reinstate Latin Jazz Award," *New York Times*, June 8. https://artsbeat.blogs.nytimes.com/2012/06/08/grammys-reinstate-latin-jazz-award, accessed April 5, 2014.

McMains, Juliet. 2015. *Spinning Mambo into Salsa: Caribbean Dance in Global Commerce*. New York: Oxford University Press.

Meredith, Bill. 2007. "The Latin Tinge: Latin Jazz Is Pounding, Pulsing, Grooving—and Under Appreciated." *Jazztimes* (November): 66–70.

Miller, Herbie. 2007. "Syncopating Rhythms: Jazz and Caribbean Culture." Jazz Studies Online. http://jazzstudiesonline.org/?q=node/596.

Miller, Ivor L. 2000. "A Secret Society Goes Public: The Relationship between Abakuá and Cuban Popular Culture." *African Studies Review* 43, no. 1 (April): 161–188.

Miller, Ivor L. 2009. "Bongó Itá: Leopard Society Music and Language in West Africa, Western Cuba, and New York City." In *Bridging Diasporal Sacred Worlds: Black Music Scholarship and the Americas*, edited by Samuel A. Floyd Jr. Berkeley: University of California Press.

Monson, Ingrid. 1994. "Doubleness and Jazz Improvisation: Irony, Parody, and Ethnomusicology." *Critical Inquiry* 20 (Winter): 283–313.

Monson, Ingrid. 1995. "The Problem of White Hipness: Race, Gender, and Cultural Conceptions in Jazz Historical Discourse." *Journal of the American Musicological Society* 48, no. 3 (Autumn): 396–422.

Monson, Ingrid. 1996. *Saying Something: Jazz Improvisation and Interaction*. Chicago: University of Chicago Press.

Monson, Ingrid. 1998. "Oh Freedom: George Russell, John Coltrane, and Modal Jazz." In *In the Course of Performance: Studies in the World of Musical Improvisation*, edited by Bruno Nettl with Melinda Russell, 149–168. Chicago: University of Chicago Press.

Monson, Ingrid. 1999. "Riffs, Repetition, and Theories of Globalization." *Ethnomusicology* 43, no. 1 (Winter): 31–65.

Monson, Ingrid. 2000. *The African Diaspora: A Musical Perspective*. New York: Garland Publishing.

Moore, Robin D. 1997. *Nationalizing Blackness: Afrocubanismo and Artistic Revolution in Havana, 1920–1940*. Pittsburgh: University of Pittsburgh Press.

Moreno, Jairo. 2004. "Bauzá–Gillespie–Latin/Jazz: Difference, Modernity, and the Black Caribbean." *South Atlantic Quarterly* 103, no. 1 (Winter): 81–99.

Moreno, Jairo. 2016. "Sonorous Specters: On Some Recent Histories and Economies of Afro-Latin Jazz." *Journal of Latin American Cultural Studies* 25(3): 397-417.

Morton, Jelly Roll. (1938) 2005. *The Complete Library of Congress Recordings* (interviews by Alan Lomax). Rounder Records.

Narváez, Peter. 1994. "The Influences of Hispanic Music Cultures on African-American Blues Musicians." *Black Music Research Journal* 14, no. 2 (Fall): 203–224.

Navarro, Mireya. 2000. "A Master of Latin Jazz Is Rediscovered at 79." *New York Times*, December 30, B1, B6.

Nicholson, Stuart. 2001. "Europeans Cut In with a New Jazz Sound and Beat." *New York Times*, June 3, section 2, 1, 28.

Oliver, Paul. 1991. "That Certain Feeling: Blues and Jazz . . . in 1890?" *Popular Music* 10, no. 1 (January): 11–19.

O'Meally, Robert G. 2001. "He Inspired Jazz in the Concert Hall." *New York Times*, May 27section 2, 20.

Ortiz, Fernando. (1935) 1984. *La clave xilofónica de la música cubana*. Havana: Editorial Letras Cubanas.

Ortner, Sherry. (1984) 1994. "Theory in Anthropology since the Sixties." In *Culture/Power/History: A Reader in Contemporary Social Theory*, edited by Nicholas Dirks, Geoff Eley, and Sherry Ortner, 372–411. Princeton: Princeton University Press.

Padilla, Felix M. 1985. *Latino Ethnic Consciousness: The Case of Mexican Americans and Puerto Ricans in Chicago*. Notre Dame: University of Notre Dame Press.

Pastras, Phil. 2001. *Dead Man Blues: Jelly Roll Morton Way Out West*. Berkeley: University of California Press.

Pérez. Louis A., Jr. 1999. *On Becoming Cuban: Identity, Nationality and Culture*. Chapel Hill: University of North Carolina Press.

Pieterse, Jan Nederveen. 1994. "Globalisation as Hybridisation." *International Sociology* 9, no. 2: 161–184.

Pinckney, Walter R., Jr. 1989. "Puerto Rican Jazz and the Incorporation of Folk Music: An Analysis of New Musical Directions." *Latin American Music Review* 10, no. 2 (Fall/Winter): 236–266.

Porcello, Thomas. 2007. "Three Contributions to the 'Sonic Turn.'" *Current Musicology* 83 (Spring): 153–164.

Porter, Lewis, and Michael Ullman. 1993. *Jazz: From Its Origins to the Present*. Englewood Cliffs, N.J.: Prentice-Hall.

Powell, Josephine. 2007. *Tito Puente: When the Drums Are Dreaming*. Bloomington, IN: Author House.

Quintero Rivera, Angel. 1998. *Salsa, sabor y control: Sociología de la música "tropical."* Mexico City: Siglo Veintiuno Editors.

Quintero Rivera, Angel. 2006. "Las músicas de América Latina." In *Latinoamericana: Enciclopedia contemporánea de América Latina y el Caribe*, edited by Emir Sader. Rio de Janeiro: Bontempo Editorial.

Quintero Rivera, Angel. 2007. "Migration, Ethnicity, and Interactions between the United States and Hispanic Caribbean Popular Culture," translated by Mariana Ortega Breña. *Latin American Perspectives* 34: 83–93.

Radano, Ronald M., and Philip V. Bohlman, eds. 2001. *Music and the Racial Imagination*. Chicago: University of Chicago Press.

Raeburn, Bruce Boyd. 2007. "The Spanish American War and New Orleans Jazz." *Jazzeitung*. In German at www.jazzzeitung.de/jazz/2007/01/heute-marchingband.shtml.

Raeburn, Bruce Boyd. 2012. "Beyond the 'Spanish Tinge': Hispanics and Latinos in Early New Orleans Jazz." In *Eurojazzland*, edited by Luca Cerchiari, Laurent Cugny, and Frank Kerschbauer, 21–46. Lebanon, N.H.: Northeastern University Press.

Regis, Helen A. 1999. "Second Lines, Minstrelsy, and the Contested Landscapes of New Orleans Afro-Creole Festivals." *Cultural Anthropology* 14, no. 4: 472–504.

Roach, Joseph. 1996. *Cities of the Dead: Circum-Atlantic Performance*. New York: Columbia University Press.

Roberts, John Storm. 1972. *Black Music of Two Worlds*. New York: Praeger.

Roberts, John Storm. 1979. *The Latin Tinge: The Impact of Latin American Music on the United States*. New York: Oxford University Press.

Roberts, John Storm. 1999. *Latin Jazz: The First of the Fusions, 1880s to Today*. New York: Schirmer.

Rodriguez, Andrew. N.d. "A Fork in the Road." Unpublished manuscript.

Román, Miriam Jiménez, and Juan Flores, eds. 2010. *The Afro-Latin@ Reader: History and Culture in the United States*. Durham: Duke University Press.

Rose, Al, and Edward Souchon. 1978. *New Orleans Jazz: A Family Album*. Baton Rouge: Louisiana State University Press.

Rouse, Don. N.d. "New Orleans Jazz and Caribbean Music." http://www.prjc.org/roots/nojazzandcarribe.html, accessed February 13, 2008.

Russell, William. 1994. *New Orleans Style*, compiled and edited by Barry Martyn and Mike Hazeldine. New Orleans: Jazzology Press.

Sakakeeny, Matt. 2008. "Instruments of Power: New Orleans Brass Bands and the Politics of Performance." Ph.D. diss., Columbia University.

Santoro, Gene. 2000. "Latin Jazz." In *The Oxford Jazz Companion*, edited by Bill Kirchner, 522–533. New York: Oxford University Press.

Saxon, Lyle, Edward Dreyer, and Robert Tallant. (1945) 1987. *Gumbo Ya-ya: Folktales of Louisiana.* Gretna, La.: Pelican Publishing.

Schafer, William J. 1977. *Brass Bands and New Orleans Jazz.* Baton Rouge: Louisiana State University Press.

Schmeisser, Iris. 2007. "'Un Saxophone en Mouvement'? Josephne Baker and the Primitivist Reception of Jazz in Paris in the 1920s." In *Cross the Water Blues: African American Music in Europe,* edited by Neil A. Wynn, 106–124. Jackson: University of Mississippi.

Schuller, Gunther. 1958. "Sonny Rollins and the Challenge of Thematic Improvisation." *Jazz Review* 1, no. 1 (November): 6–21.Schuller, Gunther. 1968. *Early Jazz: Its Roots and Musical Development.* New York: Oxford University Press.

Schuller, Gunther. 1989. *The Swing Era: 1930–1945.* New York: Oxford University Press.

Serrano, Basilio. 2007. "Puerto Rican Musicians of the Harlem Renaissance." *Centro Journal* 19, no. 2 (Fall): 94–119.

Serrano, Basilio. 2015. *Puerto Rican Pioneers in Jazz 1900–1939: Bomba Beats to Latin Jazz.* Bloomington, Ind.: iUniverse.

Sher, Chuck. 1997. *The Latin Real Book.* Petaluma, Calif.: Sher Music.

Singer, Roberta L. 1982. "My Music Is Who I Am and What I Do: Latin Popular Music and Identity in New York City." Ph.D. diss., Indiana University.

Singer, Roberta L. 1988. "Puerto Rican Music in New York City." *New York Folklore* 14, nos. 3–4: 139–149.

Sinnette, Elinor Des Verney. 1989. *Arthur Alfonso Schomburg: Black Bibliophile and Collector.* Detroit: Wayne State University Press.

Smith, Pamela J. 1986. "Caribbean Influences on New Orleans Jazz." Master's thesis, Tulane University.

Stanyek, Jason. 2004. "Transmissions of an Interculture: Pan-African Jazz and Intercultural Improvisation." In *The Other Side of Nowhere: Jazz, Improvisation and Communities in Dialogue,* edited by Daniel Fischlin and Ajay Heble, 87–130. Wesleyan: Wesleyan University Press.

Starr, S. Frederick. 1995. *Bamboula! The Life and Times of Louis Moreau Gottschalk.* New York: Oxford University Press.

Stearns, Marshall. 1956. *The Story of Jazz.* New York: Oxford University Press.

Stewart, Jack. 1991. "The Mexican Band Legend: Myth, Reality, and Musical Impact; A Preliminary Investigation." *Jazz Archivist* 6, no. 2: 1–14.

Stewart, Jack. 1994. "The Mexican Band Legend: Part 2. *Jazz Archivist* 9, no. 1 (May): 1–17.

Stewart, Jack. 1999. "Cuban Influences on New Orleans Jazz." http://www.arhoolie.com/titles/7032c.shtml, accessed February 19, 2008.

Stewart, Jack. 2007. "The Mexican Band Legend: Part 3." *Jazz Archivist* 20 : 1–10.

Stokes, Martin, Jonathan Webber, and Shirley Ardene, eds. 1994. *Ethnicity, Identity and Music: The Musical Construction of Place.* Oxford: Berg.

Suarez, Virgil. 2002. *Latin Jazz.* Baton Rouge: Louisiana State University Press.

Sublette, Ned. 2004. *Cuba and Its Music: From the First Drums to the Mambo.* Chicago: Chicago Review Press.

Sublette, Ned. 2008. *The World That Made New Orleans: From Spanish Silver to Congo Square.* Chicago: Lawrence Hill Books.

Szwed, John. 2005a. *Crossovers: Essays on Race, Music and American Culture.* Philadelphia: University of Pennsylvania Press.

Szwed, John. 2005b. Liner notes to *The Complete Library of Congress Recordings by Alan Lomax.* Rounder Records (CDROUN1888 / 0 11661 1888 2 2).

Taussig, Michael. 1987. *Shamanism, Colonialism, and the Wild Man: A Study in Terror and Healing*. Chicago: University of Chicago Press.

Taylor, Arthur. 1993. *Notes and Tones: Musician-to-Musician Interviews*. New York: Da Capo.

Thompson, E. P. 1977. "Folklore, Anthropology, and Social History." *Indian Historical Review* 2, no. 2: 247–266.

Thompson, Robert Farris. 2005. *Tango: The Art of Love*. New York: Vintage Books.

Tomlinson, Gary. 1992. "Cultural Dialogues and Jazz: A White Historian Signifies." In *Disciplining Music: Musicology and Its Canons*, edited by Katherine Bergeron and Philip V. Bohlman, 64–94. Chicago: University of Chicago Press.

Tsing, Anna. 2005. *Friction: An Ethnography of Global Connection*. Princeton: Princeton University Press.

Vega, Ray. 2000. "Letter to the Editor of Downbeat Magazine." August 7. http://groups.yahoo.com/group/latinjazz/message/3394.

Walker, Daniel E. 2004. *No More, No More: Slavery and Cultural Resistance in Havana and New Orleans*. Minneapolis: University of Minnesota Press.

Walser, Rob. 1999. *Keeping Time: Readings in Jazz History*. New York: Oxford University Press.

Warner, Michael. 2002. *Publics and Counterpublics*. New York: Zone Books.

Washburne, Christopher. 1997. "The Clave of Jazz: A Caribbean Contribution to the Rhythmic Foundation of an African-American Music." *Black Music Research Journal* 17, no. 1 (Spring): 59–80.

Washburne, Christopher. 2001. "Nuyorican Son." *Current Musicology* 67–68: 452–486.

Washburne, Christopher. 2001–2002. "Latin Jazz: The Other Jazz." *Current Musicology* 71–73: 409–426.

Washburne, Christopher. 2008. *Sounding Salsa: Performing Latin Music in New York City*. Philadelphia: Temple University Press.

Washburne, Christopher. 2010a. "Celia Cruz at the Apollo." In *Ain't Nothing Like the Real Thing: How the Apollo Theater Shaped American Entertainment*, edited by Richard Carlin and Kinshasha Holman Conwill, 226–228. Washington, D.C.: Smithsonian Books.

Washburne, Christopher. 2010b. "Latin Music at the Apollo." In *Ain't Nothing Like the Real Thing: How the Apollo Theater Shaped American Entertainment*, edited by Richard Carlin and Kinshasha Holman Conwill, 220–225. Washington, D.C.: Smithsonian Books.

Washburne, Christopher. 2012. "Latin Jazz, Afro-Latin Jazz, Afro-Cuban Jazz, Cubop, Caribbean Jazz, Jazz Latin, or Just . . . Jazz: The Politics of Locating an Intercultural Music." In *Jazz/Not Jazz: The Music and Its Boundaries*, edited by David Ake, Charles Garrett, and David Goldmark, 89–110. Berkeley: University of California Press.

Washburne, Christopher. 2016. "An Introduction to Eddie Palmieri: A Revolution on Harlem River Drive." Red Bull Music Academy. http://daily.redbullmusicacademy.com/2016/05/the-note-eddie-palmieri-intro.

Watkins, Glenn. 1994. *Pyramids at the Louvre: Music, Culture, and Collage from Stravinsky to the Postmodernists*. Cambridge, Mass.: Belknap Press.

Watkins, Glenn. 1995. *Soundings: Music in the Twentieth Century*. New York: Schirmer.

Watrous, Peter. 1997. "The Jazz Is 'Lite,' the Profits Heavy: Radio Stations Enjoy Rising Ratings as Music Purists Fume." *New York Times*, June 5, C13.

Werner, Otto. 1992. *The Latin influence on Jazz*. Dubuque, Iowa: Kendall/Hunt.

Williams, Martin T. 1967. *Jazz Masters of New Orleans*. New York: Da Capo Press.

Williams, Martin T. 1970. *The Jazz Tradition*. New York: Oxford University Press.

Williams, Martin T. 1992. *Jazz Changes*. New York: Oxford University Press.

Woideck, Carl. 1996. *Charlie Parker: His Music and Life*. Ann Arbor: University of Michigan Press.

Wynn, Neil A., ed. 2007. *Cross the Water Blues: African American Music in Europe*. Jackson University Press of Mississippi.

Yanow, Scott. 2000. *Afro-Cuban Jazz*. San Francisco: Miller Freeman Books.

Yglesias, Pablo. 2016. "The Oral History of Eddie Palmieri's Harlem River Drive." *WaxPoetics*. http://www.waxpoetics.com/blog/features/the-oral-history-of-eddie-palmieris-harlem-river-drive, accessed June 1, 2017.

Yúdice, George. 2004. *The Expediency of Culture: Uses of Culture in the Global Era*. Durham: Duke University Press.

Index

Figures are indicated by *f* following the page number

For the benefit of digital users, indexed terms that span two pages (e.g., 52–53) may, on occasion, appear on only one of those pages.

CPSIA information can be obtained
at www.ICGtesting.com
Printed in the USA
LVHW082219150721
692862LV00008B/505

9 780197 510841